THE COMMUNION OF THE CHRISTIAN WITH GOD

Lives of Jesus Series

LEANDER E. KECK, *General Editor*

THE COMMUNION OF THE CHRISTIAN WITH GOD

Described on the Basis of Luther's Statements

by WILHELM HERRMANN

Edited and with an Introduction by
ROBERT T. VOELKEL

FORTRESS PRESS
PHILADELPHIA

Library of Congress Catalog Card Number 78-154491

ISBN   0-8006-1270-1

2720B71   Printed in U.S.A.   1-1270

FOREWORD

In a time when a premium is placed on experimentation for the future and when theological work itself values "new theology," the reasons for reissuing theological works from the past are not self-evident. Above all, there is broad consensus that the "Lives of Jesus" produced by our forebears failed both as sound history and as viable theology. Why, then, make these works available once more?

First of all, this series does not represent an effort to turn the clock back, to declare these books to be the norm to which we should conform, either in method or in content. Neither critical research nor constructive theology can be repristinated. Nevertheless, root problems in the historical-critical study of Jesus and of theological reflection are perennial. Moreover, advances are generally made by a critical dialogue with the inherited tradition, whether in the historical reconstruction of the life of Jesus or in theology as a whole. Such a dialogue cannot occur, however, if the tradition is allowed to fade into the mists or is available to students only in handbooks which perpetuate the judgments and clichés of the intervening generation. But a major obstacle is the fact that certain pivotal works have never been available to the present generation, for they were either long out of print or not translated at all. A central aim, then, in republishing certain "Lives of Jesus" is to encourage a fresh discovery of and a lively debate with this tradition so that our own work may be richer and more precise.

Titles were selected which have proven to be significant for ongoing issues in Gospel study and in the theological enterprise as a whole. H. S. Reimarus inaugurated the truly critical investigation of Jesus and so was an obvious choice. His *On the Intention of Jesus* was reissued by the American Theological Library Association in 1962, but has not really entered the discussion despite the fact that questions he raised have been opened again, especially by S. G. F. Brandon's *Jesus and the Zealots.* Our edition, moreover, includes also his previously untranslated discussion of the resurrection and part of D. F. Strauss's evaluation of Reimarus. That Strauss's *Life of Jesus* must be included was clear from the start. Our edition, using George Eliot's translation, will take account of Strauss's shifting views as well. Schleiermacher's *Life of Jesus* will be translated, partly because it is significant for the study of Schleiermacher himself and partly because he is the wellspring of repeated concern for the inner life of Jesus. One of the most influential expressions of this motif came from Wilhelm Herrmann's *The Communion of the Christian with God,* which, while technically not a life of Jesus, emphasizes more than any other work the religious significance of Jesus' inner life. In fresh form, this emphasis has been rejuvenated in the current work of Ernst Fuchs and Gerhard Ebeling who concentrate on Jesus' own faith. Herrmann, then, is a bridge between Schleiermacher and the present. In such a series, it was also deemed important to translate Strauss's critique of Schleiermacher, *The Christ of Faith and the Jesus of History,* for here important critical issues were exposed. Probably no book was more significant for twentieth-century study of Jesus than Johannes Weiss's *Jesus' Proclamation of the Kingdom of God,* for together with Albert Schweitzer, Weiss turned the entire course of Jesus-research, and undermined the foundations of the prevailing Protestant theology. From the American scene, two writers from the same faculty were included: Shailer Mathews's *Jesus on Social Institutions* and Shirley Jackson Case's *Jesus: A New Biography*. There can be no substantive dialogue with our own theological tradition which ignores these influential figures, though today they are scarcely read at all. Doubtless other works could have been included with justification; however, these will suffice to enliven the theological scene if read perceptively.

In each case, an editor was invited to provide an introductory essay and annotations to the text in order to assist the reader in seeing the book in perspective. The bibliography will aid further research, though in no case was there an attempt to be comprehensive. The aim is not to produce critical editions in the technical sense (which would require a massive apparatus), but a useable series of texts with guidance at essential points. Within these aims, the several editors enjoyed considerable latitude in developing their contributions. The series will achieve its aim if it facilitates a rediscovery of an exciting and controversial history and so makes our own work more fruitful.

The republication of Herrmann's most famous book is intended not only to expose important links between certain recent theological work and the past, as indicated above, but also to stimulate a rediscovery of Hermann in his own right. The editor has provided an Introduction in which, appropriately, he sketches the context of Herrmann's work as a whole rather than summarizing the argument of the book or assessing it in detail. His annotations to Herrmann's text, printed at the back of the book, allow the reader to see something of the shifts in Herrmann's thought. Notes added by the Series Editor are identified: [LEK].

The editor, Robert Voelkel, is Chairman of the Religion Department of Pomona College. Having received his B.A.

at the College of Wooster (1954), he studied at Edinburgh as a Fulbright student in 1954-55, and earned his B.D. at Union Theological Seminary in New York in 1957. He then combined teaching and campus ministry at Wooster for two years before undertaking graduate study at Union. Since receiving the Th.D. in 1962, he has been on the faculty of Pomona College. In 1968-69, he pursued post-doctoral research in Marburg, Germany.

In 1968 Dr. Voelkel published *The Shape of the Theological Task* (Westminster Press) in which he interprets Herrmann's significance for theological work in today's contexts. The interplay between theology and problems of culture continues to be a major research interest. His contribution to the present volume, therefore, carries forward long-standing concerns, grows out of extended study of Wilhelm Herrmann himself, and opens the way for renewed appreciation of a major figure in modern Protestant theology.

LEANDER E. KECK
The Divinity School
Vanderbilt University

CONTENTS

FOREWORD v
INTRODUCTION BY ROBERT VOELKEL xv
SELECTED BIBLIOGRAPHY lxiii
THE TEXT OF *The Communion of the Christian with God* lxv

INTRODUCTION

§ 1. The present situation of Protestant Christianity . 1
§ 2. The difficulty of the position is overcome by the
　　　piety of those not under bondage to law . . 6
§ 3. The exposition of what personal Christianity is is
　　　the common task of all parties in the Church . 8
§ 4. The impossibility of uniformity of doctrine in
　　　Christianity 10
§ 5. The feature of unity in the New Testament and in
　　　the Christian community generally is the com-
　　　munion with God that is mediated through Jesus
　　　Christ 14
§ 6. The true objectivity of Christian knowledge . . 16

CHAPTER I

THE RELATION OF THE CHRISTIAN RELIGION TO MYSTICISM AND TO THE FORMS OF RELIGIOUS OBSERVANCE INVOLVED IN MYSTICISM

§ 1. The uncommunicable element in all religion . . 19
§ 2. The Catholic choice of this incommunicable ele-
　　　ment as the common essence of religion . . 21
§ 3. Mysticism and its significance for Catholicism . 22

PAGE

§ 4. A want of clearness in the Protestant attitude to mysticism 25

§ 5. The enduring significance of mysticism for the Christian life 27

§ 6. Why, within the Christian community, the way of mysticism must be abandoned 29

§ 7. The unsatisfying element in the doctrine of the two natures in Christ is correlated to mysticism . 32

§ 8. We get free from mysticism and scholasticism when we get beyond the legal conception of religion . 37

§ 9. We part company with the older Protestantism . 40

§ 10. The difficulty and practicability of our undertaking 44

§ 11. The longing of the Christian for an objective reality to support his faith is made effective in Luther's Christianity 48

§ 12. The elements of Luther's theology which belong to the past 51

CHAPTER II

THE ESTABLISHMENT OF OUR COMMUNION WITH GOD THROUGH THE REVELATION OF GOD

§ 1. The conception of revelation as communicated knowledge about God and the piety founded on this notion 57

§ 2. Revelation as a fact inside our own experience, but distinct from ourselves, convincing us of God's working upon us 59

§ 3. The Person of Jesus as the only revelation convincing one who perceives the necessity of unconditional obedience 61

§ 4. The Person of Jesus is the most important element in the sphere of reality which we can reflect upon 64

§ 5. It is not through a historical judgment that the Person of Jesus becomes a fact we ourselves establish 66

PAGE

§ 6. The personality of Jesus, by its own power, makes it possible for us to grasp it as an element of our own sphere of reality   71

§ 7. The peculiarity of the Christian religion is rooted in the consciousness of this fact in our own experience   78

§ 8. The saving fact is the personal life of Jesus when it is grasped by us as a reality   80

§ 9. The simplest features of the portrait of Jesus which is to be got from the tradition   84

§ 10. The claim of Jesus to be the Redeemer and the proof of its truth   93

§ 11. The Person of Jesus as the revelation of God . .   97

§ 12. The objective grounds of our certainty that God communes with us   101

§ 13. The subjectivity of an arbitrary profession of faith   105

§ 14. The power of the Person of Jesus over our heart is the vital principle of our religion . . .   108

§ 15. The mystic, traditional, and rationalistic objections   111

§ 16. The impossibility of giving expression to the new life in communion with God in representations that are devoid of self-contradiction . . .   116

§ 17. The Christianity of children   117

§ 18. Adult Christianity   119

§ 19. The easy Christianity that renounces self-knowledge and reflection and accepts the conceptions of others   124

§ 20. The possibility of a confession of the Divinity of Christ   126

§ 21. Defects in the old Protestant doctrine of the work of Christ and the way of salvation . . .   129

§ 22. The value of the doctrine of the substitutionary penal sufferings of Jesus   135

§ 23. Luther's criticism of the thought of a substitutionary satisfaction   137

§ 24. The receiving of forgiveness through Jesus . .   140

PAGE

§ 25. The true idea of the Deity of Christ and Christological dogma 142
§ 26. Luther's attitude to Christological dogma . . 146
§ 27. The connection of Luther's peculiar idea of the
Deity of Christ with his view of redemption and
with the Christian knowledge of God . . . 172
§ 28. The advancement of Christian piety by means of
Luther's thought 179
§ 29. Communion with God and Christ through the
imagination 184
§ 30. The mediation of true communion with God by
means of the Christian community . . . 189
§ 31. The difference between this Christian religion and
mysticism 195

CHAPTER III

THE EXERCISE OF OUR COMMUNION WITH GOD IN RELIGIOUS FAITH AND MORAL ACTION

§ 1. Turning to God is wrongly supposed to begin in
prayer 202
§ 2. The form of the personal life in which a communion
with God can take place 205
§ 3. Our turning to God begins in the use of His act of
beneficence, that is, in faith 212
§ 4. Faith is not experienced by the renewed man as a
work of his own 214
§ 5. Luther rises superior to this error 216
§ 6. The reappearance of the Catholic idea in Protestant
Christianity 221
§ 7. We get free from it by personal forces . . . 224
§ 8. The relapse into the old view accounted for by the
force of criticism inherent in faith, especially
in regard to miracles 230
§ 9. Worldly religion hardens the orthodox notion of
faith 236

CONTENTS

PAGE

§ 10. True faith in itself communion with God and not merely a preliminary condition for communion . 241

§ 11. Submission to God only in pure trust . . . 243

§ 12. The place of forgiveness of sins in the life of faith 246

§ 13. Repentance as an element in the life of faith . . 253

§ 14. The element of contemplation in faith . . . 256

§ 15. Faith fleeing the world 258

§ 16. Luther's idea of the freedom of a Christian man . 265

§ 17. Christian humility 267

§ 18. The fear of God 270

§ 19. Love to God or to Christ 272

§ 20. The historical and the exalted Christ in the life of faith 281

§ 21. Communion with God as an experience and as an act 296

§ 22. Moral activity in communion with God . . . 298

§ 23. Faith as the power to will the good 300

§ 24. Faith as the impulse to will the good . . . 306

§ 25. Luther is defective as regards this point . . . 310

§ 26. The inner connection between love to God and love to our neighbour 313

§ 27. The foundation of a Christian system of ethics . 317

§ 28. Eternal life in bearing the cross and in one's moral calling 320

§ 29. The consequences of this further development of Luther's ideas 328

§ 30. The prayer of faith 331

§ 31. Prayer and willing resignation 337

§ 32. Prayer for earthly blessings 338

§ 33. The new birth 342

§ 34. Baptism and the new birth 349

§ 35. Science and the thoughts of faith 353

§ 36. Our attitude among the theological parties of the present day 356

SUPPLEMENTARY NOTES TO THE TEXT 357

INDEXES 369

INTRODUCTION

Robert Voelkel

Wilhelm Herrmann was born in 1846 into a pastor's home in Melkow, Prussia. His study took him to Halle from 1864 to 1870 where he heard Julius Mueller lecture and where he lived for two and a half years in the home of F. A. G. Tholuck. Here he also came in contact with Martin Kaehler. His academic work included a thorough study of Kant and a Latin dissertation on Gregory of Nyssa. The latter was sent to Albrecht Ritschl whom Herrmann also met in Tholuck's home. After several years as gymnasium teacher he was called to Marburg as professor in 1889 and remained there in spite of three calls elsewhere until his retirement in 1916. He died in 1922 after several years of failing health.

Herrmann and Protestant Theology in Wilhelminian Germany

Herrmann lived in a period of German and European history the full import of which is well recognized, but the real meaning of which is under debate. The revolutions of 1848 signalled the political restiveness of the European peoples caught between the pressures of economic growth, the struggle of a feudal order to retain its control, rising nationalism, and liberal demands for equality. Living in Prussia and middle Germany before his move to Hesse, Herrmann was a member of the state which helped to frustrate the liberal aims of the Frankfurt parliament and on at least one occasion he spoke with appreciation of the efforts of the Hohenzollern royal house toward the unification of Germany. He served in the armed forces during the Franco-Prussian war.

Yet Herrmann also lived to see the demise of the German empire in the revolution of 1918. Here the fissures in German political life were fully revealed and questions about the political and social future of the nation were posed. The challenge to the German *Geist* was concretely manifest and distinctly felt. What the liberals throughout the nineteenth century had raised as the rallying cry for the drive to national unity, and the Hohenzollerns had so effectively exploited in their dynastic politics, was now called dramatically in question. Furthermore, the bankruptcy of war and empire was declared by a people weary of killing and unclear about aims of conquest or national honor. Herrmann's lifetime spanned the years between 1848 and 1918 and the meaning of his work is in no small measure to be read from the meaning of this age.

In the narrower context of intellectual history where Herrmann's professional work lies, it is also appropriate to ask about the meaning of this age. His birth was almost coincident with the revolt of the young Hegelians—Feuerbach, Kierkegaard, and Marx—against the master. His death was almost coincident with the second edition of Karl Barth's commentary on the Romans, often seen as the inauguration of a new era. In fact from the perspective of Barth it is possible to interpret this age in which Herrmann lived as the closing chapter of a long story begun following the Reformation, climaxing the work of the great Idealists, especially Schleiermacher and Hegel, and tragically ending in the nihilism of Nietzsche. Figures like Franz Overbeck, the skeptical and critical church historian of Basel, are celebrated as sensing the ills of the age. Feuerbach, Kierkegaard, and Marx are looked to as honest critics in whose hands the triumphant system of Hegel fell to pieces. And the senselessness of a destructive war is seen as a sign of social decay and pretension.

In short, Herrmann is often seen to have lived in that era when the pride of modern man was defeated by history. And the great irony is seen in the fact that it was precisely this modern man who had put such faith in history. Hegel had made it the court for judging the world. Schleiermacher had made it the scene for religious self-realization. But both were to be disappointed. For to reason, as Hegel had proclaimed it, history presented the absurdity of trench warfare and the posturing of Wilhelm II. To piety, as Schleiermacher had fostered it, history presented the chance to resist war for national honor, and pious men had stood in Wilhelm's ranks. The prophetic voice of Barth announced the judgment of God upon the man who has faith in history and admonished him to turn to God's revelation in his Word. Only this stands fast amidst the turbulence of human events.

Such an interpretation of history, however, arises from history itself. It was forged in the peculiar world of post-World War I Germany in the peculiar tradition of the German intellectual world. Furthermore, it was formed against the background of German culture and the particular interweaving of Christian doctrine, the educational system, critical university study, and the problem of national identity specific to this setting. Since, however, the brilliance of German theological learning had so much influence upon worldwide theological study in this century, such an interpretation has found a wide reception. Moreover, the prominent role played by Germany in the upheavals of the twentieth century and the tragic dimension these upheavals highlighted could not but reenforce the Barthian position. Especially is this so when many of its champions proved to be the heartiest opponents of Hitler's evil system.

Now, however, we stand in the last third of the twentieth century with the period of the two world wars at a little distance. Before us opens the prospect of a pluralistic world with a non-European majority posing a myriad of problems seemingly defying a unified solution. Furthermore, Anglo-Saxon culture does not square so easily with this interpretation of history. The theologian who stands in this culture has reason to ponder the hermeneutical problem of dealing with the German theological tradition, and part of this problem is to determine what significance the age prior to World War I has for him. Understanding Herrmann depends upon it.

Perhaps we do well to look for a moment at three figures from this age who would not have seen it as the end so much as a beginning: Karl Marx, Charles Darwin, and Friedrich Nietzsche. Marx proclaimed a shift from idealistic speculation to scientific materialism. He wedded theory to practice in such a way as to be the herald if not the founder of modern day political technology. Darwin set out a view of man and his origins which has a pertinence today when the impact of environmental controls and the biological revolution have only begun to be felt. Nietzsche with more tragic and aristocratic overtones celebrated the birth of a man who stands above men of the past because he refuses to try to transcend them. Heidegger for one has seen this work as the necessary prerequisite for a transformation of philosophical inquiry.

The common note struck by Marx, Darwin, and Nietzsche is a resolute and courageous disavowal of a transcendent refuge. And if they occasionally speak with pathos, they are yet willing to avoid absolutes. They take history so seriously that they are willing to be subject to its risks. Such willingness to sacrifice the transcendent can be called the spirit of science, and it is no accident that Darwin practiced science and Marx spent so many years constructing *Das Kapital* as scientifically as he could. Surely it is a scientific world in which we live where the premium is upon critical judgments and applicable techniques. And surely it is to misread this world as a strutting of human pretensions rather than to see it as a disavowal of all unitary visions with their pretense of transcendence.

Coming to terms with this scientific world was what Wilhelm Herrmann's whole career was about, and he cannot be correctly interpreted but in relation to it. It infected his personality and his teaching style as well. Even though he was a man whose religious life was stamped by the Lutheran pietism in which he was raised and the religious intensity of the *Erweckungsbewegung* he knew in Tholuck's home, and even though the power of his personality gripped his students, Herrmann recedes into the background behind his thought. His student and admirer Wilhelm Schmidt testifies that one did not get close to him. He was not really approachable except in the formality of his office hours, and he strictly avoided propagandizing his students. He focussed instead the full force of his personality upon the matter at hand.[1]

Yet it would be a mistake to see Herrmann as unambiguously modern. Like so many figures who lived in his age Herrmann carried some cultural baggage from the past which is not wholly consistent with the thrust of his thought. His warm piety did not escape notice. It was reflected also in his seeming feeling of mission in his teaching. The cutting edge of his critical denunciation of doctrinal orthodoxy was applied to save bright young men for the service of the church. He detested creedalism because it threatened to cut the nerve of faith upon which

1. F. W. Schmidt, *Wilhelm Herrmann, Ein Bekenntnis zu seiner Theologie* (Tübingen: J. C. B. Mohr, 1922), p. 2.

the church itself was built. Furthermore, he does not come down to us pictured as a prophetic figure with the verve and power of Ernst Troeltsch. Like his fellow disciples of Albrecht Ritschl, Adolf Harnack, and Martin Rade, Herrmann was basically conservative in temperament.

Here is highlighted a basic tension in the theological world of Germany before and after the turn of the century. Albrecht Ritschl (1822–89), professor in Bonn and Göttingen, set the tone for theological work in the Protestant faculties during Imperial times. His training as an historian and Biblical critic under F. C. Baur inclined him to look at the details of the Christian tradition with less emphasis upon speculative or systematic schemes of interpretation. He became convinced that the true heritage of Luther had been obscured by Pietism in the Lutheran church and that this was consistent with tendencies which had manifested themselves often in the church and led to Roman Catholic errors. He also saw the peculiar power of the Christian religion to derive from Jesus' sense of vocation and the influence this had on the community of his followers. They were turned from the values of the world to values of love in the realm where the world was forever conquered—the kingdom of God.

Ritschl's own influence is to be seen in the awareness of scientific standards for theology. Harnack and the amazing production of scholarly works he accounted for can be seen as the legitimate outgrowth of Ritschl's teaching. Those about Harnack pointed with pride to his appointment as head of the Royal Library and noted with satisfaction that it was he who was instrumental in the founding of the first of the modern research institutes, the Kaiser Wilhelms Gesellschaft. Martin Rade, editor of the famous periodical *Die Christliche Welt,* always conceived this journal as one of articulate criticism within the church, above the party strife and loyal only to scientific ideals. In tune with this was Ritschl's own quest for the essence of Reformation faith taken up as the search for one's true Protestant heritage.

However, the full implications of the scientific enterprise were not always clear to the Ritschlians. To raise critical historical questions is to expand horizons. And as the horizons are expanded the terrain is seen in new proportions and new perspectives. Thus to ask questions about the nature of the Christian tradition and the Protestant heritage in the realm of historical research is to find eventually that the context in which these questions are placed has changed. It may well be that the one who has asked the questions in the first place finds himself questioned in the process. Furthermore, the questioning process may necessitate attitudes and actions which are political and social in character. Thus he may find himself drawn into a drama of controversy the outcome of which is by no means secure.

It remains a fact that Herrmann did not enter the arena of social and political struggle, that Harnack remained a confidant of the Kaiser, and that Rade suffered with the inability of *Die Christliche Welt,* and the association of friends which was organized about it, to keep out of narrower ecclesiastical politics and broader state and national affairs. Also the movement of religious socialism looks now to have been much more provincial than its leaders then could understand.

In the world of theological scholarship the *Religionsgeschichtliche Schule* worked at expanding the horizons of those who asked about the essence of Christianity and the heritage of Protestantism. The traditions of the Bible were seen in comparison with the surrounding religious world of the ancient Near East. Beyond this the whole question of the cultural relativity in religious life was posed. Troeltsch as the systematic advocate of the school began with historical researches to open up the complexity of

Protestantism, to highlight its close relationship to the medieval Catholicism, and to wrestle with the fact that religious community, as this is inseparably part of Christianity, means social doctrines and social attitudes themselves historically conditioned.

Troeltsch was led beyond this to assess the normative questions implied in the Ritschlian method. What is implied in the particular focus upon this particular tradition about its absoluteness and its priority in the history of men? Indeed what is implied in historical research itself about normative judgments and what leads one out of the relativity of historical events to some sort of transcendent position of evaluation? In addition Troeltsch had a keen sense of the cultural dissolution threatening his own world and the challenges to the social order of Germany and the provinciality of Europe in the modern age. That he found no solution to these problems reduced in no way their relevance.

The Burden of Herrmann's Theology

Herrmann, instead of looking to the broader dimensions of world history and cultural relativism, focused upon the real significance of the Ritschlian method for distinctively Christian theology. His work took the form of polemic first against orthodoxy which he saw to compromise the very faith it sought to defend but second and most importantly against rationalism which he saw only to perpetuate orthodoxy's errors in the name of enlightenment. The center of his attack was upon metaphysics, and recent research has shown that it was indeed Herrmann who taught Ritschl in his later years to direct his guns also against metaphysics.[2] Thus it was Herrmann who was

2. Hermann Timm, *Theorie und Praxis in der Theologie Albrecht Ritschls und Wilhelm Herrmanns* (Gütersloh: Gerd Mohn, 1967), p. 98, n. 12.

specifically responsible for a distinguishing characteristic of the Ritschlian school as it has been remembered.

The two forms of Herrmann's polemic, however, are not to be seen as operating on the same level. The attack on orthodoxy was a lifelong battle—one which did not end with Herrmann's death. It was fought in the particular setting of theological education in Germany and has about it the personal character of specific historical events. The theologians who are involved in this struggle with him can in certain measure be seen as the spokesmen for ecclesiastical interests in the university. The students who heard Herrmann's side of the story did so in the context of their own vocational training to be servants of the church. Thus the issue of faith was seen from the side of faith's concrete expression in the life of the community of faith—specifically the *Landeskirchen* of Germany.

In his attack upon rationalism Herrmann drew the issue of faith into connection with the intellectual tradition of formalized theology as this has come to be practiced in the universities of Western culture. Thus the clear distinction Herrmann saw between faith and the exercise of metaphysics had to be drawn before the analysis of faith could be correctly made and the proper intellectual responsibility for faith assumed. His first major book which brought him to his professorial chair is addressed to this problem. It is called *Religion in Relationship to Knowledge of the World and to Morality*,[3] and it is subtitled "A Foundation for Systematic Theology."

In substance this book is a detailed treatment of Immanuel Kant's thought with interest in showing that the impulse to religion comes from man's practical reason as

3. *Die Religion im Verhältnis zum Welterkennen und zur Sittlichkeit* (Halle: Max Niemeyer, 1879).

he seeks concretely to manage his life in the world.[4] Although the exercise of pure reason draws man into levels of greater abstraction, the practical reason disciplines him to specific actions in specific situations. To secure the validity of judgments made by the practical reason recourse is often taken to universal schemes of understanding in which is rooted a scheme of universal validity. Such is the path to classical metaphysics. But this involves a fundamental misunderstanding of the reasoning process by which one arrives at specific judgments. The service of Kant has been to distinguish between pure reason which opens up ever new configurations of concepts for comprehending experience and practical reason which relates comprehension to human willing. Therewith is the problem of universal validity no longer seen as one to be settled by pure reason; it can only be settled in an inquiry which examines carefully the nature of willing and thus the process of action.

Kant himself was thus led to a metaphysic of morals. Herrmann chose to see this and its ancillary interpretation of religion as the last bastion of the very rationalism Kant had sought to destroy in his critical philosophy. For it looked upon human willing and action too abstractly seeking a rational solution for an historical problem. In the context of Herrmann's own thought a basically Kantian stance needed to be supported by further explication of the exercise of human willing in the course of history. Thus he can be seen moving more and more out of the school of neo-Kantians represented in Marburg by the philosophers Hermann Cohen and Paul Natorp into fellow traveling with

4. A full discussion of this work and its place in Herrmann's thought can be found in Peter Fischer-Appelt, *Metaphysik im Horizont der Theologie Wilhelm Herrmanns* (Munich: Chr. Kaiser, 1965). The same author has a shorter essay written as the introduction to his edition of some of Herrmann's essays: *Schriften zur Grundlegung der Theologie* (Munich: Chr. Kaiser, 1966), Part I, pp. xv-li.

the philosophers of life—notably Bergson and Dilthey.[5]
From them he draws terms which make it possible to
articulate his own notion of human action in history. This
involves self-realization as one is drawn to moral responsibility by the men one meets. In this context the whole
question of universal validity takes on rather different
colors.

It is drawn into connection with religion where the
fundamental commitments of one's life manifest themselves
in concrete expression. Metaphysics thus is not the way
to religion but the way out of it. It is an ersatz solution
in which the real difficulty of the problem of universality
is avoided. For this problem is a specific moral problem
faced by specific men in specific situations in such a way
as to define their specific self-expression.

These themes are fully expressed in the last of Herrmann's major works, his *Ethics*.[6] Here he argues that
ethics may not properly be divided into philosophical and
theological ethics. Moral action is so closely tied up with
the nature of religion that it may not be discussed without
reflecting upon why one is drawn to faith and precisely
how one exists historically. By the same token the question
of ethics arises in classical Greek culture with the Sophists
and their famous critics, and no discussion of ethics in the
context of theology can ignore the roots of the problem
itself. It is precisely as man reflects upon the question of
whether he ought to be something different from what
custom dictates that he searches for a point of reference
from which to judge his actions. And the answer to this
search in the idea of the good (Plato) or in the doctrine of

5. A thorough outline of the various ways Herrmann argued this
point may be found in Theodor Mahlmann, "Das Axiom des
Erlebnisses bei Wilhelm Herrmann," *Neue Zeitschrift für systematische Theologie* 4 (1962): 11-88.

6. *Ethik*, 6th ed. (Tübingen: J. C. B. Mohr, 1921). The first edition appeared in 1901.

nature (Aristotle) determines fundamentally the course of philosophy. Implied in this analysis, but not drawn out by Herrmann, is the claim that metaphysics is not central to the philosophical task but only one attempt to solve the question of ethics, and a mistaken one at that. It is in religion that the question of ethics finds its answer; not in religion conceived as doctrine but in the experience of faith.

Faith is the central notion in Herrmann's theology. And there is an irony to this. For it is the notion of faith which has been pressed into service to defend a theological tradition in which the Christian gospel is interwoven with the very metaphysics Herrmann criticizes. Classical Christian theology deriving from the Alexandrian fathers and influential in Western Christianity through the work of Augustine is an amalgam of Judaeo-Christian symbols and the broad Platonism of the Hellenistic world. The many varieties within classical Christian theology are known to any student of the history of doctrine, but common to them all is the idea that truth disclosed in the specific events of Hebraic history culminating in the life, death, and resurrection of Jesus of Nazareth is truth fundamentally constitutive to the world. Access to this truth may or may not involve the independent exercise of human reason, but it must involve a fundamental commitment to the traditions of Judaeo-Christian history and the institutions which formulate them and also keep them alive. None of the truly great theologians saw this commitment apart from a basic change in the man's life who made it, a change akin to the repentance Jesus himself had called for. Faith, *credo,* and human perfection were intertwined.[7]

7. The whole burden of Herrmann's thought in relation to classical Christian theology is argued in detail in my book, *The Shape of the Theological Task* (Philadelphia: Westminster, 1968).

Herrmann in speaking of faith is responding in certain measure to a sham form of this classical theology represented by latter-day Protestant confessionalism. The irony of his focusing upon faith was that he took the most cherished weapon of the orthodox of his day and turned it upon them. Yes, faith is indeed the point, he could say to those who sought to stem the tide of modern critical thought, but it must be correctly understood. And when it is, one will see that modern critical thought is not to be feared but to be welcomed.

Of course, it was not irony alone which motivated Herrmann. By using the concept of faith he moved from the level of his attack upon orthodoxy to the level on which he met rationalism. For it is faith which most clearly captures the experience of the Christian, and the choice of this conception to denote this experience despite its later fate was almost demanded.

With these observations we have arrived at the second of Herrmann's three major works, the one which is here reprinted. And in trying to bring out its importance in Herrmann's thought and for continuing theological labor, we must reflect upon the fact that it appears now in a series devoted to classical lives of Jesus. A cursory reading is not even necessary to see that this is in no way a life of Jesus as one might expect. Not only is but a bit of it concerned with the question of the historical Jesus; there is also a most brief set of references to the kind of scholarly literature that is relevant. Nevertheless it appears in this series not just by the capriciousness of the series editor. It is, from Herrmann's standpoint, extremely appropriate.

Herrmann knew that the question of the nature of the Christian religion could not be answered without specific concern with the sources of that religion. And yet he also knew that no one could come to terms with these sources who had not carefully laid down the boundaries within which it is possible to understand religion. Thus Herrmann's contribution to the study of the life of Jesus stands between his other two major works. The implications of his critique of metaphysics as well as his idea of ethics as the problem of how one is called to self-realization over against the customary demands of his environment must both be kept in mind as the reader turns to Jesus. By the same token it is in looking at the figure of Jesus that the ethical question receives its answer and the metaphysical quest can be abandoned.

So Herrmann avoided writing a story of the life of Jesus. He wrote instead a book defending Ritschl against certain of his detractors. Although the polemical tone of the book is softened in its later editions—including the one from which this translation was made—and although Herrmann's attitude toward Ritschl became more independent and critical,[8] the basic intention remains the same. The historical Jesus had always been the locus of the Christian religion for Ritschl and it remained so for Herrmann. What

8. The extent to which Herrmann was "estranged" from Ritschl is at issue when James M. Robinson argues that the extensive changes between the first edition of this book in 1886 and the second edition in 1892 reflect Herrmann's disenchantment with his former teacher and his increasing involvement with Schleiermacher. For this point of view Robinson is in part dependent upon Otto Ritschl's biography of his father. Cf. James M. Robinson, *Das Problem des Heiligen Geistes bei Wilhelm Herrmann* (Marburg: K. Gleiser, 1952), p. 16. This is found confirmed in Herrmann's work of 1906 entitled *Christlich-protestantische Dogmatik* in the famous series *Kultur der Gegenwart*. Robinson says, "The estrangement from Ritschl reached its high point in the *Christlich-protestantische Dogmatik* (1906), in which Ritschl's positive theological performance is not considered at all and Schleiermacher rules the field completely." This is not quite accurate in light of that section in Herrmann's essay "Die Lage und Aufgabe der evangelischen Dogmatik in der Gegenwart" published in 1907 where Ritschl's distinct contribution in supplementing Schleiermacher's insights is discussed. Cf. *Schriften zur Grundlegung der Theologie*, I:20-24. I would look upon Herrmann's development as reflecting his refining his theological position and making more discriminating judgments of his intellectual forebearers.

this entails for the theologian is an historical exercise: returning to Jesus to find out exactly what he signifies. So might one suspect that it was the historical Jesus related through the story of his life which was primary. And so thought those critics of Ritschl who, fearing historical criticism and its destructive work, tried to turn instead to the regenerated Christian or to the religious man in general and with psychological and descriptive tools lay the basis for theological insight.[9] Not only is this a barren path founded on a fundamental mistaking of the Christian religion, thought Herrmann, this is also a gross misunderstanding of the implications of Ritschlian theology.

It is not the story of Jesus' life to which the theologian returns but his redeeming and reconciling action by which men are moved to call him Lord. From this perspective the way one turns to look at Jesus is closely bound up with what one will finally see. Or as Herrmann might also have phrased it: to look at the Jesus of history requires real awareness of what it means to be historical. One finds this out when he is called to faith.

This point can be most closely seen when one takes seriously the subtitle of this book. For it is to Luther that Herrmann turns in order to develop his point of view, and it is statements of Luther copiously collected which give shape to the book itself. Luther had insisted upon the fundamental importance of justification by faith because he understood so clearly from his own experience the centrality of faith in the Christian religion. His attack upon the Roman Catholic church from which he finally retained so much in the way of doctrine and cultural outlook came

9. When this book was first written the critics of Ritschl who seemed most in Herrmann's mind were F. H. R. Frank of Erlangen, R. A. Lipsius of Jena, and C. E. Luthardt of Leipzig. These men were quite different in character and intellectual interest. For Herrmann they had in common a misunderstanding of faith.

precisely because faith was at stake. Herrmann argues that it still is, for the Protestant church even though it loyally mouths the assertion that faith and not works justifies man has in fact betrayed Luther's insight long since.

The forces which Luther battled against in articulating his doctrine of justification derive from a fundamental mistake in interpreting the Christian religion. This mistake may perhaps be a result of the fact that the Neo-Platonic tradition became so important in early Christianity. But that is only an occasion for the expression of the basic misunderstanding of religion which Herrmann labels mysticism. The Roman Catholic church whose piety is really mystical is thus an occasion for its institutional expression and the doctrinal orthodoxy which reenforces it. Mysticism is the drive for unity with God—direct unity in connection with which the means to this unity finally become irrelevant and are cast aside. Luther's emphasis upon justification by faith, however, demands that the means by which one comes to faith never become irrelevant and are never cast aside.

The force of this argument can be clearly seen, I think, when we reflect upon the two basic flaws in mysticism as Herrmann conceived it. The first involves a basic misunderstanding of human life. Unity with God which one may experience inwardly as contemplation or ecstasy detaches him finally from the totally historical character of human existence. Although Herrmann does not do so, one might, I believe, focus upon the highly dialectical nature of the language of a mystic such as St. John of the Cross as evidence of the basically ahistorical character of mystical piety. When the midnight of the soul is in fact its moment of illumination, then ordinary language by which men manage historical events has really been negated (or perhaps *aufgehoben*). In fact, however, human life is historical coming-to-be in the context of other men and the natural conditions which surround us. Like Marx, Darwin, and Nietzsche, Herrmann chose to face this fact squarely and not to try to negate it in mystical transcendence. His Kantian understanding helped him see that mysticism could be supported by metaphysical speculation, and he found it no accident that classical orthodoxy and Neo-Platonic mystical forms go together.

Historical life, where personal centers of consciousness take shape as men interact with one another in specific places and moments of time, is where we live and is that of which we must take account. To do less is to open the doors to intellectual dishonesty, to say nothing of moral laxity. Precisely such dishonesty has accompanied the orthodox tradition with its mystical piety. In the present day it is especially manifest in those who would try to neglect the very tool which human historical life has forged for its own self-understanding: historical-critical research. So do the orthodox misuse the possibilities of their own historical moment when they try to defend ancient traditions and secure them by demanding subscription to them in faith.

Furthermore, this basic misunderstanding of human life in its historical character is reflected in the way the figure of Jesus has appeared in classical theology. He is not the one who lived in the Judaism of the Roman Empire having fellowship with his disciples and preaching the coming of the kingdom of God. He is an idealized form of the perfect man through whom the pious in contemplation or devotion may reach beyond for unity with God. When such unity is reached, he is really no longer necessary and can be discarded. Luther who found himself captivated by Christ calls such procedure fundamentally in question. Through him we, who live in an age where intelligent people are just not willing to overlook the problems caused by traditional material, may have some help in understanding faith. And as a first step we must discard mystical piety.

Perhaps the second flaw in mysticism is even more deadly. For it is really a misunderstanding of what is meant by the term God. And here Herrmann modulates richly on the themes of Paul and Luther. God is only appropriately spoken of as one who is spoken to. The word "God" is a personal name used by one personal being in response to another. Thus it is only available to one who has been called to full personal being himself. For man this not only involves his historicity; it brings him into full historical existence. On the one hand, it happens only in the concrete context of human community at particular moments and in particular places. On the other hand, one senses the full concreteness of moments of human life only when the interaction of persons makes him aware of the uniqueness and mystery found in other consciousnesses and calls him to full possession of his own inner life. The mystery of personal encounter is necessary for the appropriate use of the word God, because it is the necessary condition for one's perception that he is fully dependent upon another in order to be truly himself.

It can be seen immediately that the use made of the figure of Jesus in mysticism leads finally not to God himself but to an ersatz God feebly supported by metaphysical speculation. Jesus in his own personal being, precisely as the historical character he indeed was, stands at the center of the Christian religion and when he is pushed to the side, there is no God and use of the term is deceptive. Put another way: if God is not the gracious personal redeemer revealed in, with, and under the figure of Jesus, then he is not.

The centrality of the figure of Jesus in understanding the meaning of God is one facet of the Pauline and Lutheran scheme which Herrmann represents. The rest is in large measure included. For the grace of God brings one to faith, and in the experience of faith one finds freedom.

Faith is that wonderful trust in the possibilities of the present moment seen now as the encounter with a being whose purposes are even loftier than our own and who meets us as we are called to full personhood ourselves. In this event he is a personal creator and would be betrayed were we to leave behind the precise historical context in which the encounter takes place. God fades into the ghostly realm of images and abstractions the moment one seeks to escape the concreteness of his own selfhood and the larger context in which the experience of self-possession takes place. Whether this might happen in contemplation, prayer, or theological system-building makes little difference.

The particular historical context of God's gracious reconciliation with man includes Jesus of Nazareth whose inner life founded the community of faith and the living continuity of this community through time which is the body of Christ. So it is that Herrmann insists that no one can really come to the figure of Jesus unless he be called to faith by men of faith. In the community of Christians the inner life of Jesus is realized. God is a living God, and men of faith are living through time and in space. Faith is active in love.

It was this living God to whom Luther was trying to do justice in his doctrine of justification by faith—the living God who is active in his grace where the Word is preached and where faith issues forth in love. Although Luther's insight took the form of a polemic against good works and did not realize itself in a theological construction which was thorough enough to analyze the historicity of human life and the interpenetration of God's personal nature and man's personal self-realization, his understanding of faith and his resistance to Roman Catholic mystical piety preserved the true Pauline and Biblical traditions. He sensed as have few others the relationship of deity, grace, trust, freedom, new life, the nature of Christian community, and the centrality of the figure of Jesus.

To return to Luther for the equipment necessary to see the place of Jesus in Christian faith is beneficial. For the Protestant and the Ritschlian, it is also necessary to re-capture Luther's insights from a church which has recon-structed classical orthodoxy on Protestant soil and fallen into the flaws of mysticism no matter whether this be expressed in conservative or liberal theological forms. In the process he can admit that in Luther's day the times were not ripe for a full understanding of the implications of his insights and that only with the tools of modern critical science can they be fully worked out. This Ritschl sought to do in asking on the one hand about the histori-cal heritage of Luther and on the other hand by trying to reconstruct the doctrines of justification and reconciliation. In the middle he placed the figure of Jesus and the com-munity of faith. They must remain in the middle thought Herrmann without either one absorbing the other.

So it is that Herrmann's book on the life of Jesus is a book in defense of Ritschl based upon the texts of Luther. For the figure of Jesus is only available in its true form to the man of faith who has been called to faith in the context of human community. But what does he find when he looks at Jesus with the proper equipment? This is the question which remains for Herrmann to answer. And he tries to do so.

One sees in the picture of Jesus something which any honest searcher can find. He finds a man who living in the context of Judaism claims to be the Messiah. Perhaps with more sensitivity than the merely interested observer he sees that Jesus does not use this claim for self-aggrandize-ment or self-righteousness but combines it with humility and a demand for self-giving love. Thus he comes into conflict with the vision of the kingdom of God which pious

Jewry cherished and the terms of this conflict leading to his death make clear the moral power of his personality. Like many others, he is hardened to the woes which history has put upon him, but he is master over them in creating history.

However, this is as yet only the external aspect of the picture of Jesus and without the internal power of his personality it would make him merely a prototype for human self-realization. As such he would be the means to an end and not the ever-present source of grace which one experiences in faith. The internal power of Jesus' personality derives from the completion of his historical role in his death. And as he articulated this to his disciples he was able to see in its horror not a moment of testing or an ordeal to be courageously faced but precisely the redemption of all men. By virtue of this men call him sinless, for the love of fellow men was so central to his own understanding of his historical role that he could only look at his death to see what indeed it would accomplish for others. His own ideals were not beyond his own accomplishment. He was an embodiment of them.

It is this unique sinlessness which fixes Jesus forever in the Christian tradition and its faith. Though we may find our own failings glaringly revealed in our contact with ordinary men, this is not by virtue of their perfection. Precisely the personal trust and responsibility we feel in genuine encounter with others may form the standards by which we judge their inadequacies. In encounter with Jesus and his inner life, however, we are aware of his personal perfection and call him Lord. The Christian community as it preaches Jesus lives by his inner life in the picture which the New Testament brings to it and in its compelling presence in its midst.

In faith one need not have fear of historical-critical research into the figure of Jesus. This is not because nothing can be found, but it is because one must hope that much will be found out about Jesus that will show him even more to be a child of his times. The narratives of miracles will be revealed as appropriate only to the earliest community and as means to articulate the real "miracle" of Jesus, his redeeming power. By the same token, historical research disarms the sayings of Jesus of their law-giving significance in the realm of ethics.[10] They are no longer seen as universal judgments to be lifted out of the context of his eschatological expectations into relevance for the experiences of the modern world. With the aid of historical-critical research all aspects of Jesus' life can be seen as meaningful in faith only as a reflection of his inner life from which faith derives. Thus can the full dimensions of historical responsibility be opened for us who live in times which are radically different.

The fact of Jesus the man of Nazareth is of prime importance. This fact, however, is an interplay between the circumstances of the first century in which Jesus lived and the consequence of his interacting with these circumstances. And this interplay is seen in its fullness only when the experience of a man today opens him to perceive its dimensions. For this reason, when Herrmann speaks so forcefully about the fact upon which faith is grounded, he combines this with terms like "the personality of Jesus," his "person," and the "figure" (*Bild*) of Jesus. Striking on the one hand at the psychologizing of religion he saw involved in the enterprise of certain of Ritschl's critics, he yet, on the other hand, participated in the growing concern for discerning how experience (*Erlebnis*) is entailed in historical understanding.[11]

Thus the figure of Jesus, or portrait, depending on how

10. *Schriften zur Grundlegung der Theologie*, I:217-20.
11. Cf. Mahlmann, *op. cit.*

one translates the very important word *Bild,* is significant as it brings impulses to faith today from the life of Jesus ages ago. At this point, however, Herrmann runs into certain difficulties illustrated clearly by his debate with Martin Kähler.[12] It was Kähler who had reflected upon the fact that many who pursued the historical Jesus in order to find the basis for their religion overlooked the very character of the sources they had to examine to fulfill their quest. These sources, the New Testament, had as their intention the proclamation of Christ. For this reason they retained only those remembrances and only those events which suited their purposes. Not only are the gaps left too many to give the quester after the historical Jesus sufficient material, but the material which remains is thoroughly stamped by the kerygmatic intentions of the gospel writers. The historical Jesus is in fact only to be found as the Biblical Christ.

What Kähler wished to do was to justify in certain measure the suspicion of both traditional and uneducated Christians that the exponents of radical criticism in the theological world were setting up intellectual criteria for faith which in fact limited its scope. Did one have to equip himself with all of the techniques of modern historical-critical research to come to faith? Were all the dogmas of

12. The second edition of Kähler's *Der sogenannte historische Jesus und der geschichtliche, biblische Christus* (Leipzig: A Deichert, 1896) contains a long argument with Herrmann. This was stimulated by Herrmann's comments on the first edition published in 1892 in "Der geschichtliche Christus der Grund unseres Glaubens," *Zeitschrift für Theologie und Kirche,* 2 (1892): 232-73. This is now to be found in Herrmann's *Gesammelte Aufsätze* (Tübingen: J. C. B. Mohr, 1923), pp. 295-335, and in *Schriften zur Grundlegung der Theologie,* Part I, pp. 149-185. Some comments are also found in *The Communion.* Kähler eliminated the sections of his book devoted to the argument with Herrmann from its later editions, one of which has been translated into English by Carl E. Braaten as *The So-Called Historical Jesus and the Historic, Biblical Christ* (Philadelphia: Fortress, 1964).

the past only available to the one who could see their truth in the context in which they arose? And the answer to these questions was "no." Although Kähler in no way appealed to the authority of the ancient traditions of the church for their sake alone, he did wish to make the point that what these traditions expressed was in fact true.

The emphasis upon the work of Jesus as Son of God was a direct outcome of the fact that his life and death effected salvation. The earliest disciples who basically shaped the kerygma of the church were not really interested in reflecting upon the person of Jesus apart from this total work he accomplished. They ignored the years of childhood because they were irrelevant. What dominated their view was the resurrection, and Jesus' messiahship is meaningless to them except as he is the one who has been raised.[13] Even the modern critic must admit that both the gospel literature and the epistles of Paul are dominated by the event of the resurrection.

Furthermore, the resurrection as the manifestation of God's power and redemption in Jesus gives a unity to all of the Biblical material. Now as always the church must look to the witness of the earliest disciples for one Word of God. This need not obscure the fact that this witness is diverse and various. Such a fact has been known from the beginning. But precisely in its diversity, this witness speaks the saving Word which one must hear not only as he is accustomed or as it is most comfortable for him but as it is spoken by God the Lord.[14] Christian orthodoxy is correct in its suspicions that reduction of the Biblical kerygma by means of historical critical tools destroys its character as the Word of God, even though the means for expressing these suspicions in a doctrine of verbal inspiration is an error as well.

13. Kähler, *op. cit.*, pp. 103 ff.
14. Ibid., pp. 198-99.

Herrmann's picture of Christ, thought Kähler, is merely a capricious reduction based not upon an understanding of the nature of the Bible but upon dogmatic presuppositions. His choice of messianic consciousness in Jesus as a means for interpreting his death is really backward. One must begin with the kerygma of the resurrected one and from it understand his death and messiahship. It is further capricious to assume that the traditional picture of Jesus which has been prominent in the church for centuries can be set aside in the modern world without reflecting upon its normative significance for Christianity from the beginning. Better would be the way of those in modern theology who speak of *Heilsgeschichte*.[15] This allows one to use historical-critical tools but forces him to see Jesus in the context of a history which begins with God's gracious action in Israel and continues through his gracious action in the present day preaching of the church.

More is at stake here, thought Kähler, than just the issue of Jesus and his historical life. The fundamental character of salvation is threatened in Herrmann's thought. The power of God's grace is seen in his redeeming action. If this power is to be experienced only in the overpowering influence of Jesus' inner life which comes from the Biblical picture, then it is really not secured against a fundamental scepticism and resignation in the world.[16]

Kähler finds it open to subjectivism and weak idealism. The real power of the kerygma of the church is precisely what it proclaims: God's redeeming action in raising Jesus from the dead. Or, as Kähler puts it using two terms special to Herrmann: the ground of faith is its content.[17]

It is clear that Herrmann can respond to Kähler on the issue of the power of God's grace. For he chose to distin-

15. Ibid., p. 184.
16. Ibid., pp. 166, 185.
17. Ibid., p. 171.

guish between the ground and content of faith in the interest of showing that faith must be the personal experience of every man drawn into the power of Jesus as Christ. Jesus is the ground of faith as the one from whom the community of faith arose. And he continues as its Lord by virtue of the fact that the community returns to its source or ground for the preservation and renewal of its life. But the content of faith varies from Christian to Christian as the impact of the inner life of Jesus alive in the community is felt in a variety of historical moments. To obscure this distinction is to misunderstand the full dimensions of faith and to cut the tie between religious experience and moral action which Herrmann found so crucial.

At the basis of this difference between these two lies a different understanding of history. Herrmann sees history not only as the medium within which one lives but as the setting for his own moral action. Thus historical-criticism is not the servant of an historical metaphysics which tries to bring the historical process under a unified vision but the product of a heightened moral conscience. So is Herrmann not impressed with the fact that Christians through the centuries have been, and that simple pious men today still are, traditionalists. Surely it is possible to be morally sensitive in traditionalist culture, but it is morally insensitive to try to superimpose traditionalism on an age where it is fundamentally questioned. This is precisely what he finds Kähler doing,[18] even though Kähler is not afraid of historical-critical labor itself and is fully adept at taking part in it.

Grace in history is effective precisely in the more acute way that historicity is experienced. Its power is found in the increase in human freedom which comes in faith. There is no decline in the importance of grace when one

18. Herrmann, *Schriften*, I:162-71.

articulates it in terms of personal encounter. The man of faith knows that he is called outside of himself by one who is independent from him. Without this he would remain subject to the given of his life and not drawn to full consciousness and responsibility. Perhaps it is Kähler who has underrated the power of grace in bringing it too closely into connection with the message of the church and securing it against the vicissitudes of history by identifying its affects with a particular sequence of events.

Such an argument would take us far too much into Kähler than is here intended. However, we cannot leave him without indicating that his critique of Herrmann has scored important points and must be taken seriously. No one can deny that Herrmann's outline of the essential features in the picture of Jesus is open to question. Furthermore, the Ritschlian echoes are so distinct that one cannot help but acknowledge the validity in Kähler's suspicion that dogmatic and not critical concerns exercised considerable influence upon Herrmann. And aware as he was of the ramifications of the work of Johannes Weiss on the New Testament notion of the kingdom of God, Herrmann is vulnerable to the charge that his picture of Jesus is not really responsive to problems caused by scholarly research. This vulnerability increases if we move from Herrmann's day to our own and survey the way foundations he thought secure have been eroded. The pivotal points located in Jesus' messianic consciousness and his interpretation of his death to the disciples at the Last Supper must now be acknowledged as almost entirely insecure. Kähler is certainly correct in saying that the experiences of the post-resurrection community color entirely the presentation of the figure of Jesus in the New Testament. And Kähler's observations about the way the church has seen a unity to the Bible in the Word of God are historically accurate and worthy of serious consideration by the one who approaches the Bible as a segment of the church's tradition.

Herrmann's Legacy in Bultmannian and post-Bultmannian Theology

The debate between Kähler and Herrmann has continued into the present day. Not only has it been colored by the results of many specific works of New Testament research; it has also been affected by a quite different theological climate prevailing since World War I. Under the leadership of Barth the Biblical and classical theological traditions have been revived. Primary to this revival is the notion of the Word of God as God's own self-disclosure in Jesus, the Biblical witness, and the preaching of the church. No less significant has been the uncertainty European men experienced in twentieth-century history and the resonance which eschatological themes from the Bible and the Christian past have found. Since the recovery from World War II, the theme of secularization has come more and more to the fore as churchmen have found themselves increasingly in the flow of fast moving cultural streams. Thus the dimensions within which the question of the historical Jesus must be placed are now large enough to include the question of history itself and the knotty issue of how the obscure events of early Christian history are related to the unique claims for universality found in church proclamation.

In large measure the Herrmann-Kähler debate has been carried on within the Marburg school surrounding Rudolf Bultmann and most lately led by Ernst Fuchs and Gerhard Ebeling. Here the insights of Kähler have not been lost— as for example when the kerygma is seen as central to the New Testament and when Jesus is seen to be living as he is preached.[19] Moreover, the influence of Barth is consid-

19. Cf. Kähler, *op. cit.*, p. 194.

erable, evidenced in the fact that the Word and preaching have a basic significance in the thought of the Bultmannians which they did not have for Herrmann. However, whereas Barth deviates consciously from the intentions of his teacher,[20] Bultmann self-consciously attempts to salvage Herrmann's notion of faith. And it is the Herrmannian tradition which is carried forward by means of a theology of the Word. Thus radical Biblical criticism, rather than undermining the figure of Jesus upon which Herrmann depended, in fact continues precisely the line of attack he started. But it does so by assessing the proper significance of the New Testament seen as kerygma.

This can be clearly seen in Bultmann's book on Jesus.[21] Using merely the preaching of Jesus as an eschatological prophet—which is all that radical criticism allows—Bultmann notes that it is really the decisive character of this preaching made possible by the atmosphere of eschatological expectation in Judaism which vitalizes the Old Testament notion of God's will being the only source of human realization. It is only when one is called to face the imminent judgment of God that he is delivered from legalisms and abstractions made normative for human behaviour. In this deliverance he knows the meaning once again of the word "God." It comes to his lips as a personal word for he himself has faced decisively the question of his own existence and has found in the one who raised the question for him the presence of God.

The church which preaches the Word of God does so, however, not as Jesus did. It preaches the Word of the crucified one in the power of his resurrection. The end

20. See Barth's essay written on publication of Herrmann's lecture notes on *Dogmatik:* "The Principles of Dogmatics according to Wilhelm Herrmann," *Theology and Church,* trans. Louise Pettibone Smith (New York: Harper, 1962), pp. 238-71.

21. *Jesus and the Word,* trans. Louise Pettibone Smith and Erminie Huntress Lantero (New York: Charles Scribners', 1934).

which he announced as imminent has come. The decisive encounter with God is here. The kerygma of the church brings one to the moment of self-consciousness in faith which is both an awareness of sin and inadequacy and the experience of justifying grace.

Like Herrmann, Bultmann understands the experience of faith as the experience of freedom. The decisive character of the Word and the response it calls forth releases one from bondage to the world in which he finds himself placed. Just as the early Christians understood the arrival of the new age in Jesus to set them free from bondage to the evil forces of the old age, so does Bultmann understand faith as deliverance from the past into the radical freedom necessary to face the future. This leads him further into the whole program of demythologizing and into the realm of Heideggerian language.

Mythology is in fact the means in religious contexts for neutralizing the decisive transcendence of God which is experienced in moments of radical freedom. The questionable value of mythology in a world dominated by the outlook of modern society with its disinclination to look for transcendent causality only facilitates the theologian's attempt to take the Pauline and Johannine notions of faith seriously. Now we can cut through the mythological language which quite naturally in the Biblical era clothed the substance of the gospel. This includes the central event of the resurrection which can be rescued from all the attempts by means of quasi-historical language to give it a fundamentally mythological significance. For the resurrection is only an event to the man of faith; transcendence is only meaningful in faith. Or, as Bultmann likes to say he learned from Herrmann, he quotes Melanchthon that to know Christ is to know his benefits.

Bultmann's program of demythologizing as well as his understanding of faith are reenforced by the use of Heidegger's existential analysis. Not only does this help him to express the fact that man is bound to his world in being thrown into it and to see the experience of faith as one of realizing authentic existence in self-consciousness. It also provides a helpful tool for delimiting the use of the term God. The existential philosopher in the pattern of Heidegger has ruled out the recourse to God for explaining the predicament of human existence and the possibilities of human realization. His is the philosophical counterpart to demythologizing just as the classical metaphysical systems were the counterpart of the mythological world-view. Here Herrmann's polemic against metaphysics hears its echo.

In dealing with history Bultmann also reflects Herrmann's position. Thus he directs a polemic against a metaphysics of history which tries to neutralize the historical nature of faith by means of raising the historical moment into a unified system of understanding. Historicity is absorbed into history. In this polemic Bultmann draws heavily upon Dilthey and Collingwood. He does not wish, however, to be drawn into the neo-Hegelianism of Collingwood. To do so would be to neglect the moral imperative which stands at the base of historical experience and which is so starkly revealed in the claims the kerygma makes upon man.[22]

These claims must be defended at all costs for without them faith loses all reality and Jesus fades into the past as a character who may be of interest to the antiquarian but not particularly to the Christian. For, Bultmann argues, in the particular content of his life and message, there is nothing which distinguishes him in any significant measure from the prophetic tradition of Judaism or from the apocalyptic world in which he lived. The "what" of his life is not responsible for the decisive character of his

22. Bultmann, *The Presence of Eternity* (New York: Harper, 1957), p. 136.

lordship. It is the "that" of his life, its eschatological importance, recognized only in faith and present in the early church only as the message of the risen lord which has religious significance.[23]

Thus, although Bultmann would not speak as Kähler did of the "so-called historical Jesus" and mean by it the figure which the Biblical critic hopes to find in the Bible and never will because the Bible does not present him, he is equally despairing of a quest for this historical Jesus. This is on the one hand because of the scarcity of the material on which to build a picture, although in principle there is no reason not to try.[24] But on the other hand, and for far more important reasons, this is not a legitimate *theological* quest. It seeks to neutralize by historical knowledge the decisive meaning of an eschatological kerygma for man's historicity.

Here we find again the relationship between faith and the Biblical picture of Jesus present in Herrmann's thought. But there are some important differences. Not only has Bultmann tried to react to the way the figure of Jesus in the New Testament has been enveloped in the eschatological preaching of the church. He has also cut the fundamental connection between Jesus' messianic self-consciousness and the experience of faith which Herrmann thought so important. This particular "what" of Jesus' life was not separated for Herrmann from the "that" of his decisive significance. True, the way he connected them is now open to question—speaking generously!

Ernst Fuchs, successor of Bultmann in Marburg, has, to-

23. *Das Verhaeltnis der urchristlichen Christusbotschaft zum historischen Jesus* (Heidelberg: Carl Winter, Universitätsverlag, 1965), p. 9; Eng. trans. in Carl E. Braaten and Roy A. Harrisville (eds.), *The Historical Jesus and the Kerygmatic Christ* (Nashville: Abingdon, 1964), p. 20.

24. Cf. Schubert M. Ogden, "Bultmann and the 'New Quest,'" *Journal of Bible and Religion* 30 (1962) : 209-18.

gether with Gerhard Ebeling, tried to take up again this question of continuity between the kerygma of the church and Jesus of Nazareth. By Fuchs' own testimony his work grew out of discomfort with Bultmann's conception of the Word.[25] For he saw the kerygmatic call to decision rooted firmly in the particular historicity of Jesus.[26] Agreeing with Bultmann that Jesus did not conceive himself to be the Messiah, Fuchs yet argues that the baptism of Jesus by John the Baptist and the subsequent death of the Baptist placed Jesus in a specific position in the eschatological drama. This place is also clearly seen in the parabolic speech so characteristic of the preaching of Jesus preserved in the gospel sources. Here Jesus steps forth as the representative of God with a peculiar immediacy appropriate to the impending final events.

Fuchs wishes not to be understood as raising psychological questions about Jesus' attitudes toward his own times and his role in them. Rather is it Jesus' understanding of time which is the key to his real historical significance and it also unlocks the secret of his place in the New Testament and the preaching of the church. For he answered obediently the demands of the moment and thus brought to speech once and for all the intimate connection between temporality and human existence, i.e., the historical character of all human life. To forget the specific and concrete circumstances in which this took place is to miss the full import of history itself. For time is not a general term indicating process and movement. It is rather the experience of facing a particular present in relationship to a particular past and future. In his setting Jesus experienced

25. *Glaube und Erfahrung* (Tübingen: J. C. B. Mohr, 1965), p. 407.

26. Ernst Fuchs, "Die Frage nach dem historischen Jesus," *Zeitschrift für Theologie und Kirche* 53 (1956): 210-29; Eng. trans. in Ernst Fuchs, *Studies of the Historical Jesus* (Naperville, Ill.: Alec R. Allenson, 1964), pp. 11-31.

the present as the presence of God and in his preaching God was present in his Word. The kerygmatic nature of the New Testament is in direct continuity with the historical Jesus. So also is preaching whenever it takes place; not by virtue of repetition or imitation but by virtue of the address of God which takes claim upon a man in the experience of his historicity.

Here Fuchs is careful not to presume that the historical process has left unchanged the notion of God prevailing in New Testament times nor to forget that man in the present day is called to decision in terms appropriate to his world. Thus he seconds Bultmann's program of demythologizing, emphasizing that the language which pictures man in bondage to powers of the cosmos and delivered from them by a redeemer is significant only as it brings the man who hears it to understand his bondage to sin in the past in light of the future opened to him. This is a future of love as he himself brings to speech new possibilities for others. In being addressed they are brought to hope and trust in God who withdraws himself from the past and is present as he calls from the future.

Thus it is the very nature of divinity and the character of faith as this arises in man's historicity which plunges Fuchs into speech about language (Sprache). He agrees with Herrmann that faith has no content apart from the experience of the man of faith. He is worried, however, that this experience will be robbed of its constitutive power when the phenomenon of the text is removed or not sufficiently justified theologically. For it is this phenomenon and the job of explicating the text in preaching which preserves the structure of grace so necessary to faith. And theology is in fact hermeneutic—the science of interpreting the text. For speech and language are not really the product of human culture but the precondition for human existence. They open up the possibilities of transcendence in the midst of existing things. It is in bringing the world to speech that the distinctively human manifests itself in history. But this does not arise out of the world itself. It happens as one is addressed—as he is himself called to the event of speech. Here he knows God as creator and redeemer.

There are several sides to Fuchs' theological enterprise. In part it may be seen as deeply involved in what James M. Robinson has termed "the new quest of the historical Jesus."[27] In this context, Fuchs marches with such as Ernst Käsemann and Günther Bornkamm outside of the boundaries seemingly laid down by Bultmann's work. The "what" of Jesus' life and preaching is reintroduced into the "that" of his eschatological role in the kerygma. And since Bultmann and his pupils are professional New Testament exegetes, this has stimulated a spirited debate over texts and interpretations.[28] It has also brought to bear upon examination of the figure of Jesus Heidegger's idea of understanding (*Verstehen*). The concern of this endeavor is to find a tool for showing that, although Jesus' life is intimately bound up with the first-century world in which he lived, and although access to specific events of his life is difficult by virtue of the New Testament sources, nevertheless his "understanding of existence" (Robinson) forms the continuity between now and then. Trying thereby to express what Herrmann meant by the "inner life of Jesus" the "new questers" capitalize on the complexity of understanding as Heidegger conceives this. For it is part of his attempt to break through the whole tradition of Western philosophy to the fundamental language character of human existence. Its complexity lies in the fact that Heidegger

27. James M. Robinson, *The New Quest of the Historical Jesus* (Naperville, Ill.: Alec R. Allenson, 1959).

28. Much of this debate is represented in Braaten and Harrisville, *op. cit.*

is trying so to relate the content, the form, and the occasion for human expression and thought that they may never be "thought" or "said" to be separate.

The upshot of this manner of proceeding is that the very tool which was to help in the job may turn out to be so complicated to operate that the job does not get done. For in the very idea of "understanding" the problem of history is included. Applied to an historical character the idea may reintroduce the difficulties which one is trying to sort out. Thus it seems wise, in the context of Herrmann's heritage to focus upon the broader issue at stake in Fuchs' work—the nature of faith and its relationship to theology.

It is at this point that Gerhard Ebeling takes up the argument. Bultmann, in responding to the "new questers," had agreed that the issue of historical continuity was relevant and perhaps even interesting. However, the role Jesus plays in the kerygma of the church following the decisive events of his cross and resurrection involves a material discontinuity extremely relevant to the theologian who, in the style of Herrmann, is careful when and where and how he speaks of God. Ebeling scrutinizes this distinction between historical continuity and material discontinuity and finds it lacking.[29]

Not only does this distinction run into logical difficulties —total discontinuity destroys the very discussion of historical relation—it also reveals a truncated view of historical understanding. To be sure, Bultmann was correct in trying to protect the theological substance of Christian faith from both the apologist who would substitute simple representation of the figure of Jesus for the *existentielle* decision of faith and the crude historian who would distinguish between historical Jesus and kerygmatic Christ to discredit the latter. But this intention can only be fulfilled when

29. Gerhard Ebeling, *Theology and Proclamation,* trans. by John Riches (Philadelphia: Fortress, 1966), pp. 32-81.

one accounts adequately for the fact that the "what" of Jesus' own life was caught up in the "that" of the eschatological kerygma. In short, the question of the historical Jesus is properly the Christological question: how does what is implied in Jesus of Nazareth's life become explicit in the theological formulations of the church?

One must be careful in processing the Christological question to recognize that theological formulations from the past are significant precisely because they show how the implicit becomes the explicit. They are not authorities for faith except as in their coming to speech again they are faith coming to speech. Thus they lead back to the ground of faith in Jesus in which the Word of God came to speech at a concrete and particular point in human history. In preaching, in faith, in Jesus' preaching and life, and in the reflective and critical exercise of theology it is the reality of God which is at stake. But God is real as he is man's gracious Lord, and when the Word of God is spoken, this is an event which fundamentally qualifies human existence. Man is called in question and established together. This is what the decisiveness of Biblical eschatology is about. This is why Jesus in his cross and resurrection is the act of God judging and redeeming men.

Both Fuchs and Ebeling reflect at key points upon the structures of existence which the theological tradition illuminates and which are part and parcel of this fundamental relationship between man and God. Both find it the bondage to sin as bondage to the past illuminated as guilt as it is removed by the gracious act of God addressing man in his Word. Both also see this expressed in theological language about law and gospel. It is Ebeling especially, however, who like Herrmann takes the discussion back to Luther and plays again the Lutheran themes.[30] He is troubled, though, and admits in a sentence or two that the

30. Ibid., pp. 79-81.

theological notions of law and gospel are themselves problematical. What, he asks, are we to do in an age when men have no inkling of the law. Their bondage is so complete that they know not that they are bound. What can salvation mean today in this context? That, Ebeling concedes, is the knottiest problem the theologian faces.

Fuchs in dependence upon Friedrich Gogarten has seen aspects of the same problem.[31] He is aware that the process of secularization which has been active since the Renaissance and Reformation has undercut the external authorities in terms of which man could concretely understand his bondage. If one can say that the New Testament means demythologizing, one can also say that Luther meant secularization in Western culture. For he brought the question of the law to which one is obedient out of the protection of holy church and into connection with the basic experience of man in his world. The resulting independence of modern man over against this world is what one means by secularization. But what then is bondage? Precisely this secularization itself! For modern man in his independence is in danger of freezing history into a technological mould. He is in danger of losing the source of his real independence in the Word of God.

Yet it would seem that this does not solve the problem which troubles Ebeling; it merely highlights it. For secularization is described only in its formal aspects. But the ontological relationship between man and his world peculiar to modern man means concretely that all aspects of his life are imbedded in this relationship. This includes language. It also is subject to the independent self-consciousness of one who looks to the world for tools to further his aims. Language is used cynically and responsibly to effect ends. Furthermore, the institutions within which language

31. *Hermeneutik*, 2nd ed. (Bad Cannstatt: R. Müllerschoen, 1958), pp. 80-87.

and speech take place are dissected, evaluated, destroyed or reconstructed. In part this happens within the traditions of man's learning; in part it happens in the give and take of social-political events. To reflect upon preaching in relationship to faith is not merely to reflect upon the event of language in a secularized world but to reflect upon the institutions within which preaching takes place.

This point can be illustrated by some remarks on a book of Ebeling's—*The Nature of Faith*[32]—which more than any other in recent theology resembles in intention Herrmann's *The Communion of the Christian with God.* A course of lectures for a university-wide audience in Zurich, this book beautifully and clearly relates faith to history, history to historicity, historicity to the particular historical moment of Jesus, Jesus to deity, deity to grace and righteousness, grace and righteousness to self-understanding and love, and love to hope. And pervading the whole course of lectures is precisely the fact that the lectures are taking place at all. They are an attempt to bring faith to speech.

Now Ebeling would be the first to protest that his theological lectures are not preaching. But these lectures are certainly closely analogous to preaching, and the line between the two seems only to depend on the arbitrary contextual difference between an ecclesiastical community with its customs of worship and lectionaries and a university lecture hall. Furthermore, the clarity and beauty of Ebeling's book arises from the clarity of the university context. Here one can expect the word to meet the situation calling it in question and yet affirming it.[33] One can

32. *The Nature of Faith,* trans. Ronald Gregor Smith (Philadelphia: Fortress, 1961).

33. I am fully aware that many, especially in Ebeling's own universities, may doubt this assumption and may be correct. In a relative degree, however, it is still true that lectures can be given and heard in the university setting and communication can effectively take place.

expect people to be listening and hearing and bringing with them a world which can stand vis-à-vis the word of faith as the law stands vis-à-vis the gospel.

Whether one can expect that in the ecclesiastical setting is another matter. Is not Ebeling's question about the meaning of law in the present day really reflective of the fact that the cultural undergirding of ecclesiastical life assumed for so many centuries to be true and universal has now been almost totally eroded? None of the presuppositions for a message of redemption are reliable. There is no consensus on moral conventions against the background of which one can speak meaningfully of duty, obligation, right and wrong. There is no common fund of piety which can provide a vocabulary for speaking of deity and holiness. There is no universal awareness that the sacred traditions of Bible and church are precious and important needing only the skilled exegesis of the preacher. And there is the added complication that people are bombarded with words on the one hand and are increasingly trained to edit out most of these words on the other as deceptive nonsense. In such a context kerygmatic theology, the notion of the Word of God, and many other idioms of classical or recent theological literature are highly questionable for dealing with faith.

The Significance of Troeltsch's Question to Herrmann

Posing such questions to Ebeling is merely a means for updating questions posed to Herrmann in his own day by one of his greatest admirers and severest critics: Ernst Troeltsch. Troeltsch appreciated the fact that Herrmann seriously and skillfully dealt with the pressing theological issue of faith by bringing it into connection with ethics. He knew that Herrmann understood the evils of simple confessionalism and had faced fully the new situation set forth for the theologian by the Enlightenment and the

Kantian critical philosophy. His criticism was thus couched in the terms in which Herrmann spoke; Troeltsch reflected upon the basic problems of ethics.[34]

These problems arise, Troeltsch argues, in connection with religious faith, human culture, and critical evaluations. They are distinctively modern in the form we face them reflecting the facts of modern Western history. The breakup of the grand synthesis of Hebraic Christian religious motifs and Graeco-Roman culture institutionalized in the medieval church and rationalized in theological notions of natural law gave birth to independent rational assessment of the possibilities and purposes of human culture in general. Troeltsch saw this crudely attempted in the Enlightenment using the remnants of the theological tradition but done with far greater sensitivity after Schleiermacher, in the early nineteenth century, articulated clearly the place of historical knowledge and sensitivity in forming a general theory of culture. In both the Enlightenment and its descendants, however, the issue of religion and its nature was placed in this larger context and theology became a facet of the history of religion.

Moreover, no theory of culture was merely a descriptive task in the simplest meaning of the word. Bound up inseparably with it was the question of value and purpose to be answered only by reference to some form of transcendental judgment. Although a most thorough analysis of transcendental judgment was to be found in Kant, Troeltsch was not satisfied with an ethic of the autonomous moral disposition as this was worked out in Kantian thought. He wanted more reflection upon the processes of history to see how objective values were produced which were not subject merely to the vicissitudes of

34. Although he referred to Herrmann elsewhere, the one concentrated source for Troeltsch's *Auseinandersetzung* with Herrmann is "Grundprobleme der Ethik," *Gesammelte Schriften* (2nd ed. Tübingen: J. C. B. Mohr, 1922) II: 552-672.

relativity. These values also were relevant to the problem of ethics, for without them all the institutions of human culture were just the neutral raw material for moral action and thus of equal importance.

Troeltsch's motivation here is not just to have the equipment for making value judgments about processes of historical development, although this interested him very much as an intellectual problem. He was also aware that without dealing with the question of objective values in human culture one could be either passive in accepting the institutions of his own culture or be superficially defensive of them. In the case of Herrmann this is not an irrelevant point, for in the substantive section of his *Ethik* he moves easily and naturally to a discussion of family, society, and state as the natural contexts in which the man of faith exercises his moral freedom. Troeltsch was suspicious that this resembled too closely the ethical posture of German Lutheranism with its doctrine of the two realms and its willingness to leave to the orders of creation responsibility for forming the context for human action. To be sure, Herrmann was not to be confused with Lutheran orthodoxy since there was no holy sanction to nature and its orders in his thought, but he operated in such a way as to show himself a clear descendant of orthodoxy assuming the "church type" of relationship between religion and culture.

The "church type" of relationship represented a compromise—not at all a bad term in Troeltsch's mind—between the other-worldly impulses of religion and the this-worldly demands of concrete living. It stood in contrast to a "sect type" of relationship in which the other-worldly impulses were apparently less compromised in a disciplined pattern of moral and community life. No real assessment of ethics in Christian theology could take place without sober examination of the role played by both church and sect types in Christian history.

In the same way, Troeltsch looked upon Herrmann's interpretation of the Christian religion and the part played in it by Jesus as truncated and fixed to his presuppositions about the relationship between church and culture. For he chose to see Jesus and faith in connection with the ideas of redemption, forgiveness of sins, the power of grace, and other notions classically represented in the Pauline epistles. To do so, however, is to fail to realize that it was in the context of the church that these ideas became normative as outlines for the picture of Jesus. The burning demand for righteousness which characterized Jesus' own preaching was institutionalized in this form in the church in connection with concrete means of grace in the sacraments and structures of authority and obedience headed by priests. The traditions of the church including the scriptures came into existence in this context and functioned there. The aspects of Jesus' own preaching which depended upon the immediacy of his own presence and his call for righteousness went somewhat underground only to emerge in the various forms of sectarian spirit found in Christian history.

Although the Reformation called fundamentally in question the authoritative structures of the church, it retained an authoritative Biblicism and transferred the Catholic compromise of nature and super-nature to one between church and state. It is this Reformation tradition in which Herrmann stands, and it should be no surprise that he finds Luther's particular form of Pauline understanding so appealing for unlocking the secrets of Jesus of Nazareth.

From this perspective Troeltsch could also register his protest with Herrmann's attempt to make Christian faith the normative measure for man's religious experience in general. Although Herrmann appeared to be arguing from the general phenomenon of man's moral consciousness to the phenomenon of religion and thus to the particular phenomenon of Christian faith, by interpreting faith in

terms of the experience of being redeemed by God's grace
in Jesus and by seeing this experience mediated by a particular historical community, he was in fact rendering all
of man's moral and religious experience subject to Christianity. In so doing he was in fact reconstituting orthodox
claims of absolute truth and representing the ancient claims
of the church for hegemony in human culture. Despite his
modernity, Herrmann was indeed not modern enough.

Of course, Herrmann is not without response. He was far
from naive about the distinctly Christian stance he took—
according to the tradition of Luther. He never pretended to
be anything but a Christian theologian. Furthermore, if he
was true to his insight into the historical medium through
which faith is transmitted, he could plead that the theologian must honestly begin by being what he is and standing responsibly in the traditions of his heritage. No capricious decision to see Jesus in the way he did was at stake.
Rather was he seeking to speak about faith from the midst
of faith. No argument to convince one to have faith was
intended, for such an argument would violate the very
nature of faith.

Moreover, Troeltsch himself has not taken full enough
stock of the fact that the cultural context in which he poses
the questions of ethics and the nature of religion has a
history too. And this history is as distinctly Western as
Herrmann's even if it is not as ecclesiastical. Furthermore,
Troeltsch's characterization of religion as union with the
eternal and infinite and therefore as other-worldly is open
to examination. If it comes down, so does much of the
interpretative structure he has erected to deal with Christianity. Troeltsch's vain search for the religious a priori
may have caused him to sense this too. The course of research in the history of religion since Troeltsch and the
penetrating study by Wilfred Cantwell Smith into the term

"religion" itself would seem to bear out this form of Herrmannian criticism.[35]

All of this response to the contrary notwithstanding, Troeltsch's criticism of Herrmann deserves reflection. For it highlights something which will strike the perceptive reader of *The Communion of the Christian with God.* Although Herrmann is very careful to indicate that Luther is only relevant to his concerns as one who expressed clearly and fully his faith and not as one who wrote dogma, and although he acknowledges the way Luther was conditioned by his times and thus used the dogmas of the church less critically than we must, he still does not deal adequately with the question of Luther's relevance for the modern world. Why should one expect Luther to lead him correctly to the figure of Jesus or to communion with God? And even if he does, why would his expressions commend themselves to someone whose exposure to the Christian tradition is minimal or less? If Ebeling is correct in his suspicion that the "law" has little meaning in the present day, can Luther, whose thought hinged on the dialectic of law and gospel, be fully comprehended?

What comes clearly into focus here is the ambiguity of Herrmann's whole character. Radical and individual in thought, he was distant and conservatively pious in habit. Modern and self-consciously pioneering in shaping the theological task, he was traditional in executing it. Raising the horizons for seeing the place of the church and its theological enterprise in culture, he yet lacked the vision of Troeltsch to see what lay within these horizons. And this ambiguity has remained characteristic of the Herrmannian heritage in Bultmann, Fuchs, and Ebeling.

Contributing in large measure to the persistence of this

35. *The Meaning and End of Religion* (New York: Macmillan, 1962).

ambiguity is the place of theology and the theologian in German culture. Troeltsch's "church type" is here classically represented. The university whose ideals are scientific trains officers for traditional institutions. The church is not only one of these; it is probably the oldest and most traditional. It is supported by the financial structure of the state and its agencies permeate beyond worship and pastoral activities into the schools and other aspects of the common life. The presupposition is that the aims of church, state, and university are in harmony. And the theologian is really not uncomfortable with this presupposition. The irony of Troeltsch's own thought is that he was at home in the system too.[36]

If we are to see Herrmann's thought in the larger context of the age in which he lived, then this cultural presupposition must be placed in question. The revolutions of 1848 and 1918 lodged provisos against the view of the state included in it. Marx's whole career highlighted the problems of self-identity for the university and the scientific enterprise. Herrmann's polemic agaist unitary theological schemes in the name of faith sets out guidelines for the necessary disciplining of theology as a science. And today one must supplement this polemic with new analysis of the historical traditions in which faith is carried. Since, however, this is never accomplished outside of history, it must take full account of the social and political structures in

36. Much is often made of Troeltsch's shift from a chair of theology to one in the history of philosophy and culture when he went from Heidelberg to Berlin in 1915. Although it can be argued, as I for one would not choose to do, that this reflected discomfort with traditional theology and an interest in speaking more widely to the university audience, it should not be overlooked that Troeltsch went to his death defending the special character of the German spirit as an expression of German culture. The distinct contribution of German religious life to this culture was not overlooked. Furthermore, Troeltsch showed no discomfort operating within the German university with all the rights and privileges appropriate to an Ordinarius.

which the theologian stands. American culture with its quite different understanding of the relationship of church, state, and university offers an interesting vantage point for gaining perspective. Here the alternatives of "church" and "sect" offered by Troeltsch must be supplemented and perhaps his whole endeavor reconstructed. But it is certain that the broader horizons provided by the history of religion will play a major role. The complicated nature of theology conceived in this way is merely a function of the seriousness with which the man of faith is confronted with his historicity. For he must assume the burdens of a scientific and secularized world.

And is this not precisely the problem of the Jesus of history as Herrmann saw this and as his disciples have seen it too? For it is in a specific moment of time, in the life of a specific man in a specific place that the nature of historicity came to expression in such a way that men in a continuous tradition since him have been called to make history as well. To rob this man of his name and life is to destroy history. So also is to ignore the fundamental character of the experience of history in the present. Both represent attempts at abstraction which are defeated when one speaks unabashedly of faith in Jesus, or *The Communion of the Christian with God*.

* * *

Reprinted here is the second English edition of *Der Verkehr des Christens mit Gott* printed first in 1906. The text is a revision by R. W. Stewart of the first English edition printed in 1896. The translator is J. Sandys Stanyon. Stewart has altered the format of the first edition by eliminating the elaborate paragraphing of that work in line with the paragraphing Herrmann himself introduced with the fourth German edition of 1903. Stewart has also brought the first edition, which was based on the second

German edition of 1892, into line with the fourth German edition. This text was not substantially altered by Herrmann in later editions, although I have noted the major changes. A critical edition of this work does not exist and would entail reprinting both first and second German editions with the minor revisions made of the latter up through the seventh. Except for the beginning of the introduction these are not really extensive and are of particular interest only to one concerned about the subtleties of Herrmann's own development. The work is basically unchanged. The translation is quite literal, although it is a tribute to Herrmann's lucid writing style that it makes quite readable English. I have tried not to second guess the translator save at a point or two when it seemed mandatory.

SELECTED BIBLIOGRAPHY

An exhaustive bibliography of Herrmann's writings has been compiled by Peter Fischer-Appelt. *Metaphysik im Horizont der Theologie*. Munich: Chr. Kaiser, 1965. Pp. 215–32. It is arranged chronologically and includes notations of the various reviews of Herrmann's works as these appeared in contemporary journals. Here is also to be found a long bibliography of related works written during Herrmann's lifetime and since. Below is a selection of the most important items.

ORIGINAL EDITIONS

Die Metaphysik in der Theologie. Halle: Niemeyer, 1876.
Die Religion im Verhältnis zum Welterkennen und zur Sittlichkeit. Halle: Niemeyer, 1879.
Der Verkehr des Christen mit Gott. Stuttgart: Cotta, 1892 (2nd ed.), 1896 (3rd ed.), 1903 (4th ed.), 1908 (5th and 6th eds.). Tübingen: J. C. B. Mohr, 1921 (7th ed.).
Ethik. Tübingen: J. C. B. Mohr, 1901 (1st and 2nd eds.), 1904 (3rd ed.), 1909 (4th ed.), 1913 (5th ed.), 1921 (6th ed.).
Dogmatik. Stuttgart: Perthes, 1925.

COLLECTED ESSAYS

Gesammelte Aufsätze. Edited by F. W. Schmidt. Tübingen: J. C. B. Mohr, 1923.
Schriften zur Grundlegung der Theologie. In two volumes, edited and with an introduction by Peter Fischer-Appelt. Munich: Chr. Kaiser, 1966, 1967.

WRITINGS ABOUT THE APOSTOLIKUMSSTREIT

"Cremer gegen Harnack." *Die christliche Welt* 6 (1892): 1151–59.
Worum handelt es sich in dem Streit um das Apostolikum? "Hefte zur christlichen Welt." Leipzig: Grunow, 1893.
"Die Pfarrersfrage eine Gemeindefrage" *Die christliche Welt* 7 (1893):145–58.
"Ergebnisse des Streits um das Apostolikum" *Zeitschrift für Theologie und Kirche* 4 (1894): 251–305.

ENGLISH TRANSLATIONS (other than *The Communion*)

Faith and Morals. Translated by Donald Matheson and Robert W. Stewart. New York: Putnam's, 1904. This contains two essays: "Faith as Ritschl Defined It" and "The Moral Law as Understood in Romanism and Protestantism."

"The Moral Teachings of Jesus." In Adolf Harnack and Wilhelm Herrmann. *Essays on the Social Gospel.* New York: Putnam's, 1906.

Systematic Theology. Translated by Nathaniel Micklem and Kenneth A. Saunders. New York: Macmillan, 1927. This is a translation of the *Dogmatik.*

SECONDARY LITERATURE

Karl Barth. "The Principles of Dogmatics according to Wilhelm Herrmann." *Theology and Church.* Translated by Louise Pettibone Smith. New York: Harper, 1962.

Daniel L. Deegan. "Wilhelm Herrmann: A Reassessment." *The Scottish Journal of Theology* 19 (1966):188–203.

Peter Fischer-Appelt. *Metaphysik im Horizont der Theologie Wilhelm Herrmanns.* Munich: Chr. Kaiser, 1965.

Maurice Goguel. *Wilhelm Herrmann et le probleme religieux actuel.* Paris, 1905.

Rudolf Hermann. *Christentum und Geschichte bei Wilhelm Herrmann.* Goettingen: Lucka, 1913.

Dietz Lange. "Wahrhaftigkeit als sittliche Forderung und als theologisches Prinzip bei Wilhelm Herrmann." *Zeitschrift für Theologie und Kirche* 66 (1969):77–97.

Theodor Mahlmann. "Das Axiom des Erlebnisses bei Wilhelm Herrmann." *Neue Zeitschrift für systematische Theologie* 4 (1962): 11–88.

———. "Philosophie der Religion bei Wilhelm Herrmann." *Neue Zeitschrift für systematische Theologie und Religionsphilosophie* 6 (1964):70–107.

Martin Rade. "Am Sarge Wilhelm Herrmanns, Rede des Pfarrers." *Die christliche Welt* 36 (1922):74–76.

Martin Rade and Horst Stephan (eds.). *Festgabe für Wilhelm Herrmann zu seinem 70. Geburtstag dargebracht von Schülern und Kollegen. Zeitschrift für Theologie und Kirche.* 27 (1917).

James M. Robinson. *Das Problem des Heiligen Geistes bei Wilhelm Herrmann.* Marburg an der Lahn: K. Gleiser, 1952.

J. C. Roose. *De Theologie van W. Herrmann.* Leiden: 1914.

F. W. Schmidt. *Wilhelm Herrmann.* Tübingen: J. C. B. Mohr, 1922.

W. Schuetz. *Das Grundgezuege der Herrmannschen Theologie, ihre Entwicklung und ihre geschichtlichen Wurzeln.* Philosophische Abhandlungen 5. Berlin, 1926.

Hermann Timm. *Theorie und Praxis in der Theologie Albrecht Ritschls und Wilhelm Herrmann.* Gütersloh: Gerd Mohn, 1967.

Robert T. Voelkel. *The Shape of the Theological Task.* Philadelphia: Westminster Press, 1968.

THE TEXT OF
THE COMMUNION OF THE
CHRISTIAN WITH GOD

PREFACE

APART from the substitution of this for the former introduction, the numerous smaller alterations have reference
to the two most important objections that have been urged
against the conception of our faith here defended. It is
said to be impossible to experience the Person of Jesus as
the fact that can give to our confidence in God the calm
and strength of victory. From the opposite side I am told
that what helps us is not the Person of Jesus, as we ourselves can lay hold of and experience it as a fact. The
power that saves us lies rather in narratives about Jesus—
that is, in "facts which require faith," and not in a fact of
which we ourselves are become witnesses. The two objections are fundamentally at one in a legal conception of
religion.

For my opponents on the left wing the Gospel of Jesus
is the rule of doctrine, by the acceptance of which they
wish to become or reckon that they are Christians. They
observe truly enough that through historical inquiry the
Person of Jesus becomes for us a problem, not a reality
which can decisively determine our existence. And so they
draw the conclusion that there is nothing left for us except
that combination of amazing ideas, Jesus' gospel. But when
they conclude that through the conventional possession or
the determined acceptance of these ideas a man is a Christian, they are grievously mistaken. General ideas, the truth

of which is clear to us, may indeed be accepted by us, but they do not transform us—and conversion has always been reckoned the first effect of the dawn of Christianity in the soul—they are rather an expression of what we already are. And general ideas, the truth of which is not clear to us, because perhaps they go far beyond anything comprehensible by us, for that very reason we cannot appropriate so long as we remain what we are. If we, nevertheless, make the attempt, and imagine that it lies in our power, we do not make Christians of ourselves, but something quite different.

My opponents on the right count it part of their glory that with them the sum of doctrine is much more comprehensive, and embraces at the least all that is reported or taught about Jesus in the New Testament. In this assertion, of course, the legal character of their religion is still more sharply defined. And the most strange thing in this is that they wish to make a law for all who will become Christians the very doctrine of that Apostle who contended so hotly for the recognition of the fact that there is no law there that can make alive. They evidently imagine that the sum of doctrine constructed in this way by them ceases to be law when it gets the name "gospel."

The fact that these two tendencies are dominant in our church would be cause for despair were it the case that they really lived only by the stimulus of the dogmas they profess. They live, however, also by the mysterious force of the tradition to which, as a matter of fact, they are linked, and which, even in their abuse of it, they mean to honour. For many of them, in spite of everything, there does form itself out of the material which the Biblical tradition offers them, the spiritual picture of Jesus, which can become their one and all, when they perceive in it the approach of God to their soul, His judgment and His compassion. That must comfort us when we see our church under the power of the teachers of the law; but it must not take away from us the sense of our duty to oppose them.

They hold that they will sink in a bottomless quagmire
if what they are to believe is no longer prescribed to them.
But if it can here be shown to them that the basis of faith
can only be what produces faith as the inward experience
of pure trust, one would think that even on their minds
there must force itself the truth that faith can only be
created by a personal Spirit whose reality and power we
ourselves experience. But instead of paying heed to our
proof that we can experience this personal Spirit and its
power when we listen to the sacred tradition of the Christian community, they remain blind and deaf, and will not
budge from the position that this tradition can only become a means of redemption to any one by his declaring
himself ready to make up his mind to accept as true its
doctrines and narratives. Many are even quite willing to
point out to people particular portions of the tradition
which must be unconditionally "believed," if one means to
possess faith at all. These people often bear indubitable
marks of a true faith themselves, and yet they have obviously no suspicion that by this demand they are making
themselves faith's executioners. Doubtless those of them
who are in truth Christians have another object than that
which they formally give expression to. They wish to see
preserved the sacredness of the Scriptural tradition. They
do not notice that they themselves are profaning it when
they lay upon others as a ceremonial law what is in truth
a gift of God's grace. Nor do they reflect that the Holy
Scriptures are truly reverenced when they are, first of all,
investigated in their historically determined reality; and
when, in the second place, these books are used, just as
they offer themselves to us, so that in them we may seek
out the revelation of God. But this gives us all the more
reason to hope that the perception of this truth will soon
generally prevail. From every one who wishes to adhere
to her, the Christian community must demand that he
endeavours himself to win from the Biblical tradition the
vision of that Personal Life which alone can fill him with
perfect confidence.

The assent which our opponents demand to an extract of Biblical doctrine is, first of all, morally impossible; and, secondly, a convenient substitution for what is really necessary. But if we gain a clear insight into what the Bible ought to be for every Christian, namely, the means by which with his own vision he lays hold of the Person of Jesus, then it is easy to see what attitude towards the Christian community must be taken up by the theologian called to her service. He must be ready to impart to her, without any deduction, the Scriptural tradition, and must possess the faculty of showing the people how they can use this means to reach that one end. But, on the other hand, if the ecclesiastical authorities should be in the habit of demanding from such a man that he shall "believe" a sum of doctrine prescribed by them, be it ever so small, then they would become guilty of a tyranny which ultimately they themselves must feel to be useless and barbarous. Perhaps there are not many who will venture to cherish the hope that it is in these ecclesiastical circles that a revulsion might occur which would overcome their fast-rooted perversity. But the whole corruption of the Christian faith through the use of tradition as a ceremonial law will be rooted out if in the Christian democracy[1] there awakes the consciousness that God can reveal Himself only to those who desire to be sincere,[2] and that, therefore, the state of moral self-consciousness into which we are brought by the compulsion of a stronger personal life is also the beginning of a faith which has a truly religious character.

W. HERRMANN.

INTRODUCTION

§ 1. *The Present Situation of Protestant Christianity.*

THE work in which for the last fifteen years this book has had its share has not been in vain. He to-day who is willing to see, can find the way which, even in a world altered by science, leads those who seek God to Christ.

Of course, with all our efforts, we cannot make it clear to all Christians how profoundly our whole existence, down even to that arrangement of our habits of thought which is fixed by mere caprice, has been altered, not so much through the results of science as through the method which, in point of fact, it follows, and which is, in point of fact, unassailable. There will be many Christians for a long time yet on whose consciousness this has not dawned.

But the task for the Church and for theology which grows out of this change is now facing us in fullest distinctness. The Church must endeavour to satisfy the spiritual wants of the thousands who are able to move so freely in the traditional forms of Christianity that they can find in them the means of expression for their own religious conviction. But this does not imply that these Christians, who are not compelled by their course in life to clear up their mental attitude to what is real in the world, are to be made lords over the Church.

The leaders of the Church must not avail themselves of these docile masses in order to close the Church to others who are so controlled in their life that they are simply obeying the truth, when they regard the things of this world in a different manner. One may call those happy who do not see themselves forced out of the traditional forms of Christianity by the duty of sincerity. But the Church does not make itself indifferent to them ; if she does she will become a sect ; that is to say, she will sever herself from the historical movement of humanity. She ought to stand at their service. It is just these men who are in crying need of help if they are rightly to use the precious inheritance that is theirs and not make it an instrument of their ruin.

First of all, they need to be preserved from making the Biblical tradition a law for themselves or others, by the fulfilment of which they may inherit or appropriate salvation. For thus they block the way to God for themselves and hinder others from finding it. But they are not preserved from this depravity simply by the fact that the sacred tradition has been made uncertain for them. For that only means for each Christian to whom it happens, an addition to his burdens. He sees therein only a new task God sets him. And it will not occur to him to lay this burden upon others who have, perhaps, no time to solve such a question, being taken up with other duties.* It is by the right use of the

* [The meaning is a little difficult to follow ; it is this : People beginning to have doubts themselves are all the more vehement in demanding simple acceptance of the narratives from others. They think thus to keep the others out of the difficulties they feel themselves.—Tr.]

Biblical tradition that a Christian grows out of its misuse.

The Church must also aid the Christian democracy to see to it that the Bible holds its place. When the perception grows within the Protestant Church that the Bible is given us in order that in the stress of life and stilled in prayer we may listen to its words, if haply we may catch in it the voice of God speaking to our own hearts, then surely must perish the sacrilege that makes a law out of this gift of God's grace. Of course we have in view the fact that in our Church such a deliberate profanation of the holy place gives itself out for "positive Christianity."[3] But in the midst of the darkness, guarded as it is by ecclesiastical authorities and by the State, God sends light into many a heart, so that, in fear of the judge of the conscience and in joy in the Creator and Father, it escapes from all the vulgar arts by which the world and its potentates dress up their Christianity. Among us as well as among Catholics this profound injury to the Church, this reduction of the holy Scriptures to a rule of doctrine, is limited in its practical working by the power of the Spirit that is met with in the holy Scriptures. One who comes under the grasp of the spiritual character of Jesus wins a right appreciation of the doctrines about the Person of Jesus, so that he can find in even them that one thing great and precious to him above all else in the world, the power of this personal spirit over men who are yearning to become conscious of God. When a Christian has seen shining through the thoughts of others the fact that Christ has united them to God, these thoughts are no longer strange to him. He, therefore, cannot lay them upon himself as a rule of doctrine warring against his own thinking. For he now sees in their essential characteristics, the expression of what he himself has experienced. And the rest of what is there he puts calmly aside until it shall please God that it too shall appear as originating in Him.

This is the religious way to overcome the delusion that we ought to constitute the means of God's revelation a rule of doctrine, and that the observance of such precepts, a thing which always makes us sink into insincerity, can unite us with God. But Protestant Christians would be much more quickly set free from that most influential of Roman Catholic ideas, if among us the Church had some help to give to the millions who have become conscious of their inward dissatisfaction with many Biblical representations. Through their mental attitude these people feel themselves shut out from a Church that regards and demands as the beginning of Christianity the assent to the teaching and narratives of the Bible. Short-sighted critics may hold that for this reason the Romish Church is better suited than the Protestant to the spiritual needs of moderns. For she declares herself content with the man who, even if he does not share her doctrines at least does not contradict them. In the Protestant Church, on the other hand, the demand is made that the Scriptural doctrines shall be echoed as personal conviction. The lesser seriousness of the Romish requirement will thus make it possible for many to rest in the Church of Rome who could not remain with the Protestant communion.

But it is those spiritually asleep who, in this manner, remain inside the Church. We will, therefore, be glad that for such people attachment to the Church is made harder among us than among Catholics. Yet it is a pity, too, that it is not made easier for the sincere. How shall they make a start with talk of " facts which demand faith," when by these facts are meant the miracles reported in the Holy Scriptures, or, indeed, anything that is an event of the past and not something that can be experienced here and now ? They must feel repelled by a Church that through multitudes of its ministers spreads among the people the belief that a man does not become a Christian by reverently reflecting on what is undeniably real, but by being ready to obey a general invitation to declare as true things which are doubtfully apprehended, or, in any case, are not grasped as real by himself. Further, however, in the majority of those who are thus injured and left unsuccoured by the Church, there is developed an extraordinary want of comprehension for the Biblical tradition. They count it a meaningless thing, because they are tormented with it in a meaningless way. When, therefore, earnest Christians see how the multitude regards the Bible without reverence or piety, they imagine they must be up in defence of their holy thing and thus they become compliant tools of those very guardians of it who, by their violence, have done it most harm.

§ 2. *The Difficulty of the Position is Overcome by the Piety of those not under Bondage to Law.*

There is only one way out of this vicious circle of destruction. From the leaders of the Church, who are thrown into dismay and confusion by this tremendous apostasy, nothing is to be looked for but an even greater dependence upon State support. They feel reassured when the State gives the salary and title of professor to some theologians who take up a " positive attitude," that is, to some men who ignore as much as they do themselves the existence of such a thing as science and the spiritual requirements that science creates. But in such a matter force does nor count. Help can be expected only from a reawakening within the minds of those who have lapsed from the Church of an intelligent reverence for a Bible which has been degraded in the Church to a rule of doctrine.

Now this will happen in so far as they observe that the Bible itself, instead of making an inhuman demand on us, offers us an incomparable gift. When it becomes clear to them that the Bible introduces us to a marvellously vivid personal life that compels us to self-examination, that shakes us up, that humbles us, and yet that also fills us with comfort, joy, and courage, then they will look away beyond all that has hitherto been strange and repellent in this tradition to the redeeming vision of God that they see dawning there. They learn, too, to understand at last how good such hindrances have been for them, for thus they have been preserved from the abomination of making the Bible a law of doctrine. And they even learn at last to think with heartfelt pity of the leaders of the Church, who by their high-handed action make the Bible a stumbling-block on which many fall never to rise.

When, however, those who are thus set free by Christ begin the work of self-conquest, they are blessed by continually finding in parts of the Christian tradition that had been previously repellent to them more that is now able to enrich and rejoice their souls. Perhaps, to take an example, they may never succeed in sharing the apostle Paul's conception of the Person of Christ. But it will certainly be given them to rejoice in the fact that such thoughts did rise in a Christian soul. They see there the effect of the *one saving fact* that they themselves, just as much as the apostle Paul, have before their eyes, namely, the personal life of Jesus. This joy in the Christian tradition will spread among our people the more hearts are made to glow with the glorious knowledge that true religion, the blessed life of the spirit, is given to us only when we are willing to obey the simplest demand of the moral law, namely, to know ourselves. We must let ourselves be ready to take to heart in its weightiest characteristics that which is undeniably real, and gladly despise the suggestion that for God's sake we are to adopt the thoughts of other men. The right dependence on the Christian tradition must not, in the way the Church has up till now desired, draw its strength from want of moral insight or purity, but must result from moral earnestness alone. One may hope that this knowledge will prevail among the people, for the books in which this view is upheld are becoming more numerous and are widely read ; and further, even by "positive" theologians the convictions for which we contend are now occasionally treated as the fundamental ideas of a really Christian religion.*

The new day of Protestant Christianity can dawn only in hearts that have perceived that truly religious faith recognises no other law than the moral law of sincerity and love. The day will break when these people will joyfully make, in quite another sense, the old demand of the legal party, that nothing of the treasure of the Church's tradition shall be lost ; and when, with faith free and infinitely various in its individual forms, they take up the unavoidable duty of bringing together into one truly Christian community all who are working for the same good.

§ 3. *The Exposition of what Personal Christianity is is the common Task of all Parties in the Church.*

The unity of Protestant theology in a common peaceful task far removed from the noise of ecclesiastical party

---

* Compare the reference to this fact by Gottschick "Die Entstehung der Lösung der Unkirchlichkeit der Theologie" in the "Zeitschrift für Theol. u. Kirche," 1903, p. 94. Gottschick expresses his delight that Cremer, in his attack on Harnack, has laid chief stress on the point that the legal aspect of religion must be done away with and the Person of Jesus recognised as the basis of faith. Without any doubt Harnack too has been delighted to notice this perception on Cremer's part. For Cremer will doubtless now exercise his influence to secure that throughout the Christian Church it shall be reckoned as what it really is, namely, sin, to talk of "facts which demand faith," even though we are not of ourselves able to lay hold of them as facts. Otherwise he would be serving that false legality which like us, he hates.

strife will at last be attained if we devote our attention to that which is usually expressly conceded by
the one opponent to the other. Our opponents do
not deny our personal Christianity. Well, then, let the
endeavour be made on both sides to describe what we
understand by personal Christianity. Christians are
fully agreed as to its general meaning. It is a communion of the soul with the living God through the
mediation of Christ. Herein is really included all that
belongs to the characteristic life of Christendom—revelation and faith, conversion and the comfort of forgiveness,
the joy of faith and the service of love, lonely communion with God, and life in Christian fellowship. All
this is then only truly Christian when it is experienced
as communion with the living God through the mediation of Christ. When we believe in a man's personal
Christianity we are convinced that he stands in that
relation towards God in which all this takes place.
The reformers never doubted that Christianity in this
sense might exist, and continue to exist, even amid the
perverted teaching of the Romish Church. Of course,
they maintained that two of the Romish ideas destroyed
the very basis of Christianity. Besides the idea of the
meritoriousness of good works, the notion seemed
equally obnoxious to them that the Sacraments had a
saving efficacy, not the outcome of a religious comprehension of God's promise as expressed in their
dispensation. But although they knew the Christianity
that was under the guidance of Rome reckoned on its
own merits and ascribed to the Sacraments magical
effects, for instance, baptismal regeneration, yet they

held that even there true Christian life was to be found, the inward strength of which made all these hurtful doctrines mere external additions. And so it is among ourselves. I hold the theological teaching of Frank, Lipsius and Luthardt to be wrong; I believe I see clearly how such teaching hinders the man who surrenders himself to it from coming to Christ and through Him to God; I think I know why this is the case. But I hold these teachers themselves to be Christians, to whom I owe many a good word of faith. Still, I cannot help observing that they sometimes lapse into a theology in which little that is Christian is to be discovered. The fact is, that as theologians they are products of their age; as Christians, they are created by God in quite another fashion. By the strength of that which has come to them through no medium of doctrine, they are enabled to move as Christians even loaded with the fetters of their " systems."

This faith in the power of a personal Christianity that is awakened by God is indispensable to us who are Protestants. We must believe that personal Christianity can arise in spite of wrong teaching, and can remain alive amid obsolete ecclesiastical forms. If this be the case, then Protestant theology is bound to set forth and expound precisely this personal Christianity in which we believe all Christians to be at one.

§ 4. *The Impossibility of Uniformity of Doctrine in Christianity.*

Again, the need for treatment of this subject is seen still further when we remember that there must be

different teaching among Christians, and this not only
on matters where we may feel it necessary to make some
distasteful compromise with tradition, but also where
the question may concern the expression of our inmost
faith. The doctrine which really springs from faith
has necessarily an infinite variety of forms. The
Christian seeks to express in it the reality amid which
his faith lives. But since that reality is infinite, therefore the doctrine in which one Christian seeks to
express what his faith sees, cannot be laid down as the
limit for other believers. Different men see differently,
and therefore, since they ought to be truthful, they
must express themselves differently. All attempts at
union through uniformity of a compendium of doctrine,
large or small, are futile, even when men succeed in
building up such a structure as outlasts a millennium.
Personal, living Christianity will always follow its own
free course in unfolding its thoughts; it is inaccessible
to that spirit of legalism which controls the world. We
may see this fact illustrated in every sermon that comes
truly from the preacher's heart. That heart, deeply
moved by the Spirit of God, thinks very little of any
doctrinal theory or of any theological system ruled by
such, but reveres the free testimony of the faith of
other men. In the outpourings of such a heart, therefore, the old faith, on which the characteristically new
is climbing, will certainly be expressed in some measure;
but the man, being really taught of God, will bring
forth out of his treasure, along with the old, some new
things also, which are by no means to be understood as
the mere logical consequences of the old.

In the origination of particular doctrines, there have been many contributory thoughts all springing from the Spirit of God. But the idea of dogma as a uniform doctrinal theory is contrary to the working of the Holy Spirit. A uniform doctrinal theory seeks to dominate the thinking of the Christian community, and it demands that its own logical implications shall be developed in the thoughts of the Christian. But the Holy Spirit creates men of faith.

The actual composition of the New Testament clearly shows this. If Christians seek unity by means of unalterable doctrine, then they must give up the authority of the New Testament. For in the New Testament there is no unalterable doctrine which embraces the whole scheme of Christian thought. If in spite of this the effort be made, with the New Testament as guide, to construct a system which shall guarantee the unity of the Church, then the wonderful variety of the forms of thought contained in those Scriptures will be found to be an imperfection. Such a feeling is unavoidable if we attempt at once to teach according to Scripture, and, at the same time, to have unalterable doctrine as a condition of the unity of fellowship. He who wishes to teach according to Scripture needs rather to make up his mind that the ideal of doctrines which shall be unalterable, and equally binding upon all, is a false one. Were it a true ideal, then we should have to get beyond the Christianity of the New Testament. But we must rather intrench ourselves within it. It is no imperfection, it is rather most fitting that the Epistles of the New Testament

are letters written in view of special circumstances, and
not contributions to a doctrinal system which shall be
valid to all eternity.

Of course, unity in doctrine seems indispensable.
What would a Church be without a confession? If,
therefore, the New Testament does not furnish a
definitely framed system of religious thought, such
perhaps does lie hidden underneath the manifold
utterances of faith contained in the Scriptures? In that
case it would be the business of the theology which
desires to construct a uniform doctrine for the Christian
Church, to quarry out this hidden system from Holy
Scripture. In this way certainly a sort of average
combination of Biblical ways of thinking could be
obtained, but it would be quite unserviceable when we
had got it. For such an average combination of
thoughts, so arranged, has never existed organically in
the experience of a believing man. If we should try to
follow such a combination, we should be setting up
a law which might seem easy to fulfil, but we should
not advance a step towards the kind of thinking which
is found in Scriptural writers. What really unites
Christians one with another and with the witness of the
New Testament is not the complete identity of our
thoughts, but the likeness of our ways of thinking, and
the unity of the revelation by which that likeness is
caused.[4] Illustration of both of these points is to be seen
everywhere in the New Testament. There is, on the
one hand, the same Jesus and the same conception of
God as His Father which is inseparable from Him, and,
on the other, the same personal life redeemed by the

God who is thus manifest, or, in other words, the same
faith. Every Christian who reads the New Testament
for his edification will find these two things in it, and
take them as the proper nourishment for his soul.

§ 5. *The Feature of Unity in the New Testament and in
the Christian Community generally is the Communion
with God that is Mediated through Jesus Christ.*

We hold a man to be really a Christian when we
believe we have ample evidence that God has revealed
Himself to him in Jesus Christ, and that now the man's
inner life is taking on a new character through his
communion with the God who is thus manifest. But
if this is certain, then it is the first business of theology
to set forth and expound the communion of the
Christian with God which is mediated through Jesus
Christ.

For, in the first place, in this way alone can the
Christian be guided by the New Testament as the
principle of Protestantism demands, while, on the other
hand, the notion that it is possible for the Christian to
know and hold all the various doctrines uttered in the
New Testament is, to put it plainly, a monstrous
fiction. No Christian does so, and none can. To state
all these doctrines correctly is the business of historical
inquiry; it is an arduous task, and one that is never
accomplished with certainty. Such an inquiry is not
within the power of every Christian. The manifold
nature of the doctrines uttered in the Scriptures corresponds indeed to the real nature of the life of faith,
but it forbids a Christian to appropriate to himself

equally all the processes of thought recorded by those writers. The authority of the New Testament, which gives the needed and safe guidance to every Christian, has for its sphere something quite different from fixity of doctrine, namely, the communion of the Christian with God which is mediated through Jesus Christ. Whenever the authority of the New Testament is extended so as to belong to its doctrines, that authority is diminished. Into the place of the New Testament there inevitably step those theological products which offer a unity of doctrine not found within its pages. If, however, we have learned to fix our eyes on that which God's revelation produces in the inner life of a Christian, then, in our reading of Scripture, we shall constantly meet with an authority by which we shall be safely led and wonderfully uplifted.

Second, in the vision of the communion of the Christian with God, we see wherein Christians are truly at one. In the inner life of faith all is ruled by the one God and the one Christ. Of course, in the exposition of such a life the development of particular doctrines must be set forth ; but unities of doctrine beyond these limits are not legitimate, because not vital to faith. They are worthless dreams which arouse useless strife, and hinder the unity of the Christian Church. To fix doctrines that are thus severed from the stem of real life, and to frame them into a system, is the last thing the Christian Church should undertake, and the more important the matter worked up in this way is, the more harmful it is. But if, on the other hand, we keep our attention fixed on what God is producing in the Christian's inner life, then the manifoldness of the thoughts which spring from faith will not confuse us, but give us cause for joy. For we can then understand that the manifoldness is both necessary and valuable. Hence we must cease attempting to bind together into one system thoughts of faith coming from various sources, and to make the unity of the Church depend on any product of the kind. No confession ever arose thus which believers could unanimously and heartily accept. The Church's confession of faith ought to be the confession of real faith. But this is only possible where faith itself, or the personal life of the Christian, the life redeemed by God, becomes clearly conscious of itself. Whatever faith conscious of itself says concerning itself, its origin and the forms of its own life, that alone is the real confession of faith. In this confession Christians understand each other if the faith which God has wrought is alive within them at all. On these grounds, for a Church which desires to be really a fellowship of believers, there can be no theological task more important than that of setting forth that inner life of faith, or that communion with God in which we really find ourselves at one.

§ 6. *The True Objectivity of Christian Knowledge.*

Of course, many persons fear that if we set the problem in this way, we are going to resolve Christianity entirely into subjective experiences. Their conviction is certainly right that the inner life of the Christian faith is extinguished if we lose the Christian knowledge in which we lay hold of a certain objective reality, which is our support. It remains to be seen whether, as we proceed, our exposition will disarm this suspicion ; but the error of subjectivity by no means necessarily follows from the problem as now stated. This certainly does follow : that the knowledge of the objective Christian realities is the only nourishment on which faith is fed. It is not possible to prove to an unbeliever the truth of these things. That knowledge is inseparable from faith ; and no one can gain an insight into its truth who is not sensible to the peculiar problems of the personal life that asserts itself in the sphere of moral thought. But just because this Christian knowledge is grasped in its truth only by those who occupy already the standpoint of faith, it is all the more needful to describe quite clearly the inner life of faith, wherein that Christian knowledge has its place. If we wish to settle our differences concerning doctrine, then, above all things, we must know what we mean by the inner life of faith, or, in other words, how we represent the communion of the Christian with God. Every theological discussion which does not sound these depths is in danger of that very calamity of subjectivity which others prophesy for us. The true objectivity of Christian knowledge, its truth for believers, must be lost unless it is protected by clear views concerning the life of faith.

The path on which we here enter is the only possible way to agreement concerning Christian doctrine. Nevertheless, the objection was put forward against this treatise, when it first appeared, that it did not help men to a mutual understanding. It was said that I did an injustice to those who were against me by caricaturing their views. I earned this reproach by prefacing my own exposition with a sketch of our opponents' conception of the communion of the Christian with God. Such an undertaking is, however, worse than useless. For the slightest mistake in such a description is sure to arouse the suspicion of a desire to put one's opponent in the wrong by imputing to him what is not true. It is better, therefore, simply to set forth how the life which a Christian leads with God presents itself to the writer, and then to wait and see what positive arguments others can bring against that exposition. By this means, we may hope that the errors on either side will be clearly brought to light, and confuted in a Christian spirit. Strife over doctrines is not very profitable, until we are thoroughly agreed as to how they arise out of the organic life of faith. Until then, no one who takes part in the discussion can rightly understand either his opponent or himself. We do need positive expositions of that inner life which we know to be a Christian reality. Amid these expositions, the deepest antagonisms will inevitably come to light. Nevertheless, there remains with the truly pious man a consciousness of that unity which will gradually transform these antagonisms, let us hope, replacing them by individual expressions of an unspeakably precious common possession. Let us proceed, then, to treat of that inner life of *religion* which is common to us all.

THE RELATION OF THE CHRISTIAN RELIGION TO MYSTICISM AND TO THE FORMS OF RELIGIOUS OBSERVANCE INVOLVED IN MYSTICISM

§ 1. *The Incommunicable Element in all Religion.*

WE are all at one in the conviction that the inner life of religion is a secret in the soul, and cannot be handed over from one to another. No human being can so help another by the information he may give him that the latter shall be put in possession of what is best in religion. Each individual must experience it for himself as a gift from above. Every man to whom religion is something more than a store of knowledge or a burden of commandments, experiences at times a certain stirring of feeling within him, amid which alone he is able to gain due profit from all that is of religious significance. The man who is acquainted with these movings within knows also that he needs neither special reflection nor instruction to explain them. He has, on the contrary, so strong a sense of being possessed, as it were, that he must say, "This is God." At such a time God makes Himself felt, and sets the man in that inward condition which is blessedness. In this frame of mind the words, "God is present," are the simple expression of a simple experience. Of course, even with the most pious of men such a state could not last always, nor could it relieve every inward pain. Nevertheless, traces of the experience remain in the soul which has passed through it, and keep alive the desire for its peace. Now in this longing, or this affinity for that which edifies one religiously, in short, the impulse to order the inward and outward conditions of life so that the experience of the nearness of God may fill these more and more, lies the continuity of the religious life. But the sacred moments when we experience God's immediate presence are not the mere high-water mark to which the religious life attains. Without that experience of God all the rest is so empty and vain that it does not deserve the name of religion. Such experiences constitute the incommunicable essence of all religion. He who does not understand and warmly sympathise with the many witnesses to such a frame of mind cannot be a Christian. In this experience Christians find themselves at one with all devout men of every name.

But precisely on this account it is evident that we have not yet described what is peculiarly characteristic of Christian piety. Although we share these experiences already described with other devout persons and reverence their sacredness, yet we must not let that escape us which is peculiarly Christian. In what, however, does this consist? If we are convinced that without an experience of the mysterious working of God upon the soul no religion would be of any value whatsoever, we might easily infer that this very experience is the essential thing in all religions, and therefore also in

Christianity. And so we might regard those various qualities which are peculiar to the various religions simply as a means of preparation for that essential experience, or as a particular consequence of the same.

§ 2. *The Catholic Choice of this Incommunicable Element as the Common Essence of Religion.*

This conception of the relation between the essential and the particular in religions has played an important part in history. It forms one of the most important elements in Roman Catholicism. In the Roman Catholic Church the supernatural power of a particular Christian cultus and of particular Christian doctrines is insisted upon with great force. And yet, wherever in Catholicism religion has remained a living thing, it has always been a life of just such experiences as we have found to be essential in every devout life. Mere submission to the laws of a cultus or of doctrine certainly cannot of itself constitute religion. The kind of religion which in Roman Catholicism is really bound up with such submission is an inner life which is either indifferent to what is specifically Christian, or at most but loosely connected with it. The forms in which this inner life finds expression have no prototypes in the New Testament. They were derived from the most significant religious features of the dying civilisation of antiquity. The most conspicuous features of the Roman Catholic rule of life are obedience to the laws of cultus and of doctrine on the one side, and Neo-platonic mysticism on the other. The combination of these two features makes it possible for Roman Catholic Christianity to assume many and varied forms. At different times greater or less use of cultus and of doctrine has resulted in a varied amount of preparation for the real experience of religion. The link with the historical Christ which both preserve has served in varying degree to modify the religious experience without depriving it of its mystical character. At the same time it has been possible, where the approach to Christ has not been entirely obstructed, that the impression He makes has led on to another kind of religious experience which is really Christian, and, therefore, not mystical. Then there has been the long range of variations from the sublimest forms of Neo-platonic mysticism at the one extreme, down to that sort of acknowledgment of divine power at the other, which is based only on the faint emotion aroused by the mysteries of cultus, of dogma, and of legends. But all the forms of piety which have a place in this series have this feature in common : they are mystical. And it is in these alone that we may see and study the kind of religion which is characteristic of Roman Catholicism.

§ 3. *Mysticism and its Significance for Catholicism.*

The essence of mysticism lies herein : that its religious life exhausts itself in that long series of experiences just described. When the influence of God upon the soul is sought and found solely in an inward experience of the individual, that is in an excitement of the emotions taken, with no further question, as evidence that the soul is possessed by God ; without, at the same time, anything external to the soul being consciously and clearly perceived and firmly grasped, or the positive contents of any soul-dominating idea giving rise to thoughts that elevate the spiritual life, then that is the piety of mysticism.

He who seeks in this wise that for the sake of which he is ready to abandon all beside, has stepped beyond the pale of truly Christian piety. For he leaves Christ and Christ's Kingdom altogether behind him when he enters that sphere of experience which seems to him to be the highest. It is possible that an earnest and intimate attachment to Christ and a powerful impulse towards love of our fellow men may co-exist with this. But although this is abundantly seen, even in the great mystics of the Roman Catholic Church, yet it is none the less clear that whenever the religious feeling in them soars to its highest flights, then they are torn loose from Christ and float away into a sphere where they meet the non-Christian mystics of all ages. " How can we expect adherence to historical reality when all the powers of the imagination are let loose and regarded as the organ of union with the Deity ? The mystics within the Church sought to guard themselves against passionate, unrestrained and pantheistic piety, but they often forgot themselves, to say the least, when they rose to their highest exhortations. These always lacked their full momentum so long as they took any notice of whatever was outside of God and the soul." * Their yearning after God Himself could never endure the trammels of the historical. Thus, Roman Catholicism degrades everything that is connected with positive Christianity

* Harnack, "Textbook of the History of Dogma," vol. iii. p. 382.[5]

into a mere means of preparation for the highest plane of the religious life. On that plane itself, and in those moments when enjoyment of the highest is vouchsafed, the soul knows itself to be loosed from all external things.

If such a freedom of the soul in God be regarded as the blessed goal, then any command to hold fast by what is historical cannot count on certain obedience. For the fact that everything historical sinks into insignificance when God is really found, may so dominate the feeling of the individual that he may become totally indifferent to the dogma that formulates the meaning of the historical in Christianity. Certainly, on the other hand, the prospect of reaching such a goal may lighten the burdens imposed by the prescription of incomprehensible doctrines. If we know that when we reach the highest plane of religious experience we shall obtain religious freedom in all its fulness, we may perhaps afford to endure as a means of preparation for this, a dogma which demands the renunciation of that freedom. And then besides, since the highest joys in mysticism, as in all religion, are something utterly miraculous, the incomprehensibility of the means of preparation, of the dogma and the history worked up into it, will seem exactly suited to the case. It was on this wise, we know, that Thomas Aquinas justified the irrationality of dogma; and so, in a certain degree, made it rational. The conversion of the historical in Christianity into an incomprehensible mystery thus suits well the mystic conception of religion. Each of the two features certainly puts a strain upon the other; but this very strain serves in Roman Catholic piety as a propelling force. Devout submission to dogma and to the greatest absurdities of cultus may produce in really pious persons a state of mind in which the soul counts itself free from all external bonds, not excluding even the historical revelation of God in Christ. The masses, of course, get no further than these means of preparation, and, therefore, never arrive at a real personal experience of religion. They remain, however, in a sort of union with the others, who are truly religiously alive ; for even these latter think that in their devotion to the incomprehensible they gain a mysterious strength that lifts them up to God.

§ 4. *A Want of Clearness in the Protestant Attitude to Mysticism.*

We can understand how Roman Catholics, who have discovered the paths of mysticism and are conscious of their freedom and independence, should exult somewhat over us who are Protestants. For we are not at liberty to seek freedom from positive religion in the way which they have taken ; and yet we seem to be not a little burdened with things which we cannot comprehend. If Catholics regard our kind of Christianity as a half-way religion, their judgment is somewhat confirmed by the fact that, while, on the one hand, we are impelled towards mysticism by the same motives as they, we are, on the other hand, held back by the fundamental doctrines of our Church. And so long as we preserve what is in reality Roman Catholic dogma in a somewhat modified form, and regard the historical in Christianity only as something incomprehensible, instead of seeking in it the revelation of God which actually convinces us, ours will continue to be a half-way religion. Protestant Christians who do not sincerely undertake that search never gain the courage calmly to pass by things which, belonging though they do to the most ancient tradition regarding Christ and to the primitive form of Christianity, yet as a matter of fact do not act on people to-day as the awe-inspiring revelation of God. They take these things to heart as a law and imagine, like the Catholics, that the accomplishment of this "religious duty" or of this "faith" will help them. So long as this fundamental trait of Roman Christianity, the spirit of law, which seeks salvation in the suppression of a man's own faculty of knowledge, fetters souls among us Protestants too, the truly pious, who have the intuition that in God the soul becomes free and independent will take refuge in mysticism, despite all obstacles. A. Lasson,[6] a Protestant expounder of mysticism, declares plainly that mysticism is necessary in Christianity, because without it there is nothing left but submission to doctrines imposed by external authority. I suspect that this view is secretly cherished by many theologians. On the other hand, however, it is not quite forgotten that a consistent mysticism is fraught with danger to positive Christianity. Hence men speak of a "sound" mysticism which is to be carefully preserved. But when we ask: "What is sound mysticism?" we are told it is the conviction that we stand in actual communion with God. This conviction, however, is no speciality of mysticism, for without it there can be no religion at all. This desire to retain mysticism in Protestant Christianity is not yet explained by the wish to exalt that which is common to all religion. For mysticism is not that which is common to all religion, but a particular species of religion, namely, a piety which feels that which is historical in positive religions to be burdensome, and so rejects it. When we find that Protestant theologians who count themselves strictly orthodox so frequently desire at the same time to retain mysticism, we must conclude that they view mysticism as a saving counterpoise over against the historical. While they feel the historical to be indispensable, it is nevertheless a burden to them. This is exactly the attitude of which the classical examples are the mendicant orders of the thirteenth and fourteenth centuries. In them we can see a practical illustration of the antithesis just described between the irksomeness of the historical and the freedom of mysticism. The greatness of these men consists in the energy with which, as theologians and churchmen, they worked out the consequences of that antithesis. If Protestant theologians to-day think that they cannot part company with mysticism, then they really admit that they cannot free themselves from Roman Catholicism. For in Roman Catholicism mysticism is the essential life of religion.

§ 5. *The Enduring Significance of Mysticism for the Christian Life.*

A man like R. Rothe could name nothing better than the writings of the mystics as an aid to devotion

alongside of the Holy Scriptures.* If this advice be
right, then it might be supposed that the religious life
manifested in mysticism has peculiar strength and
purity. Mysticism is undoubtedly a religious phenomenon of high perfection.   It is indeed a remarkable
thing that in Rothe's judgment the Protestant Christian
seeking religious culture must be referred to Roman
Catholicism for examples of piety.[7] Yet we find it
explicable when we study the aspirations of mysticism
towards its goal, as described for example in the happy
exposition of S. Denifle. † No one who reads Denifle's
description can deny that such mysticism is good
Catholicism or that in its utterances we may see a rich
conception of religious life combined with a strength
and simplicity of language which must go to the heart
of every pious man. It would be a bad sign if a
Protestant could not use this book as an aid to
devotion. A form of religion of such high perfection
must powerfully affect every devout soul. Although
we believe that our religion is of quite another sort, yet
we must admit that we have not reached by a long way
the perfection of culture which Roman Catholicism
possesses in mysticism. But this is the only justification
for Rothe's opinion. The mysticism which he com-
mends is indeed of great value to us, yet not because
it is an element in all religion, but because it is an
admirably perfect expression of a particular kind of
religion. The speculations of Roman Catholic mysticism
are of ancient date, and yet few of these are peculiar to

* "Theologische Ethik."   Second edition, vol. iii. p. 490.

† "The Spiritual Life, or Flowers gathered from the Gardens of
the German Mystics and 'Friends of God' of the 14th Century."
Third edition, 1880.

itself. Nearly all belong to Neo-platonism. But its
faculty of making the personal life the object of observation and description exalts it to a height never yet
attained by Protestantism. To the mystics of the
fourteenth century the soul was a miracle which they
could see with their eyes; and they never grew weary
of gazing on its riches. They searched out and they
set forth all the wealth of the inner life, so far as
Roman Catholic piety could produce it. For this
reason they are classical witnesses to the Roman
Catholic type of Christianity, and as such they have a
lasting message for Christian life. But there is all the
more reason that we should be clear as to whether we
ought to take the same path.

The mysticism of all ages is intensely attractive,
because in mysticism the universal aim of all genuine
religion is clearly grasped. In religion man seeks not
simply God's gifts, but God Himself. What God
can give without giving Himself does not comfort
the soul; the soul never rests until it has pierced
through all that is not God; a soul is free when it has
risen above all that is not God. Every devout man
knows the justice of these propositions. The theologian knows how often their truth has been forgotten in
the search after worthy aids to religion.

§ 6. *Why, within the Christian Community, the way
of Mysticism must be Abandoned.*

But if mysticism is genuine religion, when it soars
thus above all aids that it may reach God Himself, the
question still remains whether it seeks God as a

Christian ought to seek Him, and whether the God whom mystics believe they find is the living God of our faith. The mystic seeks God in his own inner life. Nor is this altogether wrong. For we have not found God until He rules in our inner life. But the mystic infers from this that everything which affects us from without, not only cultus, doctrine, but also our conception of the person of Jesus Himself, are all of them serviceable only as means to produce in us that frame of mind in which God comes inwardly near us. When this condition has been attained, then we may perceive the secret voice of God, which we may hear and know to be divine, but cannot repeat in words of ours. In such moments all that is from without recedes ; when God speaks all else must be silent. The mystics knew well how to describe the freedom felt in the devout soul that is conscious it has passed through this incomparable experience. It is the joyful breathing of a soul that knows it bears the highest good within its own inviolable self. The mystic is lifted above all that fetters men and brings unrest, for he knows he has found God. But for this very reason he has left Christ behind. According to mysticism, Christ leads the man who becomes His disciple up to the threshold of blessedness. But then the mystic steps across that threshold, and, at the highest point of his inner life, he has no longer to do with Christ but with God, for when a man really finds God, he finds himself alone with Him. When we observe this outcome in mysticism, we may be tempted to count it merely one of its casual, non-essential side-growths. To do so, however, would be a mistake. The piety of the Roman Catholic is essentially such that, at the highest point to which it leads, Christ must vanish from the soul along with all else that is external. The Roman Catholic conception of Christ is of such a character that its content cannot possibly remain with a devout man in the act of communion with God. That is the reason above all others why Christian people must turn away from the path of Roman Catholic piety, which leads its eager spirits into mysticism.

Roman Catholic piety is unable to preserve a faith in the revelation of God in Christ which can definitely mould religious practice. For it is not in this or that emotion, concerning which all that can be said is that in the emotion God is touching the soul, that we perceive the Redeemer who came to us in history. God would be in such a case only a hidden, inscrutable power, and by no means that Will of Christ which we understand and trust in. If such were our relation to God and to Christ, then the Christian doctrines concerning God and Christ would exercise only a very slight influence on our religious practice, however zealously we might hold them. For it is not what we are taught concerning God that actually reveals Him, and enables us to recognise Him. We have God just in so far as He Himself comes near to us. Now if I have to say that for me this happens in a stirring of the soul in which the vision of a personal power that spiritually dominates and liberates me is entirely blotted out, then this process is for me the form of God's appearance ; and it is this that brings me all that I can grasp of God. But then, the revelation of God in history loses all its worth. The only use left for that revelation would be to instruct us and prepare each one for his individual experience of God's presence. And such mere preparatory matters it would be not merely permissible but a duty to forget as soon as the great end itself had been attained.

§ 7. *The Unsatisfying Element in the Doctrine of the two Natures in Christ is Correlated to Mysticism.*

Corresponding to this, on the other hand, is the conception of Christ which obtains in the Roman Catholic Church. There the dogma of the two natures in Christ, and the doctrine of the redeeming work of the God-man, set forth what must be presupposed if the union of the sinner with God is to be made possible. Again, in the picture of the man Jesus, the Catholic Christian sees the Way which is to lead him to God. All this is right, for it is only because we know Christ that we can have, with full clearness and certainty, a God who by His holiness holds the sinner afar off, and yet also reconciles the sinner to Himself in granting him forgiveness by His own act. It is true also that we can only come to God by following Jesus, and by earnestly seeking to be truthful and upright like Jesus.

But this is not enough. Christ is more to the Christian. We do not merely come through Christ to God. It is truer to say that we find in God Himself nothing but Christ. All these beclouded representations of an Infinite Being in whom we cannot recognise the features of the inner life of Jesus, seek to describe, not the Living God of revelation, but only a

being of whom nothing more can be said than that
He is not the world.   Now that is precisely all that
mysticism has ever been able to say of its God.   Plainly,
the representation of the world is the only thing that
moves the soul while it thinks thus of God.   Only
disappointment can ensue to the soul whose yearning
for God in such case keeps on insisting that God must
be something utterly different from the world.   If such
a soul will dwell for a while with the God thus
reached, the fact must inevitably come to the surface
that its whole consciousness is occupied with the world
now as it was before, for evidently it has grasped no
other positive idea.   Mysticism passes so commonly into
pantheism for this very reason, and, indeed, especially
in men of the highest religious energy ; they refuse to
be satisfied with the mere longing after God, or to
remain on the way to Him, but determine to reach the
goal, and rest with God Himself.   The thought that
sums up religious experience   in   such   a   manner
is necessarily pantheism.   But the whole thing is unchristian.

The Christian has a positive vision of God in the
personal life of Jesus Christ.   This vision of God does
actually set us free from the world, because it leads us
to deny self, and is grasped and realised only in connection with this moral impulse.   We are guided, however,
to this condition neither by the Church's dogmas
concerning Christ, nor yet by using Jesus' human life
as our example.   We cannot enter fully into the same
relation to God which Jesus had ; that remains His
own secret.   But we can enter into the relation to

God into which the redemption of Christ brings us only if, in our finding of God, we do not lose sight of Jesus. It is just here that both the doctrine of the Church and the use of the life of Jesus as an example prove insufficient. For the man who has nothing more of Christ than these two things must leave Christ all behind when once there awakes in him that genuine religious impulse which will be satisfied with nothing but God alone. How can he stay with Christ if he looks upon Him as only a condition, a way and means whereby to come to God? He must break through everything (even though it be adorned with the name of God like the Christ of ecclesiastical dogma) which serves only as a means, and is thus utterly different from the God whom we must find in the highest flight that our religious life attains.

Here is the limit beyond which that conception of Christ, which is embodied in the dogma and practice of Roman Catholicism, does not rise; the Christ thus conceived cannot be taken in with the soul into the inmost experiences of the religious life. When this kind of Christianity attains its goal, although it is borne forward by the most genuine religious impulse, it is de-christianised. We must get past the old dogma of the Deity of Christ to a higher conception of Christ, one which does not compel us to leave Him outside when we take religion, that is the communion of the soul with God, in all earnestness and truth.

The objection may be raised that it is just the Church dogma that gives us the representation of the exalted Christ and the doctrine of the Trinity. But in neither does it give us any pledge that when the Christian is

at the highest point of his inner life, and is conscious
that he is inwardly in the grasp of God, he will really
find Christ in God.   The Christian who is religiously
alive will always treat the idea of the Trinity as we find
Augustine did.   The reflective process which is necessary to any clear grasp of the idea of the Trinity ceases
altogether in the moments of such religious exaltation.
Augustine wrote a work of fifteen books on the Trinity,
yet, when he stood with his mother at the window of
the house at Ostia, and sought to express the deepest
sense of being in the grasp of God, he spoke not of the
Trinity but of the one God, in whose presence the soul
is lifted above itself and above all words and signs.   A
mystic who professes to hold the doctrine of the Trinity
knows that all that can be said about it belongs to those
words and signs which must shrink away back, along
with the whole world, when God makes His presence
felt.   Dante thought, indeed, that in the moment of
most exalted vision in Paradise he beheld three empty
circles.   This was a powerful expression for the thought
that religious exaltation comes to its climax in the
Ineffable.   But it certainly does not prove that the
doctrine of the Trinity will enable us to hold fast to
the vision of Jesus in the midst of our actual communion
with God.   For an empty circle and the personal life of
Christ are two things as different as can be.   The conception of the exalted Christ stands in a similar position
with the doctrine just treated.   That conception, as it
stands, by no means guarantees that in our actual
religion we shall be sure to combine the idea of Christ
with that of God.   It is possible, of course, that the

conception may arise and be cherished in such a way
that this necessary characteristic just mentioned may be
preserved. But it may also be so understood as to
nourish only an empty play of fancy, and whenever this
is the case, earnest piety will surrender itself to mysticism, and so press forward beyond such nonentities.
But this mysticism will, at the same time, lead the soul
beyond Christ.

The real facts of the case, then, are that ecclesiastical
dogma and the piety which culminates in mysticism are
bound up the one with the other, and that the Christian
Church can abide by neither. For she cannot allow herself to be placed permanently in a position where she
must be separated from Christ if she is to be lifted
into communion with God. The Christian cannot cut
himself loose from that history in which he has found
the revelation of God to himself.

If we take our stand thus within history, we may
expect as a matter of course that those who are inclined
to mysticism will think us narrow-minded. They cannot imagine how a man who yearns after the eternal
can hold fast to history.* Our only answer now to this
shall be to ask them in turn how they are sure they are
really aware of God Himself when they have those
emotions in which their whole nature seems to be exalted.
Our confidence in God needs other support than the
recollection of such purely emotional experiences can
give. We are Christians because, in the human Jesus,

---

* On this point compare my pamphlet "Warum bedarf unsere
Glaube geschichtlicher Thatsachen" ("Why does our faith require
historical facts?"). Second edition. Halle. 1891.

we have met with a fact whose content is incomparably
richer than that of any feelings which arise within ourselves—a fact, moreover, which makes us so certain of
God that our conviction of being in communion with
Him can justify itself at the bar of reason and of conscience.   Perhaps we may count upon the agreement of
the majority of Protestant theologians with us in our
exposition of mysticism as the perfection of Roman
Catholic piety.   In that case, they must be sensible of
the need for as clear an understanding of the different
nature of the Protestant's communion with God.   Our
church fellowship with each other rests upon our belief
that, amid all other differences, the same divine power
is leading us all to the same goal. This goal is not, indeed,
the mystic's emotional experience, but it is nevertheless
most certainly the communion of the soul with God.

§ 8. *We get free from Mysticism and Scholasticism when
we get beyond the Legal Conception of Religion.*

It must be the chief object of our theological
discussions to guide us to a clear understanding of
what that communion ought to be.   In the first place,
we must regard as revelation only that which brings
us into actual communion with God; and we can
regard as the thoughts of our own faith only what
comes home to us as truth within the sphere of our
actual communion with God.   Thus all that can be
the object of Christian doctrine is summed up in
religious experience, and first gains satisfactory definition
in that connection.   But, on the other hand, we can
describe as religious experience only that turning toward

God which takes place under the influence of the revelation of God within us, and can be expressed in doctrines of faith.

In observing this latter point we avoid the false path of mysticism. We quite recognise, in common with mysticism, that religious experience always culminates in the ineffable; but we maintain firmly also that the whole of the spiritual life is supported by the spiritual and definable power of the revelation of God, and, moreover, that the whole of this life consists of such spiritual processes as can be clearly expressed in the thoughts of faith. We hold that the ineffable in religion can indeed be experienced, but only in connection with that which can be put into words. Apart from this the experience would lack Christian definiteness and the consciousness of being true. Thus we escape mysticism without losing the truth it contains.

In observing the first point we avoid scholasticism. Many people find it difficult to free themselves from this Roman Catholic sort of theology, because they cannot make up their minds to be content with what is actually given them as divine revelation. Vanity and the fear of men produce a constant tendency to regard as God's revelation, and as real doctrines of faith, things which we have simply taken from the confessions of other men. This was the mistaken practice of Roman Catholic theology, and it exercises a wide influence over the heart of Christendom, even where men have not so much as heard the names of the schoolmen. The practice is not altered by transforming particular doctrines, nor by choosing apostles instead of popes as the men whose confessions we appropriate. It endures so long as people appropriate other men's expressions of their redeemed life and fancy that by so doing they become exactly like those other men. Whenever men deal thus with other men's professions of faith, even if those other men be the apostles themselves, they remain essentially Roman Catholics. Our aim should rather be to become such freemen as they were with whose professions we vainly deck ourselves. God alone can set the captives free. Theology should show us the way to Him. All the more, then, must she refuse to forge the fetters which human vanity so willingly binds about itself. On the contrary she should rather teach us to throw away these sham jewels and riches, and to flee to the revelation which can really help us out of our poverty. The most important task of theology is to open men's eyes, and lead them to see that nothing can be revelation to them except what actually lifts them into communion with God.

But one great hindrance on this true way of salvation is just that system of the thoughts of various men which theology has constructed after the fashion of the schoolmen. Such a system is dangerous to begin with, because it claims to represent complete knowledge where none of us can possibly know as a living thing more than part. And it becomes a sore temptation when it presses on us with the claim that it can help us if only we will surrender ourselves to its rule. We reject this counterfeit wealth of theology, which becomes an intolerable burden upon the earnest seeker after salvation by treating the two branches of Christian doctrine, namely, the setting forth of the revelation and the evolution of the doctrines of faith only in their divinely ordered and vital connection with the essence of religion, the communion of the Christian with God. By this breach from scholasticism, we gain for theology the opposite result from that which our breaking loose from mysticism brings about for the inner life of the Christian. There is less theology ; there is a richer life within. Our rejection of the practice of Roman Catholicism suggests the true course for the accomplishment of our task. Our object is to set forth the real communion of the Christian with God. The Christian is lifted into that communion when God turns to him and enters into communion with him ; and then, as he becomes conscious of the new reality into which he has come, his life in fellowship with God unfolds itself in the thoughts of faith concerning that reality.

§ 9. *We part Company with the Older Protestantism.*

Here, however, we come into conflict also with the aims and the methods that came to be followed in the older Protestant orthodoxy. The older theologians believed their great task was to present in their logical connection those thoughts in which the classic witnesses to Christianity had expressed their faith. We go further back. For we desire to show how those thoughts arise in the course of communion with God in the Christian soul that has been set free to enter into this experience. Thus we exhibit these thoughts, not as something handed down by tradition but as something in vital growth at the present moment, as, in short, thoughts of faith. The problem of theology, as it was then conceived, was manifestly insufficient, because it left quite untouched a question of the greatest practical importance. Here is the question: when that compendium of faith which is supposed to be necessary has been gathered from the Holy Scriptures, and has been logically arranged, and so set forth objectively, how is a man to make this his own subjective property? No one has been able to solve this problem. In spite of the long discussions on the point in treatises on the so-called Plan of Salvation,[8] the question remains unanswered. In fact, it was left with God, as a secret beyond our comprehension, to explain how the individual was to make that salvation his own which had been objectively set forth in theological doctrines.

It seemed best that it should so remain. For was there not danger in going further, and seeking to show, by a study of the processes of one's own consciousness, how salvation could be appropriated? Salvation had, of course, to be presented in a formal doctrine, which claimed to have formulated the doctrines of faith as found in Holy Scripture. But the attempt to discover the processes within the soul whereby this matter became the possession of the individual, always led to an undesirable emphasis on the human activity as compared with the objectively presented salvation. Man was to appropriate the salvation which was set before him in the doctrines of faith. But how could he do so when these doctrines were the expression of a life that he lacked. If any one tried, nevertheless, to show that a man could make such thoughts his own, it was evident that the unredeemed man had to be credited with the power to transplant himself into the new spiritual life. But what sort of a redemption is it in which man saves himself? Such was the inevitable end of the attempt, under the conditions of the older theology, to understand the processes within the soul by which the individual appropriates salvation, or becomes redeemed; the result always was that the very idea of redemption was in danger of being lost.

We are not in this peril. We will have nothing to do with the idea that the doctrines of faith systematically formulated either do or can offer salvation to men. It is, in fact, a mockery of the unredeemed man to offer him as his salvation a sum of doctrines or thoughts of which he is obliged to say that they are not his thoughts and cannot be so. The thoughts of others who are redeemed cannot redeem me. If I am to be saved, everything depends on my being transplanted into that inner condition of mind in which such thoughts begin to be generated in myself, and this happens only when God lifts me into communion with Himself. There we stand amid that truth which is absolutely closed to the unredeemed man.

Then, too, it becomes possible for us to recognise in the doctrines or thoughts set forth in Holy Scripture the free movements of that same spiritual life which has now begun in us also. Of course we do not recognise these in every idea that stands in the Bible, but this need not rob us of our peace. For the doctrines and thoughts of Scripture are not a lesson that we have to prepare as if for school. If they are taken in that sense, then they belong to that "world" which the redeemed has to overcome. For him such external laws are to be done away. He finds in his communion with the God who alone bestows and directs life another law binding him far more forcibly. If the Christian has been really lifted into communion with God, then his duty is to enjoy the new life thus given him. To this he is assisted by the witness of all the redeemed and free life within the church of God, and that witness he finds in Scripture as nowhere else. A man learns how to see this glory of the sacred Scripture when there has begun in him the same life whose rise and whose perfection are there incomparably described. Before that, the Bible is to him a book with seven seals; after that, he sees in it a means of the revelation of the grace and of the judgment of God. Before that, the thought that he is to treat the Bible otherwise than as he treats all other literature, is to him intolerable, or, at least, utterly strange. Afterwards not all the systematic investigation of the Holy Scriptures which has been developed into historical criticism will ever get him away from this position. For then he regards it as an actual miracle in history standing there before his eyes that, in the Scriptures, he finds for the new personal life that has begun in himself, and which must begin in every man in the same way, a new world which is its home. In what becomes clear to him there as revelation of God he feels himself in the grip of the law to which he must keep faithful.

§ 10. *The Difficulty and Practicability of our Undertaking.*

Thus our task is quite different from that of the older theology, so far as that theology remains on Roman Catholic lines. We have not to show how the unredeemed man is to become possessor of the ideas of the redeemed. But we are to show how he finds God and how he becomes thereby a new man, to whom these ideas remain no longer foreign. We are to bring into clear view a process which the older theology has always suffered to remain veiled. But the objection may be raised at once that any such attempt will fall directly into the worst error of mysticism. For surely what Luther says about being a child of God holds good of the inner life of religion in every case. Luther says, " If thou truly feelest this in thy heart, it will be so great a thing to thee that thou wilt rather keep silence than say aught of it."* We must recognise the full importance of this objection. The health of our religious life does indeed suffer injury if we attempt to tear away the last veil which hides it. Moreover, such an attempt never succeeds, for where religion is truly alive it is at bottom an ineffable mystery.

But it is not our intention at all to express what is unutterable. Mysticism has sought to do that ; for our part we will not try. Indeed, we affirm, on the contrary, that one group of the doctrines of faith expresses this very consciousness that the Christian life contains

* Erlangen edition, vol. xi. p. 194.

depths which cannot be fathomed.   Nevertheless, there
is something we can say concerning the way in which
man enters into communion with God.   For this experience depends on the working of objective forces
which, while they remain without significance for other
men, are yet for the Christian the expression of the
fact that God is acting on him, and of the way that
this happens.   Our exposition is concerned with the
connection of the religious life with the objective reality
around which we find ourselves.   In aiming thus at
something objective we are at one with the orthodox
Protestant theology.   But the objective reality of which
we are thinking is something quite different from the
thoughts of faith which are formulated in the common
doctrine.   These thoughts have no power to generate
the communion of the Christian with God; they are
only the expression of that sense of new life which comes
with such communion.   But everything depends on being
able clearly to grasp the objective reality which, by its
sheer bulk, produces in the Christian the certainty that
he is not without God in the world.   And how the
Christian sees this reality, and experiences its power,
can be described without either ignoring or injuring
the mystery of the inner life.

When we reject the theology whose dogmas are regarded
by the Roman Catholic Church as the necessary counterpoise to mysticism, those who cling to such theology are
apt to suppose that we are sure to fall into the same
mistake as the mysticism which breaks away from all
church limits.   But we have no intention whatever of
resolving Christianity into mere subjective feeling.   In

our view the subjective vitality of Christianity ought to
show itself in the energy with which it lays holds of and
values what is objective, namely, in the first place, the
power that can awaken and establish faith, and, in the
second place, those thoughts and utterances in which
faith makes itself known to believers.   This is just the
fault we have to find with mysticism, that it disregards
the link between the inner life of the Christian and its
real foundation, and also that it allows feelings which
have no distinct character to push aside thoughts concerning faith as if they were unessential.   The riches of
the Christian life of feeling are not to be had without
building on that foundation, nor without intimate relationship to those thoughts.   If these be wanting, the
most powerful emotions cannot enrich a man's life.
They neither give him anything new nor do they lead
him out from himself ; they leave him to experience and
to enjoy only what he has already possessed in his
previous condition.   But the man who is a Christian
always strives to rise above himself ; he must always
be looking for things to come.   Mere emotion cannot
raise us into a new life, for mere emotion leaves us
alone with ourselves and with what we have already
attained, and nothing more.   So we shall find that
the new state of feeling into which the Christian
has entered always clings to something richer than
itself, which it distinguishes from its own nature :
that is, it needs an objective reality.   Greater and
higher than all religious emotion within the Christian
there rises and towers religious thought, which
points, away past all that we have already felt

and experienced, to a boundless wealth that lies beyond.

Thus, while we insist on freedom from mysticism, we are in agreement with the old theological procedure on the following points:

(1) The subjective experiences of the Christian religion cannot be severed from the objective power which leads us into those experiences.

(2) The subjective experience of the Christian religion cannot be severed from the thoughts which Christian doctrine seeks to formulate as the contents of faith. That experience does not end in mere feeling, but comes to its perfection in those thoughts.

(3) These thoughts are much more than mere expressions of what we have already felt and enjoyed, for they express also what has been promised to us of God, who has taken possession of us and awakened our faith within us.

But we depart also from the old procedure in laying down the following propositions:

(1) The objective power which is the enduring basis of the religious experiences of a Christian is not any sum of thoughts concerning faith, however obtained, but is the man Jesus.

(2) The thoughts concerning faith arise within that communion with God into which the personal power of Jesus lifts us.

(3) It is not the possession of any prescribed sum of such thoughts, recorded though they may be in Holy

Scripture, that makes a man a Christian, but the faculty of producing such thoughts, and of cherishing them as the truth grasped by his own consciousness.

§ 11. *The Longing of the Christian for an Objective Reality to Support his Faith is made effective in Luther's Christianity.*

Should an opponent appear now after all with the objection that we are resolving Christianity into the subjective, we can only suppose that for him Jesus is not objective. Let such a man only ask himself whether the person of Jesus in its unquestionable reality is not a firmer support for his inner life than any sum of prescribed doctrine which he may, indeed, profess, but into which he cannot wholly fit his life, for the simple reason that God has not made him a parasite. That which determines our attitude is just the soul's craving after rest upon some undoubtedly objective reality, the need of knowing that we have submitted our religious life to some power which is altogether beyond any control by will or act of ours. It is a demand of God that comes home to us in this craving, and it must be obeyed. But the work to which God thus calls us does not mean that a break must be made with the past of our Church. It is precisely the vital instinct of Protestant Christianity that leads us to reject all authorities that would turn religion into a product of our own caprice; the Protestant instinct impels us to find that God who will have religion to be the product in our hearts of His will and of our own free rational obedience. Thus Protestantism began in

Luther as something quite new, and yet embracing all the best traditions of the old Church, and so it has remained in all its subsequent course so far as that course has not tended to defections and divisions. And so we wish it to remain.

In our description of the new life which is created in the Christian through the revelation of God, we shall let Luther be our guide. This, of course, does not imply that we shall here profess Luther's doctrine at every point. He lived in different conditions from ours, and therein he faithfully fulfilled his calling; but if we slavishly copied him, we should be unlike him.

To give only one illustration : Luther lived in an age when the authority of Holy Scripture as the Infallible Word of God and the authority of the dogma of the ancient Church enjoyed unquestioning recognition. And Luther held these views, these mental possessions of his time, more firmly than any other man. Hence he showed his religious energy in the very way in which he made use of these positions, then supposed to be impregnable, in order to clear the way to God for himself and others.* Had he not done so, he would not have been loyal to the faith which aims at the one thing needful, namely, to find God. Now Luther's theology arose from the combination of his new comprehension of Christianity with those Roman Catholic assumptions. In reality they had nothing to do with each other. He was not led to his new comprehension of Christianity by regarding the sacred Scriptures as an inspired law book, whose words we must follow without

* *Cf*. Harnack, " Text-book of the History of Dogma," iii. 695.[9]

question even where we do not understand them. Luther would never have gained that new comprehension simply from the reading of the sacred Scriptures. He found it, rather, amid the inward battles of a soul that could find no rest in any means of grace, because it sought the God of grace Himself, and amid such struggle he discovered records in the sacred Scriptures of what it is that can redeem a man. But he went on from the comfort that he found in his agreement with the Christianity of the New Testament, and came to place reliance on an obedience to the Scripture as a sort of law. In this, of course, he and his Roman Catholic opponents were at one. In consequence of this he imported into his doctrine much that he had neither understood as God's revelation nor had come to possess as the thoughts of his own faith. Similarly, Luther shared the Roman Catholic position with regard to the dogma of the older Church. He knew no more than any other man of his time what had been the original meaning of that dogma, and he believed firmly, like everybody else, that reverence was due to this sacred relic of the past. But while it remained for others at best a mysterious relic, Luther made of it a vessel for carrying that conception of Christianity in which his faith lived. So he had at once a far deeper relationship to the old dogma, and a stronger sense of the paramount importance of his great cause. Dogma was simply a dead weight to his opponents, but to him it was alive again with religious significance, and became an important element in the life of faith. He could not doubt that he had thus entered again into the piety

of the fathers, and so it is correct to say that the dogma
of the older Church was among the sources of Luther's
power. But that comprehension of the Gospel which
made him a Protestant and a Reformer sprang in
reality as little from the dogma of the old Church as it
did from his reverence for the inspired word of
Scripture as a sort of law. If, then, Luther is to
be our guide we must distinguish between Luther's
Christianity and Luther's theology ; for the latter
is built upon the assumptions of Roman Catholicism.

§ 12. *The Elements of Luther's Theology which belong to the Past.*

This distinction is imperative. That teaching of
Luther to which we will and can hold is his prophetic
word, in which he expresses what he has experienced,
the revelation of God as his own redemption. That
part of his teaching to which we could not hold, even if
we would, is no expression of his religious experience,
but it is his earnest effort, which cannot be too highly
praised, to find a right place and a real usefulness for
what at that date passed unquestioned amid the new
conception of Christianity which he had gained. No
one can now maintain that part of Luther's teaching in
the same way as he maintained it. For what at that
time held good without even being questioned, and
could therefore be used as a reliable means of assistance,
stands no longer unquestioned. The chariot on which
Luther's Christianity made its entrance into the Church
has become feeble and broken. If it is nevertheless to

be preserved, it certainly cannot serve any longer as a safe means of conveyance, but is at best a highly honoured burden.

The theologians who should refuse to make this distinction, and who should demand that we teach Luther's doctrine in its entirety, could not bring about now in any complete sense a reverence for Holy Scripture as a law book. They certainly could not assume that such reverence is an element in the spiritual life of those who claim to be Christians. Luther could freely assume and build upon many things which it must cost those theologians great trouble even to try to hold together. But no one nowadays has any confidence that this is really possible. No one can still hold to the idea that all words of Scripture being the word of God are infallible expressions of the truth.* But without this idea, any intention to reverence the word of Scripture as if it were a law, even where one does not view it as an expression of the truth, is an abnegation of thought. Of this every one is sensible whose religion has cost him any mental labour at all. Wherever such an one attempts to copy the theology of Luther he suffers a most painful discomfort, which is the very opposite of what Luther got from his system.

The same is to be said of the other Roman Catholic element in Luther's theology, namely, his reverence for dogma. It is true that the same reverence for dogmas is still among Protestants bound up in many ways with the mistaken conception of the Scriptures as an infallible

* *Cf.* Dieckhoff, "Die Inspiration und Irrtumslosigkeit der heiligen Schrift, 1891," pp. 59–97.

law ; but it is no longer a sure, unassailable assumption, as it was to Luther. We can no longer start from this assumption, as Luther did, when we deal with a man whom we seek to lead to Christianity. Nor, again, can we still declare with Luther that we will not argue with a man who does not admit the infallibility of the Scriptures or does not accept the Nicene Creed. If we were to do so, we should be not merely uncharitable, but untruthful. We theologians are ourselves cast out from the position of simple reverence for dogma because—and this is only putting the matter at its lowest —we have set about investigating the sources of it. Historical study of the growth of any human ideas always tends to liberate men from subjection to those ideas. And so, by the effect of such study, that which held good without question for Luther and the men of his time, in respect both of dogma and of the infallibility of Scripture, has become problematical for us and our contemporaries. Therefore, to interweave these two elements with Christian preaching now would have quite the contrary effect to that produced in Luther's time ; what then brought certainty can now only produce uneasiness if the same claim be made for it.

This must be admitted even by those theologians who are confident that with special skill they can still show valid grounds for reasserting the older Church dogma, and for reverencing the Scriptures as a law. For in any case our contemporaries are conscious that these things no longer form a firm background whereon one can reckon in Christian preaching. Conservative theologians may regard this state of affairs as a terrible declension, in which, too, they themselves more or less have a share ; but, in any case, they are called upon to help their strayed and homeless fellow men to the right way. And this they can do no longer by means of those assumptions which Luther made, because, as a matter of fact, the men whom they are to help, no longer accept those assumptions. Of course, they can direct their endeavours towards bringing men back again to the acceptance of those assumptions, and that is indeed the intention of many. But they will make no serious attempt to do this, and simply for this reason : that they are not firmly established themselves in the position where they would fain see others. Now, is the preaching of the Gospel to cease until such an attempt succeeds, or shall it go forward in the form of instruction based upon presuppositions, which, as a matter of fact, are no longer present ? The first course is impossible, and the second, while it is indeed pursued, is of little use. There may always be men among us who think they can maintain the Roman Catholic position towards the sacred Scriptures as an infallible law, and towards the older ecclesiastical dogma, and nothing is gained by arguing whether or not it is possible to hold that position in earnest ; for even such men must, in any case, admit that no one can bring the Gospel home to the men of our time as glad tidings, or as a convincing word of God, if he speaks to them from that standpoint. When such, then, is the case, we must all be equally interested in the success of the effort to free the Gospel from the connection in which it appears in Luther's theology.

I believe that this is possible if we allow Luther's system of theology to be set aside as a work accomplished for his own age, and proceed to inquire what was that communion with God into which he knew himself delivered through Christ and redeemed. Luther often spoke of this without using any of the language of Roman Catholic theology. It may, perhaps, help those who can no longer accept his theology because they do not share its presuppositions, if we describe those experiences which Luther had of the Redeemer.   And this is the more to be expected because, in his testimony concerning the one thing needful, Luther repudiates entirely the demand that, in order to become a Christian, one must begin by clear submission to some kind of prescribed doctrine.   Luther certainly regarded as self-evident certain views which we cannot make our own, or could accept only with great difficulty.   But he never demanded submission to prescribed doctrines as an essential part of religious experience.   Instead of holding such a submission to be a means of salvation, he pronounced it to be a sin. Since he thought that the way to salvation in Christ did not lie through any such performance, it is to be hoped that his weighty testimony will help the upright souls to-day, who, even for the hope of bliss, would not stain their conscience by professing to have certain ideas to which in reality they are strangers.   We shall therefore confine ourselves to those of Luther's writings in which he is occupied far more with the positive description of the Christian life than with polemical consideration of limitations laid upon that life by the

Church. In these we shall find a Luther who is at one
with himself.[10] Of Luther the theologian we cannot
say as much. How often, for example, his views
changed on the doctrine of the Lord's Supper! But
whether we turn to his discourse of the year 1518 on
Repentance, or to the sermons of the last years of his
life, we find everywhere the same portrayal of the new
life awakened in him by God, in the strength of which
he could say of himself, "My spirit is too glad and too
great for me to be at heart an enemy to any man." *
Luther's witness to that which makes a Christian to be
a Christian is a treasure not yet sufficiently valued, and
it is incomparably more precious than his theology.
The latter has had its day. Only those who are as simple-
hearted and as unconscious heirs of Roman Catholic
theology as Luther was could thoroughly enter into it;
of such persons there cannot be many now. But, on
the other hand, it will quicken and help forward, and
perhaps bring deliverance to men in whom the
yearning for God is not dead, to see how Luther came
to that communion with God which gave him a joyful
heart and a dauntless courage.

* Erlangen edition, xxiv. 16.

II.

THE ESTABLISHMENT OF
OUR COMMUNION WITH GOD
THROUGH THE REVELATION OF GOD

§ 1. *The Conception of Revelation as Communicated Knowledge about God, and the Piety founded on this Notion.*

WE may speak of having communion with God only when we are certain that God speaks clearly to us, and also hears and considers our speech in His operations.

In order to commune with us, God makes Himself known to us. The God of whose communion with men the Sacred Scripture tells, does not, for His own holiness' sake, suffer men to reach Him through any efforts of their own. He will vouchsafe this in one way alone, and that way He opens to us Himself. Now, further, if it is impossible for a man to rise unaided above all fightings and doubts into the realm of real communion with God, it is equally certain that no mere information of any kind concerning God could thus raise a man, even although that information should claim to be a divine revelation. We might indeed form a conception of God on the ground of such information. We might consent to acknowledge the reality of that revelation, and we might therefore believe our conception of God to be correct But in that case we should still have to win for ourselves the impression that the God thus revealed did actually commune with us. If we had received only information concerning God, it would still be left to us to obtain the certainty of a real communion of God with ourselves. And no such endeavour of ours could ever conquer doubt, for it is just amid such endeavours that doubt does always rise. *Information concerning God*, therefore, although it may claim to be of divine revelation, can only bring that troubled piety which lives by no delivering act of God, but by men's own exertions. God has left us in no such miserable condition, and Protestants, at least, may know this, if they will only refuse to be led aside from the one thing needful by common cries like the following: " You must believe that God made the world; that men sprang from a single pair; that God's Son became a man; that God's demand for the punishment of the guilty has been satisfied by the death of his Son; and finally that all this happened for your sake." He who determines so to believe, can only cause distress to his soul. For in such doctrines, however true they may be in themselves, we are not brought face to face with that reality which gives faith its certainty; they simply tell us something, and we are then expected by our own efforts to hold that information to be true.

§ 2. *Revelation as a Fact inside our own Experience, but*
Distinct from Ourselves, Convincing us of God's
Working upon us.

But we leave all these fruitless endeavours at religious
self-help behind, when we entirely reject the idea
that we are to believe doctrines. Untroubled by these
suggestions we must put ourselves the one question :
" Whereby shall we know that a living God is
communing with us ? " Then, when we come to see
and understand the reality which makes us certain of
this fact, we see also that the painful effort which had
been demanded of us is taken away by God's own act.
For when the Christian has once experienced the fact
that God is striving to make Himself known to him,
and when he sees how God so strives, then he begins to
see also what is true in those aforesaid doctrines.

God makes Himself known to us, so that we may
recognise Him, through *a fact, on the strength of which*
we are able to believe on Him. No doctrine of any kind
can do more than tell us how we ought to represent
God to ourselves. No doctrine can bring it about that
there shall arise in our hearts the full certainty that God
actually exists for us; only a fact can inspire such
confidence within us. Now we Christians hold that we
know only one fact in the whole world which can overcome every doubt of the reality of God, namely, the
appearance of Jesus in history, the story of which has been
preserved for us in the New Testament. Our certainty
of God may be kindled by many other experiences, but
has ultimately its firmest basis in the fact that within

the realm of history to which we ourselves belong, we encounter the man Jesus as an undoubted reality.

Of course, we may have heard about Jesus for a long time without His becoming manifest to us in His power. We can hardly put it that it is only in the vision of the Person of Jesus that our eyes are first opened to the invisible. Probably for all of us that revelation comes from those in our immediate circle, and we ought in our turn to do a like service to others. But such men, in whose earnestness and brotherly love we can trace a hidden life with God, are fragments of God's revelation. The whole revelation that God has ordained for us in our historical situation is ours only when we can see that the Person of Jesus surpasses all else that is great and noble in humanity, and that behind those whose influence upon us is strongest, He is visible as their life-giver and their Lord. The revelation of God that we get from those of our most immediate circle is not pushed aside or emptied of its value, but only deepened and perfected as we become acquainted with Jesus Himself.

The true Christian confession is that Jesus is the Christ. Rightly understood, however, it means nothing else than this : that through the man Jesus we are first lifted into a true fellowship with God. If it be asked what we are to understand by that, the reply is that for those who truly seek God it should be wonderfully simple. But it is often made difficult by those thieves amid Christendom (John x. i), who pretend to come into fellowship with God by some other way than through the man Jesus. The by-path most frequented is that of doctrines concerning Jesus which give Him the highest praise, and so form the most convenient means of avoiding His Person. By this means the only way of salvation is closed to persons without number. The divinely simple fact that the man Jesus is the Christ is made distasteful to them by the idea instilled into them that they may come into possession of much higher things, namely, a number of wonderful doctrines, the *fides quae creditur*,* by simply believing them. The result is that even among us Protestants it has become very difficult for the majority to regard the finding of God as the highest good, or even to look upon it as a wonderful gift from Him at all. Most men think it of small importance that Jesus alone makes us certain of a living God, for they imagine that of all the doctrines in which they " believe" the doctrines of the existence of God is the most elementary.

§ 3. *The Person of Jesus as the only Revelation Convincing One who Perceives the Necessity of Unconditional Obedience.*

From this there has arisen a bad practice now widely spread among us. When the question is asked : " On what depends our certainty of a Living God who works in us?" it is quite a common practice to look away from ourselves and our own particular position, and to think of as many men as possible, who stand at the greatest possible distance from us, such as the savages of New Holland or the ancient Egyptians. None of these, it is urged, have been utterly without

* " The faith which is commonly held."—Tr.

the capacity for recognising God, as indeed the apostle
Paul testifies. We are also further reminded that
Israel had the knowledge of God and enjoyed communion with Him before Christ came, and therefore it
it is finally concluded that what was possible to the
Jews must also be possible to us. Such arguments
are frequently set up in contradiction of our proposition
that for us Jesus is the revelation of God. And then
that proposition of ours looks like an exaggeration.
It seems as though, in order to reduce it to its right
proportions, we ought rather to say that we may have the
revelation of the being of God quite apart from Jesus,
but that Jesus makes some addition to that revelation,
as, for example, the knowledge that God has a Son and
constitutes one Being with Him.

Now to all this we may reply that we by no means
wish to assert, even for a moment, that the savages of
New Holland have no knowledge of God, no pulsations
of true religion, and therefore no communion with God.
But we do not know through what medium such knowledge and such communion reach them. We cannot
enter fully into the religious life even of a pious
Israelite, for the facts which worked upon them as
revelations of God have no longer this force for us.
Israel stood in communion with God as *His people;*
hence national feeling was an indispensable element
in Jewish piety; and just because the Israelite knew
what it meant to belong to Israel instead of to any
any other nation, he was able to grasp as revelations
of God those features in the course of Hebrew history
which he did so apprehend. Since we cannot feel as

Jews, the revelation which was given to Israel can no longer satisfy our need. Our position is different; we stand in such historical relationships that Jesus Christ alone can be grasped by us as the fact in which God so reveals Himself to us that everything that hides Him from us vanishes away. The knowledge of God and the religion which have been and which are possible to men placed in other historical conditions are impossible to us. Indeed, there exists in our case a hindrance to the religious life of which men were quite ignorant in olden times, namely, that deepening of the moral consciousness which has come about, and the consequent moral need. We feel ourselves to be separated from God, and consequently crippled in our faith by things which troubled the ancients very little. We cannot go back to our first simple indifference to moral demands after our conscience has once been sensible of them. Above all, the knowledge that we are bound to unconditional obedience can never die away into sloth and inactivity after it has once dawned upon us. So that when we are faced by something that wants to force itself on us as a Power over our entire life, the doubt arises in our minds whether in it we really find something we can be conscientiously willing to obey unconditionally. He who is morally free will mock at a religion that is above morality just as he pities one that is beneath it. Therefore, the only God that can reveal Himself to us is one who shows Himself to us in our moral struggle as the Power to which our souls are really subject. This is what is vouchsafed to us in the revelation of God in Jesus Christ.

He gives a fulness to our personal life which burst all other moulds of religion and allows us to find rest only in that communion with God into which He brings us.

§ 4. *The Person of Jesus is the most Important Element in the Sphere of Reality which we can Reflect upon.*

If we wish to come to God, we must not, above all things, turn our back upon the actual relationships in which we stand. The concrete reality amid which we actually live must be the nourishment of our inner life. When we take this reality to heart, then God enters our life. For the earth is the Lord's. Dreams which soar away from reality lead not to God but to nothing. They are a form of original sin, a form of untruth in which we spin a web of emptiness about ourselves, and so cut ourselves off from true life.

That is the right in the efforts that have cost honest thinkers so much toil, as they have tried to discover for human reason the activity of the Creator in the reality of nature. Those attempts belong, however, to a period of Christian life that has now been outlived. We do not apprehend ourselves as what we really are when we conceive ourselves as part of nature, for we have become conscious that our realm of life is human society and its history. Nature alone cannot show us all the reality in which we stand. She belongs to that reality, being herself a means to the existence of society; but it is in this society itself, this historical life, of which nature is thus a subordinate part and means, that we first reach the true reality, of which we must become conscious if our inner life is to have any content at all. For this reason we can no longer hope to find God by seeking Him in nature. God is hidden from us in nature because we do not find our whole selves there, we do not find there the full riches of that reality, which crowds in upon our consciousness. It is only out of life in history that God can come to meet us. In proportion as what is essential in our historical environment becomes an element of our consciousness we are led into the presence of those facts which can reveal God to us. If our souls do not awake to a clear consciousness of these facts, if we simply endure our relationship to other men, instead of living it, then the personality within us to which God desires to reveal Himself remains dormant, and we do not see the facts through which alone God can reveal Himself to us.

In that historical environment which ought to give our personal life its fulness, there is no fact more important for each individual than Jesus Christ. To overlook Him is to deceive ourselves as to the best treasure which our own life possesses. For He is precisely that fact which can make us certain, as no other fact can, that God communes with us. This assertion will no doubt give to many the impression of a manifest exaggeration. All who are accustomed to follow the orthodox method of teaching will esteem it such, but so, too, will those who think along rationalistic lines. The former think they find the support of their religious life in doctrines concerning God and Christ which are vouched for by others; the latter wish to found their inward peace neither upon authorities nor upon past events in history, but upon that eternal truth which they grasp in their own thinking here and now. Both classes must find a stumbling-block in our proposition that the person of Jesus is the fact by which God communes with us. Both are inclined to imagine that the communion with God with us is an inward experience into which external facts do not intrude. The objections they raise against our proposition are, *first*, that the person of Jesus is a fact vouched for by authorities, and, *secondly*, that it is a thing of the past. They hold that the first objection forbids us to say that, strictly speaking, *Jesus Himself* is an element of the reality in which we stand; they hold that such can be said only of the *tradition concerning Jesus*. They contend that the second objection above forbids us to say that God communes with us by this fact, *i.e.*, the person of Jesus, because this fact is a thing of the past, whereas God's communion with us must be a thing of the present. This latter contention has been specially emphasised by Luthardt; * but is evident that it will also be raised by every devout rationalist and mystic.

§ 5. *It is not through a Historical Judgment that the Person of Jesus becomes a Fact we Ourselves Establish.*

The former contention has the greater weight. Men must indeed be powerfully moved by the supposition that Jesus Himself cannot be held to be an undeniable element in our actual environment, and that it is only the story of Jesus, as vouched for by others, that can be

* See my treatise on " The Certainty of Faith and the Freedom of Theology." Second edition, 1889, p. 75. Luthardt says, against the inclusion of the past in the present religious experience, " How can what is preterite be what is present ? "[11]

called such an element. Many within the Christian fellowship find this supposition to be a very slave-chain, and for many outside that fellowship it is a drag holding them back from entering. But are the chains as adamantine as they seem ? If not, then we, too, can overcome a serious hindrance which the faith of the Reformers reached beyond, but from which they could not get free.

It is true that we should have no certain knowledge of Jesus if the New Testament did not tell us about him. Narratives by others contribute in all cases not a little to the picture we form for ourselves of historical reality. If tradition of some sort did not show us what others have experienced of human life we should lack the most valuable of the interchanges of spiritual possessions. But given this exchange, then the narrative which comes to us, either by word of mouth or in writing, is not the only fact which we incorporate into our picture of historical reality ; the content of those narratives may also become a fact for us. This happens only when we can ourselves establish its reality, and we may do this in various ways.

The most elementary form of doing so consists in extending the confidence we place in the trustworthiness of the narrator to that which he narrates. This constantly happens in our daily life, whenever we base our plans of action upon information given by others. We are guided by the content of their report just as by a reality we have grasped for ourselves. But it does not occur to us to offer ourselves as witnesses that things are really as they are said to be. Hence we can remain in this attitude only so long as we are concerned with matters of minor importance. But as soon as the contents of the information affect seriously the most important interests of life, our trust in the mental power and moral goodness of the narrator no longer suffices to assure us that what he reports is a fact beyond all doubt. If even in such a case we are compelled to take action in reliance on the report, our action takes the character of a venture. We are often obliged to act thus when the pressure of necessity does not permit of inaction ; under such compulsion we may find ourselves obliged to treat the contents of the narrative as fact. But it is obvious that no such compulsion exists when the information received in any way concerns our religious faith. If we do put confidence in the trustworthiness of a narrator, and are thus led to receive his narration as a fact among the subjects of our religious thought, then, whether the confidence be really felt or be only arbitrarily assumed, it is always very certain that the matter reported is nothing that affects the vital interests of religion. This may be clearly seen in Roman Catholicism. The historical appearance of Jesus is there really accepted on the authority of the narrators, and so we find that that appearance has nothing to do with the highest concern of religious life, namely, how a man is to find God. It serves as a stimulus to the imagination, as an example and as a symbol, but it is not to the Roman Catholic the great fact in which he sees God entering into his own life and revealing Himself to him. Whenever we find the proclamation of the appearance of Jesus thus based entirely on the authority of the narrators, it will also be observed that the Person of Jesus is put on one side so soon as the deepest religious interest comes forward for consideration.   A believer cannot base his very existence entirely on what may be given him by other men.

Our mental activity in the matter of receiving reports is certainly greater when we do not form our conception of the actual event from the narrative alone, but seek to obtain it by a combination of the narrative with something else which we know to be real.   This procedure is frequently exemplified in daily life, and it has been developed into an art in historical criticism.   The contents of the narrative are viewed in the light of the evident character of the narrator as seen through his writings, the position he occupied and its impress on him, and the culture of his age which influenced his way of looking at things.   From a consideration of these circumstances we decide how far the contents of the story may be incorporated into our picture of what actually happened.   But the decision thus reached of necessity lays claim to nothing more than probability. We are always prepared to modify our results upon more exact examination of the narrative or upon the discovery of new information.   It is obvious, then, that such decisions do not give us facts on which our religious faith could be based.   Hence it is quite explicable why historical criticism of the sacred records is so much disliked in many quarters.   If men will imagine that the reliability of the sacred records is the proper ground of religious faith, then they must necessarily be rendered in the highest degree uneasy by faithful attempts to estimate the historical probability of what is narrated in those records. We have no such anxiety ; on the contrary, we declare that the historical appearance of Jesus, in so far as it is drawn into the sphere of this attempt to establish the probable truth, cannot be a basis of faith. It is only a part of that world with which faith is to wrestle.

At this point, of course, the question arises whether we can maintain our position that the historical Christ has become for us the absolutely convincing ground of our faith in God.[12] For how is it at all possible to lift out of the mist of probability the content of a tradition that is subject to historical criticism ?

It may be said that we learn with certainty that at least Jesus lived, from the fact of the existence of His church and its historical significance, and that just as little can we question the correctness of certain features in that portrait of Jesus which his followers have preserved in the records of the New Testament. From the standpoint of the mere historian this is certainly the case. A historian may doubt much that the New Testament tells us concerning the glory of Jesus. Because it is possible to attribute it in some measure to the transfiguring enthusiasm of His disciples, it is open to the suspicion of exaggeration. But, on the other hand, the correctness of His portrait in its other features must be admitted by every one who is not prepared to adopt the absurd supposition that in the case of a man who has exerted the greatest influence on history all traces of His earthly life have disappeared. On the strength of those elements in Jesus which, beyond all doubt, are with us to-day, every reasonable man will hold the more general features of the common story of His life to be correct. Now, one might in theory hold the opinion that we have only succeeded in establishing the probability of those facts concerning Jesus ; none the less in practice, even if our interests in Jesus be only historical, we do all include His picture with its well-known features as a part of the historical reality amid which we live, and here we are evidently in no way dependent upon the authority of the chroniclers who give us those features of the life of Jesus. On the contrary, the decision which we reach that these things are facts, proceeds from our own independent activity, and is based upon that which we regard as real at present exactly as the decisions of historial criticism are. It is thus perfectly clear that we are quite in a position to detach the content of a narrative both from the narrative itself and from its author, and to regard it as an element of the reality to which we have to adjust our lives.

§ 6. *The Personality of Jesus by its own Power makes it possible for us to Grasp it as an Element of our own Sphere of Reality.*

Yet this helps us little. The historian may succeed thus in removing doubts as to the historical reality of some person long since dead ; but if he seeks to base his faith in God upon this, his argument collapses immediately. Once again a doubt lifts its head, one which perhaps can have no meaning for the mere

historian. There comes back the feeling that it is a
fatal drawback that no historical judgment, however
certain it may appear, ever attains anything more
than probability. But what sort of a religion would
that be which accepted a basis for its convictions with
the consciousness that it was only probably safe? For
this reason it is impossible to attach religious conviction
to a mere historical decision. Here Lessing is right. If,
notwithstanding all this, the person of Jesus is so
certainly a fact to us Christians that we do see in Him
the basis of our faith, and the present revelation of God
to us, this conviction is not produced by a historical
judgment.* The calmness with which Christendom
holds by the historical reality of Jesus has certainly not
been won by the forcible suppression of historical
doubt. Any such effort would be made contrary to the
dictates of conscience, and it could give no man peace.
It is something quite different which removes all doubt
from the picture of Jesus ; if we have that picture at all,
we have it as the result, not of our own efforts, but of
the power of Jesus Himself.

In the Christian fellowship we are made acquainted,
not merely with the external course of Jesus' lot in life
and of His work in history, but we are also led into His
presence and receive a picture of His inner life. For
this we are certainly dependent, in the first instance,
upon other men. For the picture of Jesus' inner life
could be preserved only by those who had experienced

* I will abstain from giving the names of all who, nevertheless, say
that this is my view. The misrepresentation will go on. For in our
Church it is as useful to the rationalists as to the " positives."[13]

the emancipating influence of that fact upon themselves. The personality of Jesus remained hidden from all others ; it could only reveal itself to such as were lifted by it. Such men were able to understand and to retain the utterances of Jesus which were expressions of his peculiar power. Hence the picture of his inner life could be preserved in His church or " fellowship " alone. But, further, this picture so preserved can be understood only when we meet with men on whom it has wrought its effect. We need communion with Christians in order that, from the picture of Jesus which His church has preserved, there may shine forth that inner life which is the heart of it. It is only when we see its effects that our eyes are opened to its reality so that we thereby experience the same effect. Thus we would never apprehend the most important element in the historical appearance of Jesus did not His people make us feel it. The testimony of the New Testament concerning Jesus arose within His church, and its exposition is the work of the Church, through the life which that Church develops and gains for itself out of this treasure which it possesses. Something similar is the case with every personality ; one must stand within the sphere of life which it created or influenced in order to be able to understand its innermost reality. So if we would understand what is most important in history, we must look not only to the records but also to the men whose actual present life expounds those records to us.

What we are thus seeking is certainly the hardest part to grasp in the whole sum of the historical reality

of Jesus; nevertheless it is just this which sets us free
from the mere record, because it presses in upon us as
a power that is present through its work upon us. He
who has found the inner life of Jesus through the
mediation of others, in so far as he has really found it,
has become free even of that mediation. He is so set
free by the significance which the inner life of the man
Jesus has for him who has beheld it. If we have
experienced His power over us, we need no longer look
for the testimony of others to enable us to hold fast to
His life as a real thing. We start, indeed, from the
records, but we do not grasp the fact they bring us
until the enrichment of our own inner life makes us
aware that we have touched the Living One. This
holds true of every historical personality; the inner
content of any such personality is laid open only to
those who become personally alive to it, and feel themselves aroused by contact with it and see their horizon
widened. The picture of a personality becomes visible
to us in this way, and cannot be handed over to us by
any communication from others; it must arise within
ourselves as the free revelation of the living to the
living. It is thus, therefore, that the inner life of Jesus
becomes part of our own sphere of reality, and the man
who has experienced that will certainly no longer say
that, strictly speaking, he can know only the story of
Jesus as a real thing. Jesus Himself becomes a real
power to us when He reveals His inner life to us; a
power which we recognise as the best thing our life
contains.

Any conscientious reader of the Gospels will be

constantly questioning whether the events actually happened as they stand in the narrative. Of course, we can forcibly suppress this doubt, and many a Christian will think it an inevitable necessity to do so. But such suppression will not help him. Help lies for each of us, not in what we make of the story, but in what the contents of the story make of us. And the one thing which the Gospels will give us as an over-powering reality which allows no doubt is just the most tender part of all : it is the inner life of Jesus itself. Only he who yearns after an honest fulness for his own inner life can perceive the strength and fulness of that soul of Jesus, and whenever we come to see the Person of Jesus, then, under the impress of that inner life that breaks through all the veils of the story, we ask no more questions as to the trustworthiness of the Evan-gelists. The question whether the portrait of Jesus belongs to history or fiction is silenced in every one who learns to see it at all, for by its help he first learns to see what is the true reality of personal life. We must allow the abstract possibility of the view that the historical portrait of Jesus was constructed in good part by men who were able, like ourselves, to fashion visible symbols of religious and moral ideas, and if we look at it thus we shall feel we are in a superior position, for what we can thus explain does not enrich us, but shows us what we already possess. But we cannot think thus of the total picture of Jesus' inner life, for it compels us to simple reverence.[14.]

The man who has had this experience can with heart-felt confidence allow the historical criticism of the New

Testament writings to have full play. If such investigation discovers contradictions and imperfections in the story, it also discloses by that very fact the power of the personality of Jesus, for that personality never lets the contradictions and imperfections of the story disfigure the clear features of that which it gave to men, namely, Jesus' own inner life. It is a fatal error to attempt to establish the basis of faith by means of historical investigation. The basis of faith must be something fixed; the results of historical study are continually changing. The basis of our faith must be grasped in the same independent fashion by learned and unlearned, by each for himself. Howsoever the story may come to us, whether as sifted and estimated by historical criticism or not, the same results ought to follow, and may follow, in both cases, namely, that we learn to see in it the inner life of Jesus. Whether faith then arises in us or not depends on whether this personal spirit wins power over us, or we hold ourselves back from Him. Thus in a moral experience there becomes clear to us what it is that can be the basis of our faith. So far as establishing our faith is concerned, historical work on the New Testament can bring us no nearer, and neither by this nor by any other means can we compel any other man to recognise even the bare reality of that which has an effect upon ourselves so powerful as to give us courage to believe on God.

But, nevertheless, historical work on the New Testament is not without value for faith. In the first place, it shows us how small a foundation those writings afford for a historical account undertaking to set forth as the result of scientific processes what the Person of Jesus shall signify for the Christian. In shattering such hopes it destroys certain false props of faith, and that is a great gain. The Christian who imagines that the reliability of the records as historical documents gives certainty to his faith, is duly startled from his false repose by the work of the historian, which ought to make it clear to such a man that the possession of Christianity cannot be obtained so cheaply as he thinks. Secondly, historical work is constantly constructing afresh, with every possible new modification, whatsoever results can be obtained from the records. By this means the Christian believer is constantly called upon to compare afresh that portrait of Jesus which he carries within him as absolute truth, with the relative truth obtained by historical research. And this helps us not to forget that the most important fact in our life cannot be given to us once for all, but must be continually laid hold of afresh with all our soul. And it helps us also to increasing knowledge of the inexhaustible treasures of the inner life of Christ, and to growing acquaintance with the ways of His sovereignty over the real world. Of course, we lose this advantage entirely if historical research is made to serve the ends of apologetics instead of remaining true to its own laws. It must make us thankful to feel that we have got beyond the temptation to misuse science in this way. For when we speak of the historical Christ[15] we mean that personal life of Jesus which speaks to us from the New Testament, as the disciples' testimony to their faith, but which, when we perceive it, always comes home to us as a miraculous revelation. That historical research cannot give us this we *know*. But neither will it ever take this from us by any of its discoveries. This we *believe*, the more we experience the influence that this picture of the glory of Jesus has upon us.

§ 7. *The Peculiarity of the Christian Religion is Rooted in the Consciousness of this Fact in our own Experience.*

It is, therefore, possible for us to apprehend the historical Person of Jesus as an element in that reality which gives its fulness to our life. If we are to become Christians and attain to a real communion with God, it is necessary that we should so apprehend it. To have gained such an apprehension of Jesus by no means implies that we have attained a peculiarly sublime altitude in the Christian life, it is rather the most elementary thing in Christianity. We must experience the personal life of Jesus to be a real force, first of all by the way in which Jesus' disciples behave to us, and then, when we are ripe enough, in the tradition of the New Testament,[16] and then, out of the joy and amazement that such a thing as the personal life really meets us in the world, it becomes possible for the Christian religion to develop. No matter how carefully we may have been trained from our youth up in a well-ordered system of Christian doctrines, that is not Christian religion, for in that case communion with God is not vouchsafed to us, but is a task set for us. This communion, on which everything depends, is ours only when God Himself so enters into communion with us that we can say to our souls that we mark God's working upon us in undeniable facts, and that we feel His Presence. Clearly this can become ours only through realities which we ourselves perceive to be such ; not through that which others have experienced and tell us about, but only through that which we ourselves experience. No one is ever awakened to true religion by allowing himself to be persuaded that religion in the heart must begin with an absolutely unhesitating confidence in narrators. Those men who have entangled others in such a dream will reject it for themselves if they are afterwards awakened. If religion consisted in accepting universal thoughts concerning God and the world which we could never have arrived at for ourselves, then, indeed, it might begin with unconditional confidence in the doctrines and narratives of other men ; but if no man can be religious without the consciousness that God communes with him personally, then religion can only be kindled in such an experience in a man's own life as makes upon him the impression that God is thereby communing with him. The nature of the experiences amid which a man becomes conscious of God's working upon himself just where he stands, decides what will be the nature of that man's religion. We, for our part, become conscious of God's communion with us most distinctly by the fact that the Person of Jesus reveals itself to us through the power of His inner life. On this fact alone is based the peculiarity of the Christian religion.

§ 8. *The Saving Fact is the Personal Life of Jesus when it is Grasped by Us as a Reality.*

For this reason, always, there is nothing so necessary in Christendom as the preaching of Christ, for to learn to see Him is the way of salvation for a Christian. But we do not help men into that way of salvation if we tell them, on the strength of New Testament narratives and doctrines, that Jesus as the Son of God was born of a virgin; that He taught this and that; that He wrought many miracles and even raised the dead; and that He Himself rose again, and now, having ascended to the Father, rules with almighty power. Such a story is no gospel, be it never so impressively told. These things, received with childlike simplicity, may certainly draw men's attention to Jesus and give them an impulse to seek Him for themselves; but we certainly have not in these statements that Person of Jesus Himself which is able to redeem us. If, therefore, those doctrines and narratives are presented to men as the main thing in which they must believe in order to find the Redeemer, they are certainly deluded. Such statements are a great hindrance to men to-day, for the majority can no longer accept these things with childlike simplicity. The most that can happen is that assent may be wrung from them in anxiety for their soul's welfare, and in terror excited by a violent sermon. Then they strain themselves to believe, and yet remain inwardly uncertain. Such strain and uncertainty hinder them from coming to Christ, for only they that are of the truth hear His voice.

It is therefore a matter well worth consideration whether those doctrines and narratives ought not to be used in a different way from what has been customary. They are to be taught as forming part of the witness of the New Testament to Jesus, but not to be set before men with the demand that above all things there must be assent to them. If we do so demand, then we are not preaching the gospel ; we are simply proclaiming a law ; nor is it even a good law, for to the Pharisee it will be easy and to the upright man intolerable. We ought rather to say to men in preaching : " those men who found the way to God through Jesus did actually believe such marvellous things concerning Him." Let us by all means have this testimony of the disciples earnestly made known ; but for this very reason, if we are seeking the same redemption which they found, we are not to take it for granted that everything which influenced the disciples, and affected them as something undoubtedly real to them, must influence us in the same way. If we do expect this, then the very testimony of the disciples will prevent us from seeing that which is to us, in our present position, the accessible and sure basis of salvation. Moreover, we who are seeking redemption in Jesus are by no means to undertake, as if it were quite an easy task for us, to hold the same exalted beliefs about Him which they as redeemed men held. That would be to begin at the top, and to find the basis and ground of redemption in what is really its fruit. We have not to try to clamber up on high all by our own strength, but, like the disciples of old, we are to let ourselves be overpowered and uplifted by something which is real beyond all doubt to ourselves as we are to-day.   And what is thus real ? We answer, first, the fact that disciples did so speak concerning the power and glory of Jesus. It is a fact that they did testify thus, and this ought to point us to Jesus Himself, and warn us why we are powerless to give such a testimony.   But then, secondly, another reality is the inner life of Jesus, which rises up before us from the testimony of the disciples as a real power that is active in the world when He reveals Himself to us by His power. This happens when we see ourselves compelled to recognise this spiritual power as the only thing in the world to which we utterly surrender in reverence and trust.   In this experience we lay hold of Jesus Himself as the ground of our salvation. If Jesus Himself is to redeem us we must be placed under His power, and only that which overwhelms us with the force of undoubted reality has power over our inmost life. But the power to raise us out of our previous nature, that is, a redeeming power, can be found only in something that opposes and transcends the experiences in which we have hitherto been wrapped up.

The only thing of importance is to elevate above everything else that present experience in which we and others feel that the power of Jesus really exercises an inward compulsion upon us and lifts us out of ourselves. Therefore we abandon the thoughtless habit of simply saying to men that they must see the saving facts in things that they can grasp only as the contents of other

people's stories.   For only something which inwardly
transforms him can constitute a saving fact for a man
who wishes to rise out of his spiritual weakness.   And
this effect can be exercised on a person only by something he has himself experienced, and not by something
that is merely told him.   Therefore, we call the inner
life of Jesus the saving fact.   For we to-day, just as
disciples of every age, can grasp it ourselves as a reality.
For in it we ourselves meet the Personal Spirit, who in
all that He does to us confirms the claim tradition
makes for Him that He is the Saviour of the world.
Will we willingly surrender to the spiritual power whose
influence we thus perceive to be all around us ? Or will
we treat this incomparable thing as an every-day matter
and in laziness forget it and turn our backs on it ? This,
at last, is the real test-question of faith.   And it passes
over immediately into the other question, whether or
not we are willing to be sincere.

Whenever the Person of Jesus touches us as a fact
that is real to ourselves, then we are hearing the gospel.
Not every one, indeed, can see the personal life of Jesus.
We see it only when it pleases God to reveal His Son
in us, and this can happen to us only when, with minds[17]
intent on exercising our moral judgment and satisfying
our religious need, we come in contact with the biblical
tradition regarding Jesus Christ.   But when this revelation does take place, then, under the impression which
Jesus makes upon us, there arises in our hearts the
certainty that God Himself is turning towards us in
this experience.   If we now ask : " How is it possible
that so mighty an utterance should be spoken to us in

the fact that Jesus stands before us, as an undeniable part of what is real to ourselves?" or "How can this fact become for us the intimation wherein God discloses Himself to us in His reality and power?" these questions can be answered only by the fact itself, and by what it undeniably contains. At this point, instead of saying to himself "Believe everything," a man who wants to be saved must rather say : "Believe nothing but what you see yourself to be an insistent fact."

§ 9. *The Simplest Features of the Portrait of Jesus*[18] *Which is to be got from the Tradition.*

We begin by considering what will be admitted to be the historical reality concerning Jesus by a man of our time whose interest in Him is purely historical. It may be that here and there an earnest student of history, through no merely dull misconception, may question the records concerning Jesus, and declare them to be a legend in which an actual spiritual movement manufactured a historical background for itself. Yet even then the chief point will still remain the same for him as it is for us. A historian has the right, and perhaps the duty, of declaring the results of the investigation for which he is responsible. But there is always the possibility that he, too, in moments of inward reflection upon the story on which he ventures to pass this judgment, may have his eyes opened to see the consistent and clear portrait of a Personal Life that has no equal. Indeed, he may become so possessed by that portrait that it shall become impossible for him to regard it as a product of the poetical imagination. For, in truth, such a product would only present to him what he himself could produce. In that case his judgment as a historian concerning the story becomes limited by his present experience of the story's effect. Nothing else could so influence his historical judgment without doing violence to his conscience. Nothing but that definite picture given by the records when read as they stand, and so making a powerful impression upon him, could possibly have the right to limit his freedom of historical judgment. This always happens when the inquirer becomes a Christian. But even if he does not get so far, the fact remains unquestioned that the Christ of the New Testament shows a firmness of religious conviction, a clearness of moral judgment, and a purity and strength of will, such as are combined in no other figure in history. If we wish, then, to make these features of His character more distinct, we have a right to begin from those parts of His story which are not, as a rule, called in question even by those who do not know Jesus Himself.

All men are willing to allow that Jesus did actually appear in the history of the world in which we live. It is admitted that many hundred years ago He claimed to be the Messiah of Israel ; that through His peculiar conception of His work as Messiah He drew upon Himself the hatred of His people, thereby incurring His own overthrow, and, finally, that notwithstanding this, He died confident that He had won the victory. If we saw nothing more in Jesus than this we should admit the facts, though we should pay no further heed to them. But we become more attentive when we perceive what it meant for a man to claim to be the Messiah of Israel. Such a man necessarily conceived that his existence and his work made the world complete, and that in his person the purposes of God's creation were summed up. The mere vital energy of such a man compels our admiration. If along with this he had shown a mind overpowered by a fevered imagination, if he had been emotional and had sought for honour among men, we should have counted him made of common clay, a visionary, like many whom we know. But the story of Jesus describes to us just the opposite case. His speech is notably temperate, clear, and reasonable. He is neither conceited nor overbearing, but constantly surprises us with the impression of His humility of heart. If Jesus had simply taken up the Messianic ideal of Israel, and had His purpose not ranged beyond the spiritual horizon of the Jewish people, then His character as Messiah would have displayed no feature worthy of special note. For it is quite possible to imagine that among a people whose religion formed so large a part of their life, a highly gifted man might fancy himself called upon to realise the *certain goal* for which all were ardently longing. But on close inspection the will of Jesus is seen to be by no means the mere blossom of the Jewish hope for a Messiah. In the work that He undertook, He rose above all that Israel had looked upon and hoped for as the highest good, and He was quite conscious that He was disappointing the hopes He aroused. Jesus certainly claimed, as was expected of the Messiah, that He would establish the Kingdom of God among men, and that He would thereby make the world complete. But there is no trace of political hopes, no summons to the use of force. The decisions to which he compels men concern their own inner life ; for by the Kingdom of God he means God's true lordship over personal life, especially in men's own souls, and in their communion one with another. The members of the Kingdom of God, as Jesus understood it, are those men only who are fully subject to God through boundless confidence in Him and unbounded love for their neighbours. In the fact that these spiritual considerations did rule His own being, and that they were germinating in those few individuals who grouped themselves around Him, Jesus saw the dawn of the end of all things.

Let us review those features of the portrait of Jesus which we have thus obtained. First of all, we have the outward course of His Messianic work, which tells us little of His inner life that can claim special significance. It has only two striking features : one, the conflict into which Jesus comes with pious Judaism and its Messianic hopes ; and the other, the remarkable assurance which He maintained over against the opposition of the world, and in His death. These two points need to be made more clear, and we shall make them so if we realise the peculiar nature of Jesus' life-work and his attitude towards it. It is clear without further argument that He must have regarded His work as bound to succeed, seeing that He staked His life upon it. As soon as a man makes it consciously the goal of his life to secure the realisation of all that Jesus understood as the Kingdom of God, so soon also must that man advance to the further conviction that this realisation will actually come to pass. No one can be forced to advance in moral development up to a grasp of the idea that the personal life of man reaches its perfection in perfect love, and in a trust in a God who is the very power of that love ; but the man who does grasp that thought is sensible also that nothing can interfere with its right to be realised. Convinced of this right, many men have become hard as steel against those forces of destiny which shattered their outward existence. Jesus had such a consciousness, the consciousness of the soul that has come to know its own eternal life, and in such possession he was like the martyrs who have answered the summons of the moral ideal He brought into the world. That feature of His personal life stands out grandly in the recorded story. And, in truth, it is no small matter if we let this personal power of the good in the figure of Jesus work upon us and move us to reverence ; for no man can be redeemed by Him who does not bow in true reverence before that personal, living goodness which exists in its original purity in Him alone.

Jesus is thus placed at the head of all those men who have joyfully suffered for the sake of the good. But to see this is by no means to reach that peculiar feature of His inner life which must work upon us as a fact if he is to redeem us. Jesus is separate from all men who seek to follow Him in self-surrender to the good, not simply as their never-equalled prototype, but also by the attitude which He assumes towards that ideal of perfect life which He reveals to men as their highest good.

In the first place, Jesus shows us the portrait of a man who is conscious that He Himself is not inferior to the ideal for which He sacrifices Himself. We do not gain this impression, of course, simply from isolated expressions which have been handed down to us as a testimony to His sinlessness. Such expressions taken by themselves have little force. But certainly the fact that Jesus thought of Himself as sinless stands out powerfully before us when we remember what He said and did at the Last Supper with His disciples. In face of a death whose horror he keenly felt, He was able to say that this death He was about to die would take away the burden of guilt from the hearts of those who should remember Him. He was able to look away from the death whose approach troubled Him to the moral need of men held captive by the consciousness of guilt, so deeply did He feel the horror of that need. And so mighty within Him was the consciousness of His own purity, that He clearly saw that the impression which His death would cause would loose the spiritual bonds of those who had found Him and could remember Him. Jesus could not have spoken as He then did if He had been conscious of guilt within Himself. In that hour when the conscience of every man who is morally alive inexorably sums up his life, this man could conceive of His own moral strength and purity as that power which alone could conquer the sinner's inmost heart and free him from the deepest need. And this He did, not after the manner of an enthusiastic visionary, but as a man to whom the deepest moral knowledge gave a most tender conscience.

He was the first to declare distinctly that the command
to love is not simply one of the commandments but
that it is the whole moral law, because it determines
the disposition which is the condition of righteousness,
and which therefore alone gives moral worth to human
action. He led His disciples above all to recognise
that such a life of love is the highest good for man,
or, in other words, the possession out of which
springs everything else that gives the heart true joy.
Through this thought, one which no prophet of Israel
had grasped, Jesus brought moral knowledge among
men to its culmination. He has brought it about that,
as far as His influence extends, every man feels guilty
whose heart is not wholly given up to love, but still
seeks something else for itself besides heartfelt fellowship with others and joy in personal life. But at the
same time He had to measure Himself by that same
standard, had to say to Himself that He must find an
all-conquering joy in the life and freedom and strength
of His own love. He could count Himself inwardly
pure only if He persevered in incessant effort to be
pure. He must have felt the ties of duty in such a
way. Nevertheless, even standing where He did at
that Last Supper, He said confidently that His Personality would lift away the burden of guilt from the heart
of every man to whose heart His death should come
home as a message. In view of this, any one who feels
the appeal of Jesus to his own conscience, must receive
the impression that Jesus actually was what He claimed
to be. Jesus has indeed been, by His suffering for the
sake of what is good, an example which many have

followed ; in this further respect, however, He is incomparable, that He first saw what is good in all its glory, its fulness, and its power, and that He nevertheless had not to feel ashamed of what He was compared with what He knew, and what He said. In all other cases, the very men whose goodness usually raises us give us such a conception of what is good that we measure their own moral shortcomings by it. Jesus alone has had the conviction that it was not so with Him, and the man who learns to know Him admits that conviction to be correct. He awakens in us the deepest understanding of duty, and He remains at the same time Himself the highest standard for our conscience. This incomparable moral strength of Jesus must become clear to us in the simplest features of His appearance in history, in the manner in which He claimed to be the Messiah, and in the way in which He went to His death.

When we see this, then our eyes are opened to the glory of the rest of the tradition concerning Him ; we see in it all the wonderful fact that it constantly gives us fresh views of other and yet other sides of the eternal life of a human soul. Such a tradition is incomparable, and that not because of its contents only ; its very existence is a miraculous fact, for it comes to us through the minds of men who did not experience in their own lives such untrammelled life in the good as He had. In spite of this, the tenderest features of such a life have been preserved in their narratives, and have become the true spiritual food for mankind. Jesus is for us a fact in His moral glory, in those inner movements of His soul which include the deepest moral knowledge, the never failing creative strength of the moral purpose and the bliss of this self-knowledge ; He is a fact for us which we do not accept for others' sake, but which we see for ourselves. He has thus become an integral part of all that is real to ourselves ; and He fills with light all the world in which we stand. Jesus differs, then, from all men who follow Him by His conscious rising always to His own ideal and because He compels us to admit that He does rise to it. But before everything else, when the moral vitality of Jesus has taken hold of us, another element of the traditional portrait of Jesus becomes clear and certain to us, and one that has in itself nothing to do with moral greatness, and that taken by itself must stir up unresolvable doubts.

Jesus intended to do more than make the best ideal clear for men, and more than live it out before them. As the Messiah, He claimed not merely to set men a task, but to give to them God's perfect gift. He was confident that He could so influence men that they would be able for a life of power. The Jesus who thinks thus of Himself and who looks on humanity with such a confidence in His power to redeem them from the terrible misery in which He sees every one round about Him, stands as a fact before us, a fact that has no equal.

The dying Buddha puts his confidence in the truth of his teaching ; he leaves to his disciples the admonition that they may forget him, but they are to keep his teaching and the way that he has shown them. Plato says the like of Socrates. Now in the whole wide range of history there are no other figures, apart from Jesus, which so surprise us with originality of moral strength as do these two. But while these two hid themselves modestly behind the teaching for which they lived and died, Jesus knows no more sacred task than to point men to His own Person. His life and death proclaim the conviction that no man who desires true life can do without him; every one must concern himself with Jesus, and must take to heart the fact of His Personality.

§ 10. *The Claim of Jesus to be the Redeemer and the Proof of its Truth.*

But Jesus has also put us in a position to judge of the right of this claim of His. We can understand in its actuality the redeeming power that he attributes to Himself. This is certainly not the case with the redeeming power that modern formal Christianity professes to see in Him, while all the time giving a more faithful reverence to ancient formulas of faith from which the living Spirit has fled long ago. It is said that redeeming forces proceed from Him, which are, however, to be distinguished from Himself, and from the impression His personal life makes on the spirits of men, and that the mysterious operation of these forces sets free the soul. If we are told that this is the case, we must reply that such forces can in no case become to us a fact which shall master our inmost souls. Men may talk of such force, but the talking helps no one whose conscience Jesus has quickened. Of course, a

million voices out of the Christian church loudly
proclaim this very theory a way of salvation; we are
to be saved by certain powers which are organically
connected with the worship and sacraments of the
Church. If, however, we know what it means for us
that we can keep our minds fixed on the Person of Jesus
and His power over us, these cries will not trouble us.
Even if such a thought had crept into the records
concerning Jesus, and claimed to be part of His own
teaching—thank God, it is not the case—but if it were,
then we should certainly regret the fact, but we should
not let it influence us. We should with easy conscience
declare such a doctrine to be an error of the narrator.
For it would contradict that which is our sole concern,
that which, in Jesus, has become for us as an undeniable
fact. It is for us a fact that Jesus stands before us in
history claiming to be Himself alone salvation for all
men. We have no right whatever to imagine in
addition any mysterious powers by means of which
Jesus is to bring about our redemption. He Himself
" is made unto us redemption." We can only understand His assertion in that sense. Any teaching must
be a matter of utter indifference to us which tells of
mysterious redemptive forces which are to proceed from
Christ, and which for that very reason are not Christ
Himself. Such teaching can produce no proof of its
truth; it remains one of those mere assertions which
ramble in plenty through empty heads. But for the only
assertion that we find Jesus make there exists a proof.

Jesus asserts that the advent of the Kingdom of God
is bound up with His own appearance in history, and

that this Kingdom of God makes men blessed. We cannot be grateful enough for being made to notice[19] how completely, in Jesus' preaching of the Kingdom, it is something to come. We are now in a position to see rightly how simply and profoundly Jesus understood what He called by the name the Kingdom of God. Even on historical grounds it is probable that by the phrase He thought, in the first place, of God's sovereignty. But for those who have begun to understand the inner life of Jesus in its characteristic majesty, it is a certainty that this alone is what Jesus chiefly meant by the words. He placed his whole desire in perfect surrender to God. He took the great commandment in earnest; and, if He did so, he must have done so most especially in His attempt to formulate the end of all willing as expressed in the idea of the Kingdom of God. The longing for the Kingdom of God must mean, in Jesus' life, perfect surrender to God, or love to God with all the heart and soul. Therefore, what he understood by the Kingdom of God was the experience of the complete sovereignty of God. For this it is worth while to sacrifice one's whole life. But this can be done only in the confidence that the sovereignty of God can transfer pain into joy, and utter loss into inexhaustible wealth. We can gain the confidence that the Kingdom will come some day. But it is impossible to possess in the present day what Jesus summed up as the Kingdom of God. We know that we ought to be in a state of entire submission to God, but we are not in it. We can heartily pray for the coming of the Kingdom of God, knowing, as we do, how everything within

us begins to become new when we feel the nearness of
God.   But we are, indeed, far from the commencement
of a life in power.   We are ever sinking back again
into darkness.   The mountains that our faith is to
remove keep growing greater.   The utter sovereignty
of God remains, therefore, a future for us, and the
blessedness which is to come to us from it is still
the goal of our hope and desire.   We cannot approach
it by the quiet progress of inward evolution.   Only a
miraculous transformation of our whole existence can
bring us to that goal.   But it is possible even now to
set our course in its direction, and to be so moulded that
we shall have some experience that the sovereignty of
God is indeed blessedness.   A man whose heart clings
to Mammon, who is still taking thought for his life,
and in bondage to the fear of men, can be transported
into the Kingdom of God through no violent catas-
trophe.   He shall not stand in the Judgment.   The
Kingdom of God is sure to come ; but whether its
advent will bring blessing or condemnation to particular
individuals depends on what they have previously
become.   None can submit himself to God's perfect
sovereignty who has closed his heart against the work
of God upon him, and has sought satisfaction in other
things than the experience of God's nearness.   Jesus,
however, had this confidence in Himself, that, by the
power of His personal life, He could let men see that
God does come near them, and that that alone can
make them blessed.   Men who have learnt this now
at last look rightly with eager hope into the future.
But it is the redeeming power of Jesus that they have to

thank that they have a hope at all.   In the wonderful
feeling of self-consciousness that those who are laid hold
of by Him and united to Him have of being inwardly
changed, Jesus stands before us.   The truth of His
claims may be tested by every one who has at all learned
to see the Person, the human soul of Jesus.

§ 11. *The Person of Jesus as the Revelation of God.*

The most important thing for the man who is to
submit himself to God is surely that he should
be absolutely certain of the reality of God, and Jesus
does establish in us, through the fact of His personal
life, a certainty of God which is superior to every
doubt.   When once He has attracted us by the beauty
of His Person, and made us bow before Him by its
exalted character, then even amid our deepest doubts
the Person of Jesus will remain present with us as a
thing incomparable, the most precious fact in history,
and the most precious fact our life contains.   If we
then yield to His attraction and come to feel with deep
reverence how His strength and purity disclose to
us the impurity and weakness of our souls, then His
mighty claim comes home to us.[20] We learn to share
His invincible confidence that He can uplift and bless
perfectly those who do not turn away from Him.   In
this confidence in the Person and cause of Jesus is implied the idea of a Power greater than all things, which
will see to it that Jesus, who lost His life in this world,
shall be none the less victorious over the world.   The
thought of such a Power lays old of us as firmly as did

the impression of the Person of Jesus by which we were overwhelmed. It is the beginning of the consciousness within us that there is a living God. This is the only real beginning of an inward submission to Him. As soon as trust in Jesus awakens this thought within us, we connect the thought at once with our experience of the inner life of Jesus as a present fact in our own life. The startled sense we felt at the disclosure of actual, living goodness in His Person, and the sense of condemnation that we felt, are at once attributed by our souls to the power of God, of which we have now become conscious. The man who has felt these simple experiences cannot possibly attribute them to any other source. The God in whom he now believes for Jesus' sake, is as real and living to him as the man Jesus is in His marvellous sublimity of character. The idea of a Power supreme over all things wins a marvellous vividness for us because we are obliged to pay to Jesus the homage of believing that He must certainly succeed, even if all the world besides be against Him. The Omnipotence of which we become conscious in this way must be wielded by that same purpose which produced the life-work of Jesus.

Thus God makes Himself known to us as the Power that is with Jesus in such a way that amid *all* our distractions and the mist of doubt He can never again entirely vanish from us. We are obliged, then, to confess that the existence of Jesus in this world of ours is the fact in which God so touches us as to come into a communion with us that can endure. Of course, we learn at the same time how great the gulf is between Jesus and ourselves ; and we feel it the more keenly, the more we become alive to that strength of His character which so overwhelms us that it makes the reality of God undeniable. But for this very reason the God we recognise is not only the God of Jesus Christ. He is our own God. This follows from the fact that the Man through whom the reality of God becomes visible and certain to us stands in the attitude of friendship towards men who feel themselves far removed from God. Luther says, "If we observe His loving and friendly companionship with His disciples, if we note how He rebukes without rejecting them, this will support and comfort us in every kind of trial. And this is the best and most excellent thing we have in Christ."* This personal attitude of Jesus assures us that His God is our God ; and it thereby uplifts us into the Kingdom of God's love. Hence this fact, through which God touches us, not only relieves the impotence of the creature, which of itself can arrive at no certain knowledge of God, but at the same time it helps the sinner, who, when left to himself, tries to shut his eyes to the revelation of God, because God's nature is so strange to him. God enters into such sort of communion with us that He thereby forgives us our sins. Without forgiveness we should still remain without a free certainty of the reality of God.

We see that we have no inner life at all until we recognise the good and let it rule in our hearts ; and the clearer this becomes the more painfully are we sensible that all the forces of our existence are in

* "Luther." Second enlarged edition, xv. 470 ; l. 130.

conflict with the good. This at least holds good for
any man whose conscience Jesus has quickened. He
knows well that by no strain of will can he bring forth
in his own heart what the law that Jesus has made
clear demands, namely, love. So the very thoughts
which we know are able to set free our inner life only
throw us back again into discouragement and despon-
dency. From this inward strife, from this inability to
live in the good which, nevertheless, we see to be the
form of true life, we are saved when once we have come
to understand the fact that Jesus belongs to this world
of ours. If only he has won from us the trust that His
cause is the cause of God, then, because of the interest
He showed in men, an interest which has stood the
severest tests, we become sure that the good has a
reality and a power in our own lives. Certainly, as
soon as the law of duty is set forth and expounded to
us as Jesus does it, we recognise its unassailable right.
But unless our existence in the world bore some sure
sign that the good is not essentially foreign to human
nature, we should never be certain that our knowledge
of moral law could lift *us* to a higher life, or that *we*
could attain to the blessed liberty of a moral life.
Jesus Christ is that sign. His attitude towards us
uplifts us and makes it possible for us to trust that the
Divine Power, which must be with Him and with His
work, cares for us and makes us fellow workmen with
Him in His work which aims at nothing less than the
actual realisation of the good, and a coming of the Kingdom of God. Hence, by the conviction that in Christ
God communes with us, we are placed inwardly in a

position to overcome the opposition between our
natural life and the law of duty. It thus becomes
possible for us to believe that those very things in our
surroundings which are hostile to the good, are by God's
power being made of service for what is good. For
although our moral striving seems to exhaust itself in
vain attempts, yet we have still the consolation that we
stand in and belong to a historical movement[21] in which
the good wields ever greater sway, for Christ's work must
reach its goal, and we know through God's communion
with us that we are assisting in that work.

§ 12. *The objective Grounds of our Certainty that God Communes with Us.*

When our moral need is satisfied in this way, the
impression that in Christ we have to do with God
becomes a radiant certainty. For that is the true God
who creates infinite life within us by causing us to
rejoice in the good. God communes with us, therefore,
by the appearance of Jesus Christ in such a way that we
are perfectly certain we see Him. The rise of new
doubts as to whether God does actually come near to
us in Jesus is prevented by the Christian's experience
that as soon as he understands this Man as the message
of God to him, he finds a joy in bowing to what is
inevitable, and in self-sacrifice for the sake of others.
Our experience of the communion of God with us
happens in such a way that it effects at the same time
our moral deliverance. Without it we should not have
that certainty of faith which is present and active in

every believer, even although it be often hindered in its action by the want of inward self-possession and insight.

The rise of faith as the consciousness that God communes with us cannot be forced. It remains the incommunicable experience of the man who learns to believe ; he cannot transfer it to another. For whether a man should place confidence in another is a matter for himself alone ; it is impossible to demonstrate the necessity for such a confidence to a man in whom it does not exist. If any one would obtain this soul-emancipating trust in Jesus, he must turn to Jesus and place himself under Jesus' influence. We have certainly all sorts of reasons for dreading to do this. If some men, nevertheless, do overcome this fear and are not dismayed by the appearance of the Holy One, although they know themselves condemned before Him, that must remain the strange secret of their own inner life.

The Christian's consciousness that God communes with him rests on *two objective facts, the first of which is the historical fact*[22] *of the Person of Jesus.* We have grasped this fact as an element in our own sphere of reality, and we have felt its power. It must be admitted that unless we are to live half asleep, as it were, and to have an existence on the level of the brutes, we must face this fact as something in our lives, and must say what we will do with it. The Christian knows that every man who is morally alive must be able to see this fact, which L. Ranke thus describes : " more guiltless and more powerful, more exalted and more holy, has nought ever been on earth than His conduct, His life and His death; the human race knows nothing that could be brought, even afar off, into comparison with it."* Hence all who close their eyes to this, the most precious fact that history contains, seem to the Christian to be imprisoned in dreams, shut out from the reality which is the indispensable nourishment of the inner life. *The second objective ground* of the Christian's consciousness that God communes with him *is that we hear within ourselves the demand of the moral law.* Here we grasp an objective fact which must be held to be valid in any historical study of life. For life as studied in history, or, in other words, all specifically human life, rests absolutely upon the assumption that men know they are unconditionally bound to obey the law of duty. Now we find that in the God whose influence upon us is seen in no other experience so clearly as in the power the Person of Jesus has over us, the moral convictions that rule our inmost soul acquire the form of a personal life. In the same thoughts that ceaselessly urged us forward we trace now a friendly will that has ordained it for our redemption. God brings it about that to do right ceases to be a painful problem for us, and begins instead to be the very atmosphere in which we live. Here then we find a thought which we have a right to hold to be an objective reality for every man, and we find this very thought working in us to make us certain of God. There are no other objective grounds for the truth of the Christian religion.†

* "The Popes of Rome." Sixth edition, vol. i. p. 4.

† *Cf.* my book, " Die Religion im Verhältnis zum Welterkennen und zur Sittlichkeit " (" Religion in Relation to Knowledge and to

Any one who has let the fact of the personal life of Jesus work upon him, and who has been led thereby Morality "), Halle, 1879. It is obvious that for every man who shares this life of ours in history, the thought of duty has the significance above described. If we should cease to live this life of personal fellowship, this life of ours in the midst of history, then, of course, thoughts concerning duty would disappear from our mental horizon. On the other hand, as long as we retain even a glimmering of the idea that soul finds its true life only in personal fellowship, so long we must necessarily count it an eternal truth that we are bound by certain unconditional obligations. We could not live side by side, and know we were doing so, without assuming that we are so bound. Life in personal fellowship, that is, in every relation of mutual trust, is always conceived as implying moral obligations as the eternal conditions of our life on earth. It is not simply true that we devise a shrewd rule by which we may preserve our worldly possession for ourselves, and that we then call that rule duty. On the contrary, we know that we obtain the true good of life for the first time when we obey duty's unconditional demand. And yet when we speak of the eternal truth of morality in this sense, we certainly do not mean to assert that the human individual carries that thought about with him, which we affirm to contain the eternal condition for his personal life, just as he carries organs of sense. Of course, it will avail me nothing to point this out. Critics like H. Gallwitz (" Die Problem der Ethik in der Gegenwart, 1891," p. 229) will continue to say, as before, that I hold that moral knowledge is part of man's natural constitution. The same writer says of me : " There remains for Herrmann in point of fact nothing as redeeming power in Christ except this teaching about God, and the assertion of this even in death. Thus it is no use calling the work of Christ, thus reduced to a system of teaching, a historical fact, whose effects reach down to the present day. For according to this it is possible in Herrmann's theology to separate the idea of the love of God revealed by Christ, or the gospel of the Kingdom of God from the Person of the Redeemer, and let it go on influencing the world by its own power." I need hardly say to the reader that this summary imputes to me exactly the opposite of what I have endeavoured at length to show. I am not astonished. But I am surprised that he speaks of a common principle underlying his own and my theology. I could only feel opposed to a theology which taught what he ascribes to me.

to trust in Him, cannot help thinking that there is a
Power over all things, and that that Power is with
Jesus.   In what he experiences at the hands of Jesus,
he feels himself in the grip of this Power.   Here his
religious life begins, but this beginning is kept from
being a purely subjective experience by these two objective things, viz., by that historical fact which, when once
seen, never disappears, and by his conscience.   Through
Jesus he has not merely a thought of God supported by
proofs or authorities, but he has the Living God
Himself, who is working upon him.   The man who
has attained that is a Christian.   He is a Christian,
although he is not in a position to recognise as
truths all those things which other Christians have
professed.

§ 13. *The Subjectivity of an Arbitrary Profession
of Faith.*

Where he notes his inability to do so, he will by no
means determine, as some may expect, that he will
nevertheless profess them to be truths.   For example,
he might be obliged to insist that it by no means follows
from the new life created in him by the grace of God
through Jesus Christ that he could stand by all the
affirmations of the so-called Apostolic Creed as assertions of his own convictions.   At the same time, however, he might observe that other Christians, for whom
he entertains the greatest respect, declare that they can
heartily join in confessing that Creed as their own.
Now what will a Christian do in these circumstances

who has become conscious, in the way we have described, that God is accepting him? He will certainly not accuse his fellow Christians of professing to believe what they do not believe, nor will he at once declare to be false those portions of the Creed which he cannot see to be the truth. Perhaps he may be obliged to say they are false for other reasons; but the fact that these things are strange to him will not of itself alone lead him to deny their truth. Indeed, he has just had the experience that a fact, hitherto utterly strange to him, is now true, to his certain knowledge. But, on the other hand, when he observes that other Christians join in the Apostolic Creed, he will not be induced by seeing this to resolve to do the same. In his case such a resolve would not be an act springing genuinely out of that new life which he owes to the grace of God. If he were to make such a resolve he would act, not perhaps from cowardice or vanity, but, to put it briefly, with conscious untruthfulness. At best he would be yielding to an evil habit which would tend to drive him from that standing-ground that made him sure and glad, from the impregnable rock of historical reality and the eternal. Through a strange confusion of thought this bad habit prevails largely.

Men say that we must have firm ground beneath us, and that for that reason it is well to hold immovably to what is presented to us in the confessions of the Church, and presented to us, indeed, by the Holy Scriptures. It is certainly of the utmost importance that the Christian should be conscious of standing on objective reality, and that his view of God's working upon him should not rest merely on his own wish. But it is clear that we can have such an objective basis for our faith only in facts which force themselves upon us as undeniable elements in the reality in which we stand. Then alone can we rejoice in the truth of our faith, for in that case our religious thinking obeys the compulsion of a sacred necessity. On the other hand, we fall precisely into the error of a false subjectivity whenever we seek to appropriate, as the contents of our faith, any conceptions which we do not see arising out of the fact that God comes into communion with us. For then we do not fit ourselves to the objective fact which is given us, but follow our own arbitrary and subjective will.

The temptation to the subjectivity of such a false attachment to creeds is pressing in on us all in Christendom with tremendous force. There is but one sure protection against it, and that is the joy we have in the objective reality of the personal life of Jesus, and in His power to make us feel God working upon us. The man who is sensible of this joy knows that he is hidden in a mighty Hand ; and he is able to recognise evil in the demand that he should yield to the subjectivity of that arbitrary confession, an evil thing though dressed in an ecclesiastical garb. In view of the devastation this demand is causing, it is high time that the officials of the Church should be asked whether they ought to give it the weight of their approval. If they do so, they hold poor souls the tighter in their prison chains. The Protestant people who are refusing, in increasing numbers, to join in an arbitrary confession of the faith, are simply guarding themselves against counting anything the basis of faith which does not possess the weight of undoubted fact. They are not holding by a false subjectivity, as some would-be churchly people would maintain; on the contrary, they are athirst for the objective in religion. So we mock their need if we offer them as a ground for their faith doctrines of Scripture and propositions of the Apostolic Creed in which they cannot, by any means, find an expression of facts that are sure for them. They long for facts whose power shall come home to their inmost souls, and by which they shall see that they are not without God in the world. The inner life of Jesus and their own conscience can be revealed to them to be such facts.

§ 14. *The Power of the Person of Jesus over our Heart is the Vital Principle of our Religion.*

Luther once said that he would argue no more with any man who did not recognise Holy Scripture as the Word of God. If we were now to take such a course, it would certainly be very convenient and very pleasing to the flesh, but it would be utterly fruitless. For even where the admission was made, in most cases it would be made no longer in the unthinking fashion of Luther's day. It would be the result, as a rule, either of arbitrary resolve, or of shallowness, or of anxiety. We ought rather to say that we will argue with every man, and will only lay down our arms when we see that men have no sense of unconditional obligation, and that in them, therefore, conscience is dumb. Where such a point has not yet been reached, we are to go on talking to men about Jesus Christ, but without making the senseless demand that they shall treat as real things they cannot grasp as an undoubted reality, which, therefore, *have no power over them.* We must rather communicate to them the Biblical tradition regarding Jesus as something that has been of help to us in the hope that there the inner life of the man Jesus will reveal itself to them too, remembering that in the sphere of conscience that inner life exercises far greater power than our weak faith is wont to imagine.

If, however, it is true that the reality of the personal life of Jesus, when grasped as a reality, is understood as the influence of that God for whose sake we will forsake all else, then Jesus Himself and His power over the heart is actually the vital principal of our religion. " The Christian religion consists in the personal love and adoration of Jesus Christ ; not in correct morality and correct doctrines, but in homage to the King." * And what are we to call that joy in the personal life of Jesus with which men's hearts glow when Jesus brings them into the presence of God, and they learn there how He slays and makes alive again ? I have no other name for it but this : it is the mightiest love the soul has to give. This love to Jesus we have when once we have tasted the experience that it is through Him that God communes with us. The religious life of the Christian is inseparable from vision of the personal life of Jesus. That vision must be the Christian's constant companion, and so it becomes as he finds more and more

* F. W. Robertson, " Sein Lebensbild in Briefen " ("His life as described in his letters"). Gotha, 1888, p. 71.

that in such vision he grasps that reality without which all else in the world is empty and desolate.

It is a dangerous undertaking then, and one that needs gentle handling, to say there is such a thing as a false love for Christ. And yet this must be done. The very importance of the matter demands that it shall have firm handling. If love for Jesus is anything else than reverent joy in that personal life which makes us feel the judgment and mercy of God, then that love is but the blossom of an impure heart. We are easily impressed with the spiritual beauty of Jesus, and it arouses tender emotions in the soul; but if we do not get beyond this, we show thereby that we are not letting Jesus work upon us what He would. In these tender emotions we make ourselves virtually His equals, and remain precisely what we were before; but such emotions would be stifled if we really experienced what Jesus causes to dawn upon the sinful man who does not give play to His own vain feelings, but really gives himself into Jesus' hands. True love for Jesus is a more earnest thing; its attitude is determined by the discovery that He at once destroys all the self-contentment we had before, and that was the source whence a sentimental admiration for His spiritual beauty could flow. We have said already that the religious experience of Christians, or the experience of God's entrance with power into our own life, is inseparable from the vision of the personal life of Jesus. It is equally true to say that we occupy the attitude of true love towards Jesus only when we are raised by Him up to God and away beyond ourselves. Jesus loses nothing when with manly earnest we desire nothing else than to trace in our own souls the working of the power of the Everlasting God ; indeed, it is only then that Jesus receives the reverent love which is His due.

§ 15. *The Mystic, Traditional, and Rationalistic Objections.*

It is to be hoped that we have thus really described how God comes near in such a manner that we can say He communes with us. This will be denied, no doubt, to begin with, by all those good people who look upon a historical event only as a means of expression for a religious idea, but do not know how to use it as a message of God to themselves. With these it is easy to deal. In so far as their theory may be taken as a true expression of their mode of thought, they do not stand within the Christian community at all. For the fact wherein they apprehend God, is in their view either a state of being possessed by religious ideas, or it is an emotional experience of some other kind in which they think they can trace the nearness of God. But for the Christian community the fact is the historical appearance of Christ, as that is made comprehensible among us by the preaching of the Gospel and by practical Christian life.

There is another objection, and with this it is not so easy to deal. We may be told that what we have described as features of Jesus' personal life do not make such an impression, by any means, as to justify our assertion that he who comes to see their reality is himself thereby lifted over into a new sphere of reality.

We cannot rebut such an objection; we have rather here to guard against a misunderstanding. My power is insufficient, to speak concerning Jesus so as to make His portrait alive and powerful in the soul of the reader. If I could preach like F. W. Robertson or H. Hoffmann, I would hasten as a preacher of the Gospel to give to the community the best thing that can be given it, and would not remain an academic theologian. My task here is a more modest one, but it is not superfluous : it is to describe the inner process of the Christian religion, and, in the first place, to describe its fundamental experience. It is surely worth the labour simply to bring the Christian Church to recognise that it is the most important thing for a Christian to become inwardly certain, through facts that are objective and cannot be taken away from him, that God communes with him. This is clearly the most important thing if our salvation is to consist in our having God ruling in us. If God is to rule in us, then above all things God must become a reality for us, so that all that holds us in captivity shall be thereby thrust aside. Hence the question is whether God manifests Himself as a real Power working upon us, so that we are conscious of it just as of anything else in this world. Jesus could not give us this knowledge through His teaching alone; even the sacred Scriptures, regarded as a compendium of doctrines and information concerning God and Christ, cannot convey it to us. We can have it through Jesus only when we apprehend His personal life to be now and for us a present part of the real world, and powerful enough to compel us to see God as a real power. I have now sought to show how this can be. The records concerning Jesus show us an inner life which wins our trust through its moral sublimity and the force of its self-consciousness. No means which historical science can employ will suffice to give us full assurance that what the story offers us is an actual part of the history to which we belong. Doubt as to its actual historicity can be really overcome only by looking to the contents of what we learn to know as the inner life of Jesus.

Of course, every one endowed with ordinary human feeling can see that the tradition regarding Jesus presents to us a marvellously clear picture of personal life. But that that picture is not a work of the imagination which has gradually become adopted by many as a text for religious and moral truths, can be proved only by the effect produced upon us by the contents of the picture. We find the Person of Jesus only in the preaching of disciples who believed in Him. Is it perhaps possible that it is only the disciples we see, and not Jesus Himself? To this question no answer can be given by that science whose business is to find out what can be proved to be real. The man who does answer it must base his answer upon his own personal conviction. The Jesus, that is, the inner life of Jesus, that appears to us in those testimonies of the disciples concerning their faith, brings us face to face with a decision, to wit: are we going to exalt ourselves above this man, or are we going to bow before Him?[23] If we bow before Him, we do so because His person works in us an experience that can be produced in no man by external force. We feel that He first reveals to us what the true life of a personal spirit is, and He makes us feel how stunted and confused is our own inner life. If the portrait of Jesus tells us these things, then we need not insist on knowing it in the exact historical sense : we can accept that portrait as the historical effect of a Person who is all-powerful in His sway over us, but whose personality we cannot comprehend in its actuality. If any one will insist on some other mode of procedure, then he must hold the opposite conviction, namely, that he could produce the portrait of the personal life of Jesus out of his own spiritual resources. For our part we cannot do this, for it is He who makes us both poor and rich. We could never make an exhaustive portrait of that inner life of Jesus which so influences Christians, however many words we might say. Each man can win this portrait for himself only when he sees that in all that touches his inner life there is nothing more important than the tradition regarding Jesus and the traces of His power that meet Him in his own immediate environment.

It is the same in any other case : if a man wins our confidence, we find that the immediate impression which his personality makes upon us has far more in it for us than all that we might say to others in justification of our trust. The more powerfully the personal impression lays hold of us, the greater is the contrast between our powers of description and the impression which the memory retains. Hence we will have no belief whatever in our ability, by the skill of our description, to show others the Person of Jesus in all its power. But we will recall how it was that we ourselves were helped. As a matter of fact, the witness to the faith offered to us, partly by disciples long dead, partly by those still alive, has so reached our heart, that from it we have acquired for ourselves a picture of the inner life of Jesus as the supreme spiritual power over all things, and have thus gradually learned to understand the Jesus of the Gospels. So when we wish to help others to Christianity the chief thing is to become Christians ourselves, and so to influence them by the natural and unforced exhibition to them of what really lives within us. Thus they will come into their first actual contact with Jesus Himself, and be touched with the desire to lay hold on Him more fully. He who is of the truth will hear the voice of God in the fact that such a life actually exists. No one can render help to him who will not be silent before the facts; such a man gets drowned in his blank negation. But the man who lets himself be mastered by that power of personal life that is made manifest in Jesus gains thereby a new fulness of life, and is himself renewed and transported into a new world. Through the strength of Jesus he is made to acknowledge the reality of an Omnipotence which gives this Man the victory, and from the friendship of Jesus for the sinners whom He humbles, he gathers courage to believe that all these things mean God's love seeking out him, poor sinner as he is.

§ 16. *The Impossibility of Giving Expression to the New
Life in Communion with God in Representations
that are Devoid of Self-Contradiction.*

When Jesus has given us these things, then we are
united in our own inner life with God. We no longer
need any one to tell us that there is a God, for we
cannot see the fact of the inner life of Jesus which
is now present before our own souls without becoming
aware of God in that fact. Just as little do we need
to be told by others how God works upon us, for God
comes into communion with us in the very event which
makes us certain of Him. We find out how God works,
for we actually experience God making us feel, by the
spiritual power of Jesus, who He is, what is His will,
and what are His purposes with us. We cannot communicate to a third person by any words of ours what
God thus imparts to us. We cannot even find any
complete expression of it which will satisfy ourselves.
When we try to express it we constantly fall into the
use of conceptions which partially contradict each
other because they cannot be combined into the picture
of a single definite finished event. God takes away our
self-confidence, and yet creates within us an invincible
courage ; He destroys our joy in life, and yet makes us
blessed ; He slays us, and yet makes alive ; He lets us
find rest, and yet fills us with unrest ; He takes away
the burden of a ruined life, and yet makes human life
much more difficult than it is without Him. God
gives us a new existence that is whole and complete ;

yet what we find therein is always turning into a
longing for true life, and into desire to become new.
If God would allow us to remain what we were, then
we could comprehend and represent without self-contradiction His working upon us; but as soon as we
become aware that God is touching us in the personal
life of Jesus, in order to make us certain of Himself,
then at once we feel that we have set out upon a new
course of life.   If we only keep in touch with the inner
life of Jesus, and are lifted up to God by Him, then we
become constantly impressed anew by the fact that an
ever-new fulness is being given to our life.   We have
not the mastery over it, for it is utterly inexhaustible,
and is ever re-moulding us.

§ 17. *The Christianity of Children.*

The faith which was planted in us as children by
Christian training becomes perfected in this consciousness that God communes with us by the Person of
Jesus.   When we were children we heard of God
through other Christians.   At that time the inner life
of Jesus could not yet be the revelation of God to us.
We could not at that stage so apprehend it that we
should be compelled to see in the manifestation of
Jesus the working of God upon us.   Nevertheless, even
then God turned towards us, and so made it possible
for us to understand what others said concerning Him,
it was, all the time, the same revelation of Him,
although in another form.   Some of those who spoke
to us of God—our parents, for example, if all was as it

should be—convinced us that they saw that of which
they spoke. Their earnest love, their truthfulness and
self-control, their stronger and more mature personal
life, became to us a revelation of the God to whom
they prayed. We were brought near to God, not by
the mere instruction we received in Christian thoughts,
but by that personal life sanctified of God which found
expression in the instruction. Just so, the Church, the
community of believers, became our mother, and
opened to us the Kingdom of God. We were led to
God, in the first instance, not through the inner life
of Jesus itself, but through persons who belonged to
Him, who had been set free by Him and placed in
the presence of God. But why is it then that this
does not suffice in later life? As we arrive at riper
years our moral convictions must be reached independently ; we have to distinguish for ourselves
between good and evil. Even in respect of our faith
in God we outgrow our dependence on our surroundings.
Of course, our religious faith can never be as independent as our moral convictions are ; for our certainty
of the reality of God always depends upon our actually
seeing that God is communing with us, hence it is
impossible for us to become entirely independent of
revelation. But the growth of our moral freedom
makes necessary for us a revelation quite different from
that which can be imparted to a child. When we
awake to the consciousness of our moral responsibility,
we are compelled to collect our thoughts,[24] and thereby
free ourselves and realise ourselves inwardly as so
distinct from our surroundings that the faith of other

men can no longer be for us a decisive proof of the presence of God. *God must speak more distinctly to a man who has been thrown upon himself and isolated by the power of his moral thoughts.* Hence the Christian Church, which takes the child in her arms, points the adult to something away beyond herself. She points him to the fact which she holds in constant remembrance as the foundation for her own existence, namely, the Personal life of Jesus.

§ 18. *Adult Christianity.*

When we have been trained to moral freedom, and are thus enabled to judge our own conduct, it soon becomes impossible for us to profess the same faith in God in which we grew up as children. We can no longer depend, as the child does, on the persons about us, for we now actually measure the spiritual life of others, by ideals of which we ourselves perceive the right. We make higher demands on the foundation of religious faith, for we have learned by our new moral insight what sort of thing a truly well-grounded personal conviction is. But, above all, when we feel the stress of the moral life, we cannot help thinking that God has forsaken us. When we are obliged to admit that we have ruined our spiritual strength, and that we are a hindrance to what is good, then the thought of that Omnipotence which supports and protects us grows faint within us. For it comes upon us as an undeniable truth that our ways run contrary to that which alone can ultimately prevail. Then we are forsaken of God, in what we are making of our own life. Of course, we may try to reassert ourselves, even in such a position. We may either take those thoughts of the love of God which express the confidence of Christian faith, and try to use them to deaden and silence our own experience, wherein no trace of God's love is written. *This is the practice men are led to adopt when they are told that it will help them if they determine to accept Christian doctrines.* Or, again, we may be honest, and give up faith that a God has anything to do with us, and may still retain our faith in moral ideals, and may resolve to live for these. This is the position of men without number, who are called by their wealth and culture to be the intellectual guides of the people. Or, finally, we may join the ranks of those who fling away all that uplifts the soul, and abandon ourselves to the careless- ness of a brutish life. This last course is but the natural outcome of the other two, for both these are equally untrue. Thoughts of the love of God are meaningless to us if we feel that we are condemned by that power which alone we can think of as divine. And a man who is conscious of guilt cannot establish a faith in moral ideals, except at the cost of falsifying those ideals and deceiving himself. Such persons evade the truth that a man can only will the good by denying himself, and that he can only deny himself when he has inwardly risen above all need, but not when he is rendered unhappy and powerless in his inmost soul by the consciousness of guilt. It is not possible, then, for an adult to feel himself as thoroughly in the protection of God as a child feels unless he has a different revelation of God from that which a child has.

We can rise out of the God-forsaken condition of an evil conscience and find our way back to God only when we are able to see that God has regard to this need of ours in His revelation of Himself. Jesus brings this vision to us, for by His appearance in history He makes us certain of God, when, for conscience' sake, we cannot rest content with any mere record of the religious thoughts of other men. Every man who has come to be at all conscious of what is good may be led on to understand that God *can be* none other than the Personal Vitality and Power of Goodness; and the marvellous fact of the Person of Jesus corresponds exactly to this hope of our hearts concerning God. While from our own inner life we gain no certain knowledge that the power of the Good is really supreme in all that happens, Jesus makes us certain of it by exhibiting in His Person the living fulness and un- doubted power of a good will, and thus He gives us a vision of the power of the Good over the real. We find in Him the first person who makes clear and gives a definite character and content to those moral ideals by which we judge ourselves and others. Hence we cannot judge Him, but we feel ourselves judged by Him. If we do not know Him, our evil conscience ever confirms us in the thought that there is no God. For the con- trast between what we ought to be and what we are, between our desire for life and our feeling of nothing- ness, prevents any strong faith in God from arising within us. But if, on the contrary, Jesus has become a real fact to us, He makes us feel that the Good has a power over the real, and He makes us feel also that we are separate from that power. In this experience a man who is morally mature gains a new certainty of God which is no longer dispelled by his consciousness of guilt, but confirmed by it. We do not believe in God on the strength of what we observe in ourselves ; it is also true that we do not believe in Him because of what others tells us. Our well-meaning friends can utter no words which can avail against the reality of our moral need ; only some reality which is similarly undeniable can help us there. But now, what we cannot do of ourselves we must do for Jesus' sake, namely, lay hold of the thought that God rules in this real world of which we ourselves are conscious. We can think of ourselves as being without God ; we cannot think so of Him. By the strength of His inner life He makes clear to us both our own moral powerlessness and the reality of God. The power of Jesus over personal lives consists in the fact that when He comes to them He causes them at once to despair of their own strength and to become aware of God. But when Jesus has revealed God in such a way to men, He then uses His power over them so as to uplift them.

Jesus gathers together all His powers for the task of redemption, which is His great vocation. This vocation is to reveal to us the blessedness of the life of a man who is in fellowship with God, and also His own desire to help us and His invincible confidence that He can do so. In showing this to those who experience His power over them, He redeems them. For they gather from this that the God whom they learned to know first as

Jesus Christ's Father and as their Judge, desires, nevertheless, to be their Father.

Herein lies the true analogy between the faith of a Christian and that of a child. *We must suffer ourselves to be wholly determined, like children, by a stronger personal life, and lifted above all that we are when left to ourselves.* In this way we fulfil the commandment that we shall become as little children. On the other hand, we certainly do not resemble children if we try to copy the religious conceptions which prevail around us. For while such imitation follows naturally in the case of a child, we can only accomplish it by an act of violence against ourselves. Though we might attain the same outward result, we should be acting in a spirit entirely opposed to that of a child. The child-like spirit can only arise within us when our experience is the same as a child's; in other words, when we meet with a personal life which compels us to trust it without reserve. But a man who has awakened to moral self-consciousnes finds this nowhere else in the world. Only the Person of Jesus can arouse such trust. If such a man surrenders himself to anything or any one else, he throws away not only his trust but himself.

Now, when the fact of Jesus' personal influence upon us has led us to recognise that God reveals Himself to us and pours out His love upon us, the whole world is transformed for us. For the world wherein this has befallen us is no longer to our eyes a weary stretch of numberless and perplexing events. What we experience at the hands of Jesus tells us the purpose of all that reality amidst whose relationships His Person stands.

When we understand the meaning of His life, the particular events of our life all turn out to be efforts of God in behalf of our souls. The whole world appears to us now to be a well-ordered system whose culminating point is the Person of Jesus and His work upon us. And yet this new view of the world is by no means the end of all that is included in the thought of the Christian who has become certain of God through the reality of Jesus : he has more than an altered view of the real world : he sees also a new reality which is to take form in himself and others through that which God will make of them.

§ 19. *The Easy Christianity that Renounces Sefl-knowledge and Reflection, and Accepts the Conceptions of Others.*

But we are only raised to such life amid new reality when that fact remains present to us which alone can tell us the depths of our moral need, and can then raise us to the experience of divine life. We affirm that this fact is the inner life of the Man Jesus, and yet we cannot prove it. How could we, since every one must experience for himself that the spiritual power of Jesus destroys his confidence in self, and creates in him a trust in God, that makes him a new creature ? All we can do is to show how a man becomes inwardly changed, when he does find and understand the communion of God with his soul in the influence of Jesus upon him. But we cannot substitute any product of reflection for this fact itself which we are to experience as the turning of God towards us.

And yet, self-evident as this appears, it is, nevertheless, only with immense difficulty that we free ourselves from the contrary way of thinking. Even we who are Christians are constantly tempted to regard Jesus Christ as the pre-supposition from which our relation to God may be inferred with logical certainty. The truth is that we ought to grasp Him as a fact which is real beyond all doubt, and which convinces us, by the power of its own content, that God is turning to us in that very fact itself, in order to draw us to Himself. But then it is infinitely more convenient to put aside this vision of a fact, and to seek the guarantees of our certainty of the grace of God in thoughts concerning Jesus; for the vision of this fact, in other words, the real, personal life of Jesus, constantly imposes new labour upon our souls, and makes us find God's power in an experience which is most painful, and which utterly breaks down our self-conceit. If, instead of this, it were actually possible for us to find true blessing in such mere reflections concerning Christ, and if these could give us substantial guarantees of the presence of God, then it would be possible to avoid that painful inward process amid which we become lifted to the consciousness that God is acting upon us. The temptation to follow this view always accompanies an acceptance as a matter of custom of the doctrines of the Church concerning Christ and His work. These doctrines may, indeed, be expressions of well-grounded Christian thinking; but they become, in spite of that, a powerful temptation to us if they hinder our vision of the fact in which we are to find God entering our life, and which, therefore, ought to be the basis of our faith in Him. The same thoughts concerning Christ which in others may be a sign of their redemption, will become deadly to us if we allow ourselves to be persuaded that we must accept them in order to be redeemed. For then the fact remains concealed from us that God alone is our Helper, that our highest good is to be at one with Him, and that we are at one with Him only when we are able to trace in undeniable facts the evidence that His power is the power of love that is seeking us out and overcoming the evil within us. If our hearts no longer impel us to seek in Jesus Christ the fact in which God reveals Himself to us, then, even surrounded by the greatest wealth of Christian ideas, we shall soon come to desire, not God Himself, but security from Him.

§ 20. *The Possibility of a Confession of the Divinity of Christ.*

This danger is clearly seen in the way in which the Christian Churches use the confession of the Deity of Christ. They do not, of course, abandon the proposition that Christ is the Mediator through whom Christian people have access to God, or through whom their communion with Him is mediated. But the proposition is robbed of its meaning by what is added to it. In other words, it is regarded as self-evident that if we wish to enjoy the mediation of Christ we must first of all confess His Deity. This demand prevents many an honest man from coming to Christ, and disturbs the clearness of many an earnest Christian's faith. Its injustice can no longer be concealed. To confess the Deity of Jesus means, obviously, to confess that Jesus is God. It is clearly impossible for a man to appropriate this thought to himself so as to find any meaning in the words, unless Jesus has already led him to break with his past and to enter upon a new existence.

If we are to understand the proposition that Jesus is God, it is evidently necessary first of all that we know Jesus Himself. If we do not learn to know Him, and if we nevertheless go on using the thought that He is God, then we only possess the general idea of Divine Incarnation. A man who is not utterly devoid of imagination may do something even with this ; he may construct a philosophy of the world in which he himself plays the part of a spectator. But such a play of imagination round the thought of Incarnation and the resulting theory of the universe have no significance for a man's own personal existence. It may be said, however, that the doctrine that in Jesus God became man is, nevertheless, of service because it draws men's attention to Him. That is true, but it by no means follows that in order to become Christians we must adopt the confession of that doctrine, or even that we could do so. It can only incite us to gaze upon the Man who so influenced others that in Him they were able to see a God who had become man. In that case it is possible that we may learn and understand what moves the soul of Jesus, and feel the power of that Personal Spirit, which in all its movements reveals the power of what is good, and at the same time ventures to place itself in the midst of history. We ourselves may have to sum up the content of such experiences in the thought that God Himself can be none other than that Personal Spirit who acts upon us

through Jesus. It is what we experience in the Man
Jesus that first gives definite content to the confession
of the Deity of Christ. Redeeming power for us can
only lie in something which actually works upon us. But
the doctrine of the Deity of Christ, on the contrary, can
of itself help no one. The man who only knows that
doctrine and the name of Jesus, and who is also so
devoid of character as to repeat the doctrine after others,
is certainly not made a Christian by that. Hence it is
meaningless to say to men, "If you wish to be
redeemed by Christ you must believe in His Deity."
We ought rather to put the matter thus : "If you
wish to be redeemed by Christ, you must experience in
the fact of His Person that God communes with you."

Secondly, if we are truthfully to confess the Deity
of Jesus, it is necessary that we should have known God.
But we first see clearly what God really is when we
experience God's communion with us in the influence
which Jesus has upon us. Before God becomes a power
in our inner life and makes us a new creature we have
necessarily false notions concerning Him. By the
miracle of His appearance Jesus can overcome both our
doubts as to the reality of God and our illusions concerning Him. Has a man seen the fact of the personal
life of Jesus and does he feel in it the mighty working
of God upon himself, then in that he has the beginning
of redemption. In the vision of the God, who is
in such ways working upon us, and through submission
to Him, we break way from our whole previous
existence. Before we have known this power
of personal spirit we can form only uncertain and

confused ideas about the being of God, and therefore we cannot yet understand the expression " Deity of Christ " in a religious sense, but only in the sense of earthly dreams. And so the Church durst not say to the men she wishes to lead on the way of redemption, " Believe in the Deity of Jesus, that ye may be saved." She ought rather to say, " Do not imagine that you can either believe or understand it, for only the redeemed can do that." If we do utter the name of God as we think of Jesus it is due to the power and action of the Holy Spirit within us (compare 1 *Cor.* xii. 3). It is revealed to us that Jesus is Lord when we are brought by His personal power to the consciousness of God and to submission to Him. In the true confession of the Deity of Christ there speaks the Spirit of God which is ours through the fact that Christ unites us to God. A horrible caricature of this sacred knowledge is the assertion that one must believe in the Deity of Christ in order to be redeemed by Him.

§ 21. *Defects in the old Protestant Doctrine of the Work of Christ and the Way of Salvation.*

The demand that men shall confess a definite doctrine concerning Christ as a condition of redemption is not the only customary injury that is being done. The one question of absolute importance is whether Jesus gains a power over us through His personal life. And a second hindrance to this may easily arise from the *content* of the Church's doctrines of the Person and Work of Jesus.

This hindrance may be clearly seen in that doctrine

of the Atonement which the Reformers derived from the theology of the Middle Ages, with certain well-known alterations. According to that doctrine there was a divine nature in Jesus, and because of it the deeds which He actually did were able to remove those hindrances in God which restrained His love for sinful humanity. Since Jesus' work wrought satisfaction for God in view of the injury done to Him by sin, it becomes the ground of our certainty that God *can* forgive us, and *can* receive us again into the realm of His grace. This conclusion—that God *can* do such things for us—is, of course, the highest point we can reach on the assumption of that doctrine, viz., that Christ's work is made a work of redemption by His divine nature, a nature not fully defined, which for some reason or another, He is supposed to possess. This indefinite conception of Christ's divine nature may indeed serve us in one way, namely, by adding a sort of explanation as to how what is to us an incomprehensible procedure becomes *possible*, namely, that God should turn towards the sinner and proffer him His love. But the thought that in some mysterious way there was divine nature in Jesus cannot help us to think of God's forgiveness as something actual. Yet this alone can satisfy our longing for redemption.

As opposed to Socinianism that doctrine of the Reformers concerning the Atonement was in the right, and it may claim even to-day that it protects an important truth against rationalistic disfigurements of the Christian thought concerning the Atonement. For the Christian faith is obviously a very feeble thing if all it does is to infer that divine forgiveness goes without saying because we have learned that God is love.* Any one must have utterly misunderstood the history of Jesus' life who only gathers from it that He proclaimed such an inference as a truth which any man can grasp. If the work of Jesus be seriously studied, it will rather make the impression that the divine forgiveness of sins is not a matter of course, but is something utterly marvellous. It is therefore a merit of the Reformer's doctrine of Atonement which cannot be too highly praised, that it emphasises this impression made by the story of Jesus. Their doctrine represents the work of Jesus as simply that satisfaction given to God which makes it possible for Him to perform that act of forgiveness, which would otherwise be impossible.

But this very form of recording the important truth that divine forgiveness is not a matter of course is of little use for the end it seeks. For, in the first place, this form of the doctrine suggests that a man can see why it has become possible for God to forgive him. But the more a man supposes he has this insight, the more will he lose sight of the idea that forgiveness is for every one who receives it an act of unfathomable goodness.

Again, this orthodox doctrine of the Atonement leaves the individual in the end in the same position where he is left by rationalism, with its assertion that all Jesus did was to proclaim that God, as the loving Father, is willing to forgive. The supporters of the

* This opinion has been attributed to Ritschl ; I consider this the grossest misrepresentation of his theology which has been made.

orthodox doctrine observe, rightly enough, that such a proclamation is of no use to the sinner, for the simple reason that he cannot believe it. Over against the declaration of this thought, there stands the undeniable reality of his own feeling of guilt. The man who feels condemnation by the Eternal in his own consciousness of guilt is not so easily persuaded that acceptance of a doctrine will take away this reality from him. He finds himself in a condition which to him is an undeniable fact; and is he able to step out of that reality in which he finds himself, out of that con-demnation whose justice he sees, for the sake of a doctrine which others preach to him? Jesus did indeed speak of that love of the Heavenly Father which is prepared to forgive without reserve those who repent, but He never made to any one the degrading suggestion that it should be accepted simply on the strength of His mere statement. Jesus did not write the story of the Prodigal Son on a sheet of paper for men who knew nothing of Himself. He told it rather to men who saw Him, and who, because of His own personal life, were to be sure of the Father in Heaven, of whom He was speaking. From this fancy that the mere doctrine of the father-like love of God can help the troubled sinner, it is evident that ideas belonging to Catholic piety have sprung up again amid rationalism, and in wide circles of the liberal Christianity of our time as well as amid pietism. For this fancy corresponds to the Catholic practice, which does not minister to the inner life of the Christian thirsting for truth and reality, but requires instead that, like the Jesuits, we shall forego

altogether any inner life of our own, full of sincerity
and truthfulness.[25] A sinner who is not willing to tread
the Jesuitical path will heartily scorn the suggestion
that he either can or ought to approve of that rationalistic doctrine.   Thus Protestant orthodoxy exhibited
some of the genuine instincts of the Reformation when,
during the Socinian controversy, it fought to the bitter
end against that rationalistic dream.   But what now
must be said of the practical working of the orthodox
doctrine itself?   It rejects the rationalistic doctrine, for
it is impossible that God can forgive as a mere matter
of course.   So it goes on to say that first the work and
sufferings of Christ provided a satisfaction for the justice
of God, and then this made it possible for Him to
forgive sinners.   Thus the attempt is made to face the
fact that no sinner who is trying to be honest could by
any possibility regard God's forgiveness simply as a
matter of course.   But then, even if a sinner whose
whole soul has been broken by the feeling of his moral
unworthiness should accept this orthodox doctrine, he
still remains precisely where the teaching of rationalism
would leave him.   Even suppose the doctrine true, that
God can spare sinners the torments of hell because
Jesus suffered these in their stead, still, no sinner who
has become conscious of his need can draw from this
ability of God to forgive all men the only inference
that could relieve his own distress.   He cannot say to
himself, "Since God can forgive all men, he actually
forgives me."

Now what has orthodox theology done to bridge
over the chasm between the universal possibility of

forgiveness and that actual forgiveness of God which I need? It has proposed a doctrine of the "Plan of Salvation"; and in this we are told that various stages of help by Divine Grace are needed to bring the sinner to appropriate for himself that salvation which has been objectively provided, namely, that deliverance of God from the necessity of condemning us of which we are told in the doctrine of the work of Christ. But even this doctrine, again, may be true, and yet it will not deliver any one who accepts it from his own moral need. For the sinner will be constantly driven to ask himself whether, after all, what it says, and what may really happen with others, will actually come to pass in his own case. Repeated assurances that he will get the certainty, if he only faithfully adopts the doctrine and seeks to live by it, do not help him at all. Any Christian who has but a trace of earnest desire for life will certainly not be put off with words like these instead of food. He demands a fact which shall out-weigh the fact of his inward feeling of condemnation. Nothing can help him but a fact which shall speak to him from an undeniable event, telling him that God does forgive him, that is, forgives this particular man. The orthodox theology has not opened the way for this fact, but has blocked it.

It may well cause amazement to see pious men, who are enthusiastic for their Protestant faith, who can be nevertheless quite content with the orthodox doctrine of the work of Christ and the "Plan of Salvation," although these can by no means bring a sinner to what he needs for his redemption, even if he resolve to accept them.

This would be still quite incomprehensible, even if these men had never known Jesus from their Bibles.   Their love for Him, to which their hymns and lives bear abundant witness, justifies us in thinking that, in spite of their doctrine, they must have received their actual proof of God's forgiveness from the fact that the inner life of Jesus has confronted them as a real element in history.

§ 22. *The Value of the Doctrine of the Substitutionary Penal Sufferings of Jesus.*

On the other hand, it is quite right that men are unwilling to let go the thought that redemption has been won by the vicarious suffering of Christ.   For when once the believer has heard the message of God to him in Christ, and sees therein that God's forgiveness has come to himself, his faith naturally conceives that only through the fact of the moral Personality of Jesus, made perfect through suffering, could God enter once more into communion with men who have sinned. Nay, more ; he says with a natural impulse, as he looks back upon Jesus' work, " He suffers what we should have suffered."   Hence it might seem remarkable that more is not said in the New Testament of this idea that Christ bore our punishment.   For the misery of our feeling of guilt is ever being overcome in the knowledge that the one Man through whom we have access to the Father has, since He knew that nothing else would avail, sacrificed Himself and so taken on Himself our burden.   In the fellowship that He established thus with us, we become free.

But everything is ruined if, instead of this, we adopt the ecclesiastical dogma of satisfaction, and make the idea of substitution *the starting-point from which we are to understand Jesus, and the ground of our certainty of the forgiveness of our sin.* The man who has received forgiveness through Christ will constantly experience afresh that doubts arise from his sense of guilt, and seek to rob him of this spiritual treasure. But if he has truly found in Jesus a God who forgives him, then he will also find help against the doubts of his evil conscience by looking upon Jesus. He will see that while Jesus dispensed forgiveness, He at the same time did everything to establish the inviolable justice of God's moral order. Now here is just where the doctrine of the vicarious suffering of Jesus takes it rise: it is thus that this thought is produced in the man who has already received forgiveness from Jesus. It helps to overcome the doubts which are always springing up again as to the reality of the forgiveness which has been experienced. But it is a strange misunderstanding to imagine that it can serve to give certainty of forgiveness to one who is not already redeemed. In such a man the doctrine will only raise false conceptions of God if he propose to follow it. If he follows such a suggestion, he will conceive of God as a Being who cannot forgive at all, but who can traffic with men in matters of justice.

§ 23. *Luther's Criticism of the Thought of a Substitutionary Satisfaction.*

It is interesting to observe here how strongly Luther felt that the doctrine of vicarious satisfaction does not by any means serve to set forth that which procures the sinner divine forgiveness. The doctrine has rather to do with the thoughts that the evil conscience of the sinner prompts concerning God's attitude towards him. The doctrine of the vicarious satisfaction is intended to express the faith that these are overcome; and so it makes use of those ideas which an evil conscience would employ in thinking of God's relation to a sinful man. It teaches that Jesus wrought out precisely that which, according to the verdict of an evil conscience, God must demand from the sinner before He can forgive him. And these ideas have their rightful place if they arise in the mind of a man who has already received the forgiveness of God through Christ. For they express his experience that Christ alone protects him against all the doubts as to the reality of forgiveness which arise within him from his consciousness of guilt; but they do harm when they are supposed to express the only ground for trust in God's forgiveness. In this latter case they increase the illusion, so very convenient for the sinner, that the strained relations between God and himself can be set right by a kind of traffic in justice which the reason can see through, and thus they conceal the truth that this strained relationship can only be removed by the act of forgiveness which is indeed an incomprehensible revelation of personal love. Luther saw all this concerning the doctrine of vicarious satisfaction ; and so, on the one hand, he supported and defended it as one of the Church's precious jewels ; but, on the other, he also pointed out its defect, namely, the application of legal conceptions to the relations between God and man.

The following utterance of Luther is very instructive in this connection. It is taken from a sermon which did not appear until the last issue of his Summer-Postille, in 1543.* He says, " The whole Papacy has had no better idea what to teach concerning Repentance than that it consists of three parts, which they call Remorse, Confession, and Satisfaction, and they are unable to teach the people aright concerning any one of these. *And, indeed, as to the word ' satisfactio,' satisfaction, we have been willing to please them and let it pass* (in the hope that by gentleness we might bring them to the true doctrine); yet *on the understanding that it means not our giving satisfaction but Christ's,* namely, that He pays for our sins by His own blood and death and conciliates God. But since we have so often experienced hitherto, and still plainly see that we cannot win them at all by any gentleness, and that the longer they live the more they will contradict the true doctrine, so we must strip ourselves clean of them, and part from them, and have nothing more to do with *the words they have invented* in their schools, with which they now only seek to confirm their old error and lies. Therefore, for our part, shall this word satisfaction

* Erlangen edition, xi. 306.

continue no longer, and it shall be dead in our churches
and our theology, and it shall be handed over to the
judges and schools of the law, where it belongs, and
whence also the Papists took it." In these words it is
clearly declared that a satisfaction rendered to God for
the purpose of restoring His grace to the sinner does
not in the least concern the communion of man with
God ; that this idea came from law into theology
through the medium of the Catholic sacrament of
penance ; and, finally, that Luther had admitted it into
consideration in the doctrine of Atonement out of
friendly regard for the then prevailing mode of thought,
but that he had in view its entire repudiation.* Hence
we may clearly conclude that Luther saw, indeed, how
the idea of a satisfaction wrought by Christ had arisen
from an erroneous view of the relation of the sinner to
God ; but that he nevertheless used the idea, because
he wished to grapple with the most injurious error of
Rome on its own field of thought. He might, indeed,
have said that a man who has already received God's forgiveness in another way does not need to trouble himself
as to the accuracy of such doctrinal ideas, which he himself had employed in common with the old church ; and

* H. Schultz, in his " Doctrine of the Deity of Christ" (" Die Lehre
von der Gottheit Christi," 1881), p. 194, says, with reference to this
passage, that Luther here rejects altogether the word satisfaction, and
yet only with regard to the doctrine of repentance. But the remarkable feature of the passage appears to me to be that Luther here
rejects the word in the sense of the satisfaction wrought by Christ.
It is otherwise in xxiv. 86, where Luther says, in regard to the
mischief which the word has wrought as it is used in the Sacrament
of Penance : " For this reason, too, I am against the word ' satisfaction,' and wish it had never arisen."

yet the fact is that Luther did feel, and did say that he
felt, the incongruity of the juristic conceptions in which
that doctrine moves.

§ 24. *The Receiving of Forgiveness through Jesus.*

*According to Socinian and rationalistic teaching,
Christ simply proclaimed the forgiveness of sins; according to the orthodox doctrine, He made it possible;
in truth He bestows it on us.* In the first case, it is
enough to see in Jesus a man who proclaims a divine
truth. In the second case, it is sufficient that we conceive of a Divine Being united with Jesus, and yet other
than Himself. But in the third case, forgiveness itself
only becomes ours when we actually behold God Himself in the Christ who is an indubitable fact for us.
The only way we can receive the forgiveness of God is
this, that He makes us feel the penalty of our sin, and
yet at the same time makes us notice the incomprehensible fact that He is seeking us and not giving us
up. If we are in earnest in our hope through Christ to
receive God's forgiveness we must, in the first place, not
ask for a doctrine concerning Him, but honestly try to
reflect about Him who is indeed an insistent and undeniable reality. For we cannot reckon up by the aid of
the notions of a system of doctrine that forgiveness
which is to be a work of God upon ourselves in our own
experience. Therefore, it is not of any importance that
we try to say the highest possible things regarding
Christ. We must leave such artifice alone and simply
be ready to hear what the tradition has to say to us

about Him. If there is nothing in it that takes hold of our inner life as a reality, it is meaningless to ask any further whether or how Christ mediates to us God's forgiveness of sins.

What touches particular men who come in contact with the tradition about Christ, as being real, naturally varies in each different case. For in order not to lose connection with the Redeemer, each man can hold only to what shows itself to him as an undeniable reality. For if there is any redemption for him at all in his inner life it can surely be expected only from something that can appear in this inner life as something real. Anything that has not the strength to force its way into this inner world of consciousness as an undeniable reality is not in a position to constitute with this inner world the fulcrum of a new life.

In the second place, we can say that Christ bestows on us the forgiveness of God only if he acts on us as the revelation of God that conquers every doubt and thus lets us feel that God is seeking us in spite of our sin. The forgiveness of God is not a demonstrable doctrine, still less an idea that can be appropriated by an act of will. It is a religious experience. It must stand before us as an incomprehensible reality that the same fact that increased our grief for our unfaithfulness and weakness of will nevertheless is also preceptible to us as a word of God convincing us that He has reached down to us. The appearance of Jesus can become for us this expression of God's forgiveness as soon as we perceive in Him, as nowhere else, the nearness of God. It is not through long-winded dogmatic reflections that we reach the

thought that we receive the forgiveness of sins through
Jesus, but that comes into our consciousness as soon as we
understand religiously, or lay hold of as a work of God
upon us, the fact that the Being of this Man is part
of our sphere of existence. For then His death, as
He bore it and as He expounded it in words at the
Last Supper, becomes to us the word of God that
overcomes our feeling of guilt. The God who comes
near us in Christ reconciles us with Himself by that
death.

Our yearning to meet a personal life that shall resolve
every element of separation between us and it into pure
trust, and thus give our spirits a home, is the longing
for the living God. But we find it satisfied in Jesus in
every moment when the recollection of Him takes away
our fear of the abyss and delivers us from the confusion
and perplexity of the evil conscience. Then vanishes
from the depths of our souls the isolation in which
all our experiences were wont to culminate. We
are no longer forsaken. The personal life of Jesus
through its track in history reveals itself to us in
its power.

§ 25. *The True Idea of the Deity of Christ and Christological Dogma.*

Thus, in the work which Christ does upon us, we get
a view of His Person which can only be rightly expressed
in the confession of His Deity.* We come to understand

* *Cf.* Luther, Erlangen edition, xvii. 265 : "The man now who so
knows Christ that Christ has taken away from him all his sin, death
and devil, freely through His suffering, he has truly recognised Christ

Jesus to be the divine act of forgiveness, or, in other words, we see Him to be the message through which God comes into communion with us ; and so we recognise in His human appearance God Himself drawing us to Himself.* This thought, that when the historical Christ takes such hold of us, we have to do with God Himself—this thought is certainly the most important element in the confession of the Deity of Christ for any one whom He has redeemed. We do not reach this thought by way of a logical conclusion from that which we have experienced at the hands of Christ ; but the experience itself is such when we confess His Deity we simply give Him His right name. In what Jesus does to us, we grasp the expression God gives us of His feeling towards us, or God Himself as a Personal Spirit working upon us. This is the form in which every man who has been reconciled to God through Christ necessarily confesses His Deity, even although he may decline to adopt the formula.

as a Son of God." *Cf*. 1., 173 : " But since no one can give eternal life but God alone it follows inevitably that Christ must be truly and naturally God." Worthy of notice, too, is the expression in xlvii. 6, where Luther says it is an *essentialis definitio*, to believe that Christ bestows eternal life. Another remarkable passage occurs in xlii. 6, where Luther says that if we believe that Christ gives eternal life, that is an *essentialis definitio*, a definition of His nature.

* *Cf*. Luther, Erlangen edition, xx. I., 161 : " When I thus imagine Christ, then do I picture Him truly and properly, I grasp and have the true Christ as He pictures Himself ; and then I let go utterly all thoughts and speculations concerning the Divine Majesty and glory, and hang and cling to the humanity of Christ ; then there is no fear there, but only friendliness and joy, and I learn thus through Him to know the Father. Thus arises such a light and knowledge within me that I know certainly what God is, and what is His mind."

What the Christian has in Christ, namely, that God turns to him and is accessible to him is simply summed up in the confession of His Deity. Hence it is impossible that this confession should ever vanish from the Christian Church. But the same words, by which faith confesses that it finds God in Jesus, as its highest good, may also be used in an entirely opposite sense. Indeed, we cannot grasp the true meaning of the confession of the Deity of Christ at all unless we let that work take place upon us which God effects through Jesus in the soul of every man who comes to himself. But we may, of course, have a confession of the Deity of Christ that spares us this experience with all its inward travail. This is the case when we content ourselves with assuming that behind the human life of Jesus, and in wonderful combination with it, there stands the substance of the Deity, from whose presence we may argue that the work and sufferings of Christ possess redeeming power. Certainly it is not comprehensible how any one desires to make this assumption with inward truthfulness if he expressly excludes the idea that we must experience the redeeming power of God through the influence of the personal life of the Man Jesus. But how easily all that is overlooked by any one who regards it as of importance, for some other reason, to adopt the Christian confession! We shall see in the next chapter what sort of a soul a man must have who repeats a confession that is not his own, and asserts as a fact something which he has not found to be such. Our aim here is to show that such a conception of the Deity of Christ conceals from us what God desires to give us through Jesus.

This conception, against which we are thus complaining, is the conception found in the old dogma of the Roman Catholic Church. But does not our Church also teach the same? It is a fact that the Reformation effected no change in this respect. Consequently, Protestant theology has done little to show the Protestant Christian that he cannot live on that conception of the old church. It is true that rationalistic criticism has not failed to point out the contradictions involved in the old Christological dogma. But this has had an effect similar to that which the intellectual revival in Prussia, known as the "Kulturkampf," had on the Romish Church. Criticism has not destroyed these relics of a bygone form of Christianity, but has given them a new lease of life. For that criticism denied altogether the truth of the Deity of Christ, and so caused all those forces of faith which tend towards this idea to stream together in support of the ancient dogma which, at least, supports that truth. In laying bare the fatal inconsistency in the doctrine of the two natures in Christ, rationalistic criticism gives that doctrine the benefit of a support that helps indeed all thoughts that spring out of faith, namely this, that every such thought must seem utterly unreasonable to a non-religious thinker, unless it be deprived of its essential meaning. In the "Kulturkampf" of eighteeth-century Illuminism the reaction against dogma was carried on with an honest desire for truth, but also with an astounding lack of effort to understand the nature of the thinking that springs from faith. The severity of that criticism has therefore given the orthodoxy of the Protestant people

and their leaders a similar look to that which the
Prussian " Kulturkampf " has left behind in Catholic
circles, for we find in both, on the one hand an earnest
religious exaltation of tone, and on the other a deaden-
ing of the sense for truth and a certain primitive
roughness of party spirit.

It is no part of our task here to try to mediate
between rationalistic criticism and the popular orthodoxy which it has angered and thrown into confusion.
No abatement of hostility is possible. Each party
requires the opposite side to fight against in order to
justify its own existence. We must rather try to bring
the opponents away to quite another ground, and to
interest them in questions which cannot possibly receive
consideration amid their party strifes. In this undertaking Luther can give us help.

§ 26. *Luther's Attitude to Christological Dogma.*

In Luther's position in regard to the Christological
question nothing is so conspicuous as his enthusiastic
loyalty to the old dogma. To adduce quotations from
Luther's works in support of this statement would be
quite superfluous. What A. Harnack has stated in detail
on the matter is quite true,[26] namely, that of that
generation of theologians among whom Luther stands
out supreme, none treated the old church dogma so
seriously as Luther. To others that dogma had become
a sacred relic, honoured indeed, but having no higher
significance for the inner life than that of a point of
attachment to which an arbitrary and imperious fancy

could link whatever activities or consequences and requirements it chose. To Luther, on the contrary, the dogma expressed what his faith had actually found in Christ, namely, redemption from trouble and sin. But while Luther read the old dogma in this sense, he combined with it thoughts of which neither its authors nor those who used it after them, had any conception.

These thoughts arose in Luther's mind of necessity, because his view of the salvation which Christ brought us was different from that of the old church. He sought and saw in the Person of Jesus the fact that God was looking upon him with love, and was overcoming him; the same God, from whom he had felt separated by his own sin, and whose power, at last, had been utterly hidden from him by the sense of his own miserable condition. The authors of the old church dogma never saw these things in the Person of Jesus; and numberless Christians, even in our own Church, who cherish the same way of thinking, never make that discovery. They believe that the Person of Jesus gives them something quite different, namely, nothing but the certainty that blessedness is possible to them in the future, or, at most, the certainty that a communion with God could now be resumed. This is clearly something less than Luther had from Christ. When a fact that has become part of a man's own life is to that man a communion between God and his own soul, a communion that he had never hitherto had any conception of, then that man has something quite different from a mere doctrine that he may now be certain of the

possibility of finding God once more.   It is also evident
that only in the former case the man gets something
from Christ which can be possessed only in the form
of a purely religious experience; something, therefore,
that can have no existence except for faith.   For the
idea that the conditions have been fulfilled whereby
mankind may hold communion with God, can be
established equally well by philosophical arguments
which can be grasped even by those who are
complete unbelievers.   Just as little can it be gain-
said that we come into the most intimate relation to
the Person of Jesus when we are able to recognise the
approach of God to us in the power with which
the personal life of Jesus draws us upwards towards
God.   On the other hand, the Person of Jesus recedes
in interest from us when we see in the Divine Nature
united with that Person merely the fulfilment of the
condition required if fellowship with God is to be
possible to us.   The man who gets no further than this
has certainly an undefined idea of a Divine Nature,
whose entrance into humanity appears to him to be the
basis of salvation; but when he thinks of what moved
the soul of Jesus, he cannot make use of it as
anything more than an example.   He cannot rest
his hopes of life upon it, for that alone is a foundation
of salvation for ourselves, which works in the inner
process of our rise to the God Who is a power actually
saving us.

Hence the attitude towards Jesus which Luther
consciously held marks a step forward in the development
of the Christian religion.   We move forward in our

Christianity only when the Person of Jesus gains a higher and more comprehensive significance for our own way of feeling and thinking, and when our thought concerning our faith finds expression in terms which must seem meaningless to one who has not this faith, and which in his mouth would be untrue.

Among those new thoughts which Luther consequently combined with the confession of the Deity of Christ, may also be counted his well-known demand that the two natures in Christ of which the dogma speaks must be regarded as more closely united than men usually consider them.   The usual view was a mistake, Luther declared, into which not only heretics but the " highest theologians " fell.   He confesses that he himself formerly thought, to quote his own words, "I did well to distinguish the Deity and humanity of Christ one from the other."*   A man who stood towards Christ as Luther did, and who, at the same time, held by the formula of the " two natures," was necessarily driven to advance at least to the demand mentioned above.   He was obliged to protest against every Christology " which thinks of the Deity and the humanity in Christ as being so externally united that we may look at the one apart from the other." †   But Luther's endeavours to bring the two ideas of a divine and a human nature into closer union were in vain.‡   It could not be otherwise.   Luther was thinking of the marvellous experience of faith, namely, the fact

* Erlangen edition, xlvii. 362.

† *Cf.* H. Schultz, "The Doctrine of the Deity of Christ," 1881, p. 201.

‡ *Cf.* J. Köstlin, "The Theology of Luther," 1863 ; ii. 398 ; and H. Schultz, in the volume quoted, p. 204.

that Jesus compels us to see in Him God redeeming us; and this experience cannot be expressed by anything that our thinking can make out of the two ideas of a divine and a human nature. If such an expression were possible, then we should have to be able to see to the bottom of a mystery which in reality we can only experience as fact. So long as the Church had not come to see that redemption lies just here, namely, in one's own experience of the power which the Person of Jesus has over the soul, so long was it natural that men's minds should busy themselves with these two ideas. Constant pleasure in the effort to form some more suitable conception of the relation between the two natures gave a certain satisfaction to thought, and concealed the damaging defect that men did not rightly grasp the reality of the fact about the possibility of which they were reflecting. Even the constantly evident fruitlessness of these attempts had a high value in the circumstances, for it kept alive the impression that here men had to do with an unfathomable mystery. Luther, on the contrary, had grasped the new thought whose position reveals the worthlessness of all this painful delving in a barren soil. And yet it was one of the marks of his significance as a reformer that he clothed the new thought in the forms of the old, and so he bequeathed it as a hidden germ to those generations which should only wean themselves by long mental exercise from the forms of thought employed by the ancient church.

What Luther found in the Person of Jesus cannot be fully expressed in the forms of the old dogma, for

he had found the Personal God who, in the human
life of Jesus, turns towards those who are overpowered
by Jesus' spiritual force. This experience is not so
much expressed as concealed by the formula that combines a divine nature with the human nature of Jesus.
None the less does the new element in Luther's faith
press to the front and find clear expression in his
innumerable descriptions of what the believer means
by the Deity of Christ. It goes without saying that
the Deity of Christ was for Luther as much as for
Athanasius the basis of his salvation. He writes "now
if Deity be wanting in Christ, there is no help or
deliverance for us against God's anger and judgments."*
Again, " We must have a Saviour who is more than a
saint or an angel, for if He were not more, better and
greater than these, then there were no helping us. But
if He is God, then is the treasure so weighty that it
outweighs and lifts away sin and death ; and not only
this, but also gives the eternal life. This is our
Christian faith, and therefore do we rightly confess : ' I
believe in Jesus Christ, His only Son, our Lord, who
was born of Mary, suffered and died.' By this faith
hold thou fast, and let heathen and heretic be never
so wise, thou shalt be blessed." † Again, " We
Christians need to know this : if God be not with us in
the balance, and He do not give the weightiness, then
we sink with our little scale to the ground. Hereby
do I mean to say, that if it could not be held that God
died for us, but only a man, then we are lost." ‡ In
view of such words as these, which might be multiplied

* Erlangen edition, xlv. 315.   † *Ibid.* xlvii. 3-4.   ‡ *Ibid.* xxv. 312*f*.

without difficulty, it would be strange if any one should doubt that Luther rested his confidence in God on the Deity of Christ. But it is equally true that Luther had a richer conception of Christ's Deity than was expressed in the dogma of the elder church, as may be seen from the three considerations which follow.

In the first place, Luther does not content himself with the theory that there was a divine nature in Christ, giving to Jesus' human work the weight necessary for our redemption. In a sermon on John xiv. 23–31, which was not published until the last edition of the summer series for 1543 we read as follows: "For the devil can bear it if men cling to the man Christ and go no further; yea, *he will also let us speak and hear the word that Christ is truly God.* But then he will not have it that a heart be able to connect Christ and the Father so closely and inseparably that it shall count His word and His Father's to be one word, heart and will. Just as darkened hearts do think and say: Yes, I hear indeed with what friendliness and comfort Christ speaks to the troubled conscience, but who knows how it stands between me and God in Heaven? That means, then, that the heart has not counted God and Christ all one, but has made for itself a Christ apart by Himself and a God apart from Himself, and has bartered away the true God, who wills to be found and laid hold of nowhere save in this Christ." * Here Luther is speaking of such as do indeed confess that Christ is truly God, but are nevertheless unable to take comfort from the friendliness of the Man Jesus. With such a confession of the Deity of Christ, he says, men remain a prey to

* Erlangen edition, xii. 324.

the devil.* But, on the other hand, he believes that those are taken out of the power of the devil who are able to hear, from the friendly words of Jesus, how it stands between them and God in Heaven. Such souls do not distinguish between the mind and

---

* It has been said by "Lutherans" (*see* Th. Meinhold's book entitled "The Holy Spirit and His work upon Individuals," 1890, p. 1721) that the doctrine of the "two natures" is not made superfluous for Christian faith by the fact that the devil does not oppose it. For, say they, the devils believe in God, but we should certainly not wish to assert that therefore the belief in God is superfluous for the Christian. To this we reply that in any case the Christian does not need such faith in God as the devils may possess, or, rather, ought not to have such a faith. The Christian's faith in God means that, convinced by the revelation of God, he knows that he is surrounded by an Almighty love. And on this point any modern Lutheran may be convinced by Luther's Greater Catechism. Christian life simply is the constant victorious wrestling for this certainty. In such a strife the devil's faith, whatever it may be, can by no means help us, for the devils, with their sort of faith, never attain to the knowledge of God in His full reality, because the Father does not draw them to the Son. They must surely conceive of God as a violent and therefore diabolical Being, against whom they delight to rebel. Luther doubtless meant by these words of his that the thought expressed in the doctrine of the two natures, or the Church dogma of the Person of the God-man, is not able of itself to be the basis of the inner life of the redeemed. That bliss is wrought alone by the knowledge that in the inner life of Jesus we grasp the very mind of God Himself as love poured out upon us. This knowledge was certainly not expressed in the dogma, as we well know. Of course, Luther did connect the two, the dogma and this knowledge, as I willingly grant my opponent, but the question is whether that redeeming knowledge is to be obtained only when we have first professed faith in the Church dogma. This will be affirmed by every one who is tied to that Catholic kind of faith which does not trust in the redeeming power of the Man Jesus, who conquers the sinner's heart, but, on the contrary, ascribes redeeming power to doctrines which any man can appropriate without ever having his heart renewed. We deny this, for our redemption rests on the fact that we find God in the Man Jesus.

will of God on the one hand, and the message of the
inner life of Christ on the other, because just in the
latter do they find God letting them see His heart.
Now, *if the confession of the Deity of Christ is to have
any meaning at all, it is clear that it must in any case
mean that we connect God in our thought with the Man
Jesus.*   But Luther is not satisfied with simply thinking
of a divine nature as bound up with the human nature
of Jesus after the fashion which the Church dogma
supposes. That is indeed a connection of God with Jesus,
but it is such a connection that it is quite possible to
distinguish between God on the one hand, and the
personal life of the Man Jesus on the other.   Luther
was conscious of something different from this : he felt
that precisely in the revelation of the inner life of Jesus
he had found God working upon him, and disclosing to
him all the divine Mind.   In this experience he knew
himself redeemed ; but he knew also that God will not
let Himself be found in any other way, and so he
believed that we miss the true God altogether if we
understand by the Divine Being anything else than
that Personal Will which works upon us in and from
the appearance of the Man Jesus.[27]

Luther's mind is that when a man *finds and grasps*
the speaking and acting of the Father in the Person of
Christ, as that Christ reveals Himself in word and will,
then that man has in himself the marks of redemption.
Does the older dogmatic doctrine of the two natures
lead us to grasp the Person of the Father in the disposition which Jesus manifested towards men ?   Surely it
rather prompts us to distinguish all Jesus' words and
deeds on the one hand from the divine nature on the

other hand, which alone gave to those their effectual value. It is the direct opposite of what Luther expressly demanded ; hence our assertion is correct that Luther, in these and similar utterances, rises above that conception of Christ's Deity which the dogma expresses. We will not dispute that Luther often does use the confession in the old dogmatic sense, and that in true Catholic fashion he describes assent to it as a condition of redemption, but we deny that Luther never rose above that position.

Luther's discussions of the Deity of Christ do not always bring to the front this main principle on which the truly Christian meaning of the idea depends. He speaks, as a rule, rather of the confession of Christ's Deity as the sum of all that a Christian believes without emphasising that momentous significance of the idea. But if any one refuses to grant that for Luther the great matter was that he found God in the Man Jesus, then he must have expressly determined not to see it. To show this, let the question simply be asked whether it is likely that such a man as Athanasius could have written the following words : " This is the first principle and most excellent article, how Christ is in the Father : that we are to have no doubt that whatsoever that man says and does is counted and must be counted said and done, in Heaven, for all angels ; in the world, for all rulers ; in hell, for all devils ; in the heart, for every evil conscience and all secret thoughts. For if we are certain of this : that what He thinks, speaks, and wills the Father also wills, then I can defy all that may fight and rage at me. For here in Christ I have the Father's heart and will."* According to the

* Erlangen edition, xlix. 183, 184.

conception of Athanasius, the fact which procures
salvation is the union of the divine and human natures
in the Person of Christ ; and Luther certainly did not
give up that view, but he deepened it and perfected it.
For he did not speak simply of divine nature in general,
but he spoke out his own experience, to wit, that the
personal life of Jesus gave him a certainty of God and
a vision of the divine nature, and that we have God
before our eyes and in our hearts only when the mind
and will of Jesus lay hold of our hearts, and we understand them to be the power that is greater than all the
powers of evil.   Luther got beyond the indefinite
thought that with the entrance of Jesus into the world
the Divine Essence came into the most intimate union
with the human race, or with human nature.   He bids
any and every individual soul experience for itself that
in the Person of Jesus the Personal God Himself is
exerting His love and His creative power upon such
particular individual.   Of course, the thought which
the old church dogma expresses may be inferred as a
derivative corollary from this experience.   For let any
one stand in such a relation towards Jesus that the
reality of this Man in history touches him as the
redeeming action of the Personal God upon his own
soul, then such an one cannot help thinking that the
divine and the human nature are united in Jesus in
spite of the contrast between them.   And there may
also spring from this fact the impulse to reflect upon
the way in which the union was accomplished.   Luther
did not indeed think much of this tendency to reflection,
for he says : " As for the man who will not hold fast

by the Word, but wants to be subtle and to reckon up
how it can sound correct that God and man are one
Person—let him go on and be subtle and reckon up,
and see what he gains by it. How many a man has
become a fool by all this ! " *

Perhaps Luther himself is not wholly free from
blame for the fact that the tendency he thus tersely
describes has grown apace even in the Protestant
Church, and has matured such fancies as the modern
theory of Kenosis.[28] And yet even his doctrine of the
Incarnation had far richer contents than that of the
Greek theologians had, who meditated upon the
possibility of a union between the divine and human
natures, and formulated their dogma as the norm for
those speculations. Luther was fully conscious that
the knowledge which he had won was far superior to
that less definite knowledge on which the dogma is
based ; *he says of the Popish Church, that although she
had loyally preserved the dogma, she never imagined
" that we ought to learn to recognise God in Christ."†*
Those Christological heretics against whom the old
church had fought were by no means the worst of
heretics in Luther's eyes. He thought that rather to
be the worst heresy which distinguishes between the
disposition of God and that of Christ." ‡

The second point wherein Luther's idea of the Deity
of Christ is richer than that of the old dogma is the
following : Luther, as every one will admit, repeatedly
emphasised the fact that then only do we believe in

* Erlangen edition, xix. 15.   † *Ibid.* xlix. 126.
‡ *Ibid.* l. 197, 198.

Christ when we base all our confidence on Him, and so live through Him. He saw and said that " to believe in Christ does not mean to believe that Christ is a Person who is both God and man, for that helps nobody."* This sentence does not mean, of course, that to Luther the union of the divine with the human nature in the Person of Jesus was useless. For, indeed, he held rather the conviction that when we behold that union as a fact, we no longer live without God in the world, but are redeemed. Luther can only have meant that there is a kind of belief in that union which is worthless. Now what are we to understand thereby? We might take him to mean that a Christian must believe, not only in this, but in something else in addition, and Luther himself gives occasion for such a conclusion. In the very passage just quoted he continues : " But that the same Person is Christ, that is, that for our sakes He came forth from God, entered into the world, left the world again, and went back to the Father, this is as much as to say : herein is His Christhood, that for us He became a man and died, rose again and ascended into Heaven ; by reason of such office He is called Jesus Christ ; and to believe concerning Him that such is true, is to be and to remain in His name." Here it seems to be clearly stated that in addition to believing that Christ is a Person who is both divine and human, we must also believe that " the same Person " fulfilled His office for our sakes. And yet, however often Luther may give us occasion to suppose this to be his meaning, his idea cannot have

* Erlangen edition, xii. 163.

been entirely this. For if the right belief in the Deity of Christ needed such a supplement, then that belief could not be the actual laying hold of the God who is working upon us to our salvation, and this is what it was in Luther's opinion. *Just because Luther thought so highly of belief in the Deity of Christ, he cannot have thought it needed supplementing in any such external manner.* Again, this is impossible also for the further reason that when Luther expressed his faith in the Deity of Christ, he did not find it needful to add to the thought of the Person of Christ any special reference to His work. The Person of Jesus meant to him the mind and will of God turned towards himself, and this is visible to us only in the historical work of Jesus, *i.e.*, in His " office." That Luther, nevertheless, did appear to demand trust in the work of Jesus as something special apart from which faith in the union of the two natures in the Person of Christ was of no avail is explained simply by this, that there is a faith in the Deity of Christ which by its very character excludes a redeeming trust in the fact of Jesus' work. In attacking this kind of faith in Christ's Deity, Luther emphasises this characteristic of it, that it lacks the trust in the historical work of Christ as the redeeming act of God. But from this it does not follow that Luther always held those two things apart in this way : first the faith in the Deity of Christ, and then trust in the work that He accomplished. He certainly does that often enough when he is simply proceeding on the lines of the conceptions bound up with the old dogma. But it is not so easy to follow him here. For one is not yet in agreement with him simply by being ready to conceive that Deity and humanity are united in the Person of Jesus because others have so taught, and then in the second place by resolving to trust in the work of this Person.

It is not permissible to pass so easily over a point that marks for Luther the most profound inward experience. Luther demands trust in the work of Christ. But how does this trust in Christ come to exist which frees man from himself and from his need. Many imagine it is by resolving to think that a divine nature is present in Christ along with his human nature, and then adding to this an additional resolution to have confidence that the work of this Man has redeemed the sinner. They even venture to assert that this disposition of theirs, which they have brought about by their own resolutions, has been wrought in them by the Holy Spirit. Now Luther directly refuses to have anything to do with so empty and untruthful an undertaking, and this, thank God, we may know for certain. We have only to watch what Luther understands by that trust in Christ and in His work without which belief in Christ's Deity is to him worthless. Trust in Christ means to Luther the actual experience of redemption. And it can have that same meaning to us only when it is accomplished by no undertaking of ours, but is created in us because the Man Jesus has made us feel the power and grace of God turned towards us. In such case we experience the rise of this confidence as a transplanting into a new existence; and then only does it follow that we give up all attempts to win satisfaction by our own activity for our craving for fellowship with God. Luther counted

that the readiness to give up all such attempts was the
real evidence of right faith in the Deity of Christ.

In a sermon on Matt. vii. 15–23, which Enders con-
jectures to have been delivered on May 1, 1525, in the
church at Wallhausen, Luther contrasts the faith
in the Deity of Christ which redeems with that faith
which the devil is quite willing to see ; he says :
" There are many of you who say, ' Christ is a man
of this kind : He is God's Son, was born of a pure
virgin, became man, died, rose again from the dead,'
and so forth ; *that is all nothing*. But when we truly
say that He is Christ, we mean that He was given for
us without any works of ours, that without any merits
of ours He has won for us the Spirit of God, and has
made us children of God ; so that we might have a
gracious God, might with Him become lords over all
things in heaven and on earth, and, besides, might have
eternal life through Christ—that is faith, and *that is
true knowledge of Christ*," * He speaks of a confession
of the Deity of Christ which does not mean a confession
that we have eternal life through Him, and he says that
this is the sheep's clothing of the false prophets. Such
a confession, he declares, is suffered by the devil and
practised by the Pope. He contrasts with this what it
really means to know Christ truly ; and without any
doubt we may take it that by true knowledge of Him
he means the knowledge of His Deity. To him, then,
true knowledge of the Deity of Christ is identical with
the certainty that through Christ we have a gracious
God, that we are lords over all things, and that we

* Erlangen edition, xiii. 251–2.

have eternal life. Then in what follows he goes on to concentrate this great truth in the proposition that only then do we possess true knowledge of Christ, *i.e.*, of the Deity of Christ, when we are entirely delivered by Christ from all desire to gain fellowship with God by our own works. He is well aware that the Pope knows how to teach beautifully concerning the work of Christ, and of how eternal life has been procured for us thereby ; but he thinks, on the other hand, and rightly, too, that when Christ has brought a man so far that in his craving for fellowship with God he relies no longer on his own works, but on that alone which he finds in Christ, then that man has the true knowledge of Christ. For in reality we do so rely upon Christ when we find for ourselves in Him the Personal God who reveals to us His own inner self, and when we so experience God's coming into communion with us. Until we reach the true knowledge of Christ, we shall of necessity be always trying of ourselves to find some way of securing fellowship with God.

This richer conception of the Deity of Christ which Luther attained, stands thus inseparably connected with the newly-gained comprehension of justification by faith alone. The one is impossible without the other. When we think it our duty to confess the Deity of Christ before we have found in the Man Jesus the God who redeems us, we are attempting to base our soul's happiness on our own work, and must therefore deny the truth of Luther's doctrine of justification. It is indeed utterly impossible to make that doctrine clear to a man who has not found the communion of God with his soul in what he experiences at the hands of Jesus ; but the most complete departure from that doctrine takes place when, in order to secure salvation, a man puts on the sheep's clothing of the false prophets, or, in other words, professes to believe in the Deity of Christ before he has found redemption in the Man Jesus. In the passage above quoted, Luther concludes by saying : " Wherefore I warn you once more, and bethink yourselves of it when I am dead, that you look well to their doctrine whether they preach Christ aright ; that is, whether they do not attempt to do some of God's own work instead of Him." * *The present leaders in the Protestant Church, on the contrary, seem intent on nothing so much as to insist that they must " attempt to do some of God's work for Him," namely, must prepare a confession of the Deity of Christ, which is to be subscribed in order that we may be saved.* But Luther's Reformation doctrines only countenance such a confession of the Deity of Christ as springs naturally to the lips of the man whom Jesus has already made blessed.

The third point of superiority of Luther's view over the old dogma is this : In Luther's time all who claimed to be Christians confessed the Deity of Christ as a matter of course, much in the same way as nowadays most of us agree in believing that the earth revolves round the sun ; and Luther himself usually employed the forms of expression which really belonged to this customary belief in the Deity of Christ.[29] Hence the fact is the more surprising that he, nevertheless, could raise and answer rightly the question as to how belief in the Deity of

* Erlangen edition, xiii, 253.

Christ arises.   Those who believe in the Deity of Christ
as a matter of custom never ask this question ; they
simply say over to themselves the original doctrine, which
it never occurs to them to dispute.   Whoever did not
agree with it would be making " shipwreck of the faith."
Now, as a rule, Luther's method, too, is simply to quote
the texts which, according to traditional exposition,
testify to the Deity of Christ, to set them together, with
the teaching of the fathers alongside of them, and then
to infer from these the doctrine that Christ was very man
and very God in one.[30] But these discussions of his are
frequently interspersed with traces of his new recognition
that the Deity of Christ means more to a believer than
the mere presence of divine substance in Jesus.   And
sometimes Luther goes into the question as to how that
belief in the Deity of Christ arises which is not simply
an easy assent to traditional doctrine, but is a wonderful
experience that entirely regenerates a man.   When he
does this, he always gives an answer which confirms our
view of his new conception of the Deity of Christ.

If the Deity of Christ does not simply mean that a
divine substance underlies the human life of Jesus, but
that the personal God Himself turns towards sinners
and opens His heart to them in that human life, then
belief in Christ's Deity can only arise out of that which
the Man Jesus brings about within us.   We might easily
be persuaded to suppose that a divine substance was
bound up with the Man Jesus, and in any case we might
be persuaded of this without troubling ourselves about
the Man Himself, or experiencing the power of His personal life over us.   But, on the other hand, the certainty

that the personal God Himself lets us feel His power and
His mercy through Jesus can only arise within us when
the personal life of Jesus has such influence over us that
we must believe it. It would be a senseless undertaking
to attempt to lay firm hold of the true Christian thought
of the Deity of Christ if we did not feel ourselves to be
supported by the power of such a fact as we have described. It is possible for me to speculate on the general
idea of God without difficulty, but it is not possible in
that sort of way to gain confidence that God Himself as
a personal Spirit actually comes near to me, the individual, and shows His mercy towards me. In order to
believe that, I need some fact wherein the reality of God
and the fact of His grace actually directed towards me
shall be made sure. Luther was convinced that the
Scriptures lead us in this way to the knowledge of the
Deity of Christ. He says, " Therefore we can have no
certain proof of the Deity of Christ unless we enfold and
enclose our hearts in the sayings of the Scriptures. For
the Scriptures begin very gently, and lead us on to
Christ as to a man, then afterwards to a Lord over all
creatures, and after that to a God. So do I enter de-
lightfully and learn to know God. But the philosophers
and the all-wise men have wanted to begin from above;
and so have they become fools. We must begin from
below, and after that come upwards." * Undeniably
Luther raises here the question how we can have a
sure foundation for our belief in the Deity of Christ,
and gives as answer that only the man Jesus lets us
recognise God, and that therefore He alone can establish

* Erlangen edition, xii. 412.

in us a certainty that in Him we have to do with God Himself. And just as he here distinguishes the true knowledge of Christ's Deity from the false knowledge of the worldly-wise men, who want to begin with the presupposition that Christ is God, so also he does elsewhere. "But to know Christ in the *other and true* way means to know that He died for us, that He heaped my sins upon Himself, so that I hold all my own affairs to be naught, let go all that is my own, and cling only to the faith that Christ has been given to me, and that His sufferings, His piety, and His virtues are altogether mine. When I know this, then I must hold Him dear in return, for I must be loving to such a man." *

Here some theologians, like R. Kübel,† will say, of course, that Luther doubtless means that we can only have all this in Christ if we start from the presupposition that He is truly God. But Luther follows up the words just quoted thus : " *After this* I rise up from the Son to the Father, *and see that Christ is God*." Kübel is certainly right in maintaining that Luther regards the vision of Christ's Deity as the very kernel of Christianity ; but for a man who takes that view, the question may very well arise how we get at that kernel. Even Kübel will admit that Christianity is not so light a matter that we may expect everybody to make its kernel his own without any difficulty. Luther, at any rate, was aware that the true knowledge of Christ's Deity can only arise where the sinner, in his longing for

* Erlangen edition, xii. 249.

† *Cf.* the "Neue Kirchliche Zeitschrift," issued by G. Holzhauser, 1891, p. 47.

fellowship with God, is enabled to go thoroughly against his own nature and give up all trust in self. When Christ redeems us from ourselves, then we see God working upon us in Christ's Person. Luther did not hold to the dream that we are able to make the idea of the Deity of Christ our own so as to become redeemed, that is, that even as unredeemed men we can see its truth.

To Luther the act of believing in the Deity of Christ was no simple matter; it was an art. "Hence it is an art so to recognise this King, that He is true God and man." Thus the question how we are to reach the knowledge of the Deity of Christ attained, in Luther's eyes, an importance which, as it appears to us, every earnest Christian of our own day must come to feel far more keenly. He did not count himself relieved from considering this question by his certainty of Christ's Deity, for he knew that as a living Christian he had to wrestle for this certainty every day anew. There is one particular discussion in which he expresses his certainty thus: "Wherefore it is our boast and our glory that we know that this King is not only true man but also true God"; but he interrupts this declaration with the warning: "Yet especially must we first begin thus, and first grasp that first beginning, that He was born in Bethlehem, and then after that go on to the other result.* Luther believes that if we take this course "it will follow of itself" that Christ came forth from the Father.

Our opponents urge that if we would experience the saving power of Christ, the only true method, and the method, too, they say, that Luther followed, is to

* Erlangen edition, xviii. 178.

approach Him with the presupposition that He is the Son of God; but this is definitely declared by Luther to be the practice of the worldly-wise, who begin from above to build the roof before they have laid the foundation. No picture could exhibit more clearly than this the difference between that which forms the foundation of our faith on the one hand, and that high idea of the Deity of Christ on the other, in which the thinking of faith reaches its climax. Luther says, in his exposition of the fifth Psalm,* that Christ first works upon us as the King who delivers us from ourselves, and draws us to Himself; this He effects by His humanity. Hence Christ must be apprehended first as man, and only afterwards as God;[31]but the Man Christ to whom we cling will Himself bring it about that He shall appear to us as God.† Luther is also able to tell us why it is so hard for a devout person to take this course. He says it is hard for the flesh, for the flesh always prefers to think of the Deity of Christ rather than of the Man Christ, because it shrinks with horror from the entrance into glory through the cross. Let us remember that for Luther Christ is the only true God, and that when he speaks of a becoming filled with divine benefits, and expects such from the mighty working of the power of this God, he is speaking of the rise of faith in the soul, and it is evident that his assertion quoted above means that our flesh is always trying to make our religious experience easier than it is. In reality, we can find God only when the Man Jesus overcomes our souls, so that in His dying a malefactor's death we

* Erlangen edition, opp. ex Lat. xiv. 181–2.
† " Christus homo habitus Christum Deum sponte sua adducet."

recognise His kingly power, and experience its work
upon us. This is not pleasant to the flesh, and hence
the sinner is always trying to avoid that experience, and
to talk about the Deity of Christ right away as though
he could learn the meaning of this knowledge by simply
repeating words after others.

Thus Luther desires to hold fast by the old dogma,
but none the less he puts a new meaning into it. In
the first place, he claims that he finds the Personal God
Himself in the personal life of the Man Jesus. It was
not necessary that he should here be conscious of breaking away from the old dogma, for what he demanded
might certainly be regarded as the strongest possible
assertion of that union of the divine and human natures
to which the old dogma bore witness, and Luther actually so regarded it. Nevertheless he did depart here
from the original meaning of the dogma, for, according
to its original meaning, it did not deal with the recognition of the Personal God in the human appearance of
Jesus, but with a presupposition of a divine nature
underlying that appearance. The conception of the
divine nature which was used in this latter case was
formed quite independently of what we experience of
the Person of Jesus ; and the effect upon us which was
supposed to follow from the union of the divine nature
with the human had nothing to do with our conscious
inner life. Secondly, Luther read a new meaning into
the old dogma thus : he held that the true recognition
of Christ's Deity is inseparably connected with an entire
renunciation of all our efforts to gain redemption by
any act of ours. But the recognition of the Deity of

Christ, which is expressed in the old dogma, implies, on the contrary, no such resignation ; there has always been bound up with it the idea that the individual must perform a certain operation which God demands from him, in order that he may enter into possession of those riches which have been made accessible for all mankind by the incarnation of God. And it cannot be otherwise, for in the very act of appropriating the ideas of the dogma it is impossible to carry out that renunciation. The man who seeks salvation will stop trying to help himself only when he knows that God has helped him. Now such knowledge and certainty are implied as already possessed by such as Luther would consider to be aware of the Deity of Christ, but that certainty is not implied as possessed by all who profess the dogma. Thirdly, in Luther's understanding of the Deity of Christ is involved an interest to the human life of Jesus which the dogma utterly lacked. We can busy ourselves with the ideas of the dogma without troubling ourselves about Jesus, whereas we cannot confess Christ's Deity, as Luther confessed it, without experiencing in ourselves the power of the Person of Jesus.

Thus there can be no doubt, when we take these peculiar ideas of Luther's own into account, that to Him the Person of Jesus was of far higher importance for the inner life of religion than it was when viewed from the old dogmatic standpoint. With Luther the Person of Jesus stands in the very centre of the religious experience itself. Jesus makes him certain of God, lets him see the divine nature and life, becomes to him that manifestation of God's grace in which God enters into communion with him. He knows that he has been lifted up to God, and he traces the power of Jesus in that fact; he sees God, and he finds in the infinite power which presses in upon him nothing different from the personal life of Jesus. Viewed from the old dogmatic standpoint, all was different. There the Person of Jesus was not the medium through which a devout soul beholds God and experiences God's working. There the Person of Jesus is of importance for the inner process of religion itself, and for the uplifting of the heart into the felt presence of God, only in so far as it serves as an admonition and an example. This admonition and that example may indeed be valuable, yet they place the Person of Jesus only on the outer threshold before the door of that sanctuary wherein the communion of the soul with God is to take place. Every truly devout person seeks to lay hold on God Himself in his own religious experience, and therefore if we understand by the Essence of God anything else than the inner life of Jesus, then we get away from Jesus altogether in our moments of religious exaltation. Is that the course of religion to which the New Testament bears witness? Or do we not find that there the rule of God and the rule of Christ in our souls are equally described as the highest good, without any distinction being drawn between the two? But the confession of the Deity of Christ which the dogma demands presupposes precisely this: that the Essence of God is something quite other than the inner life of Jesus, and is to stand assured for us quite independently of the

Person of Jesus. Thus the dogma necessarily thrusts the Person of Jesus out from that very position within our religious experience which alone can give any meaning to our words when we speak of the Deity of Christ. Hence we come to the decision that in the Christological dogma and in all the systems of thought that have grown from this root, there is not in any degree expressed that idea of the Deity of Christ which belongs to the life of the Christian religion, or is, in other words, a form of our communion with God.[32]

§ 27. *The Connection of Luther's peculiar Idea of the Deity of Christ with his View of Redemption and with the Christian Knowledge of God.*

When we thus defend Luther's ideas concerning the Deity of Christ, we are met with the objection that the predicate, " deity," as we use it, has no clear meaning as applied to Christ, and that therefore we had better lay it aside.* To this objection we reply, in the first place, that we do not set much store on the mere name, "Deity of Christ,"† but that our highest interest is rather to arrive at such an understanding of the *Person* of Christ as shall make us actually certain of our redemption, *i.e.*, as shall assure us of a real communion with God in spite of the trouble and sin with which we have to fight. Now this assurance we have attained, because we have learned to understand the fact that

---

* *See* Lipsius, " Philosophy and Religion," 1885, p. 308.

† *Cf.* Erlangen edition, xlix. 21, 151, where more stress is laid upon the divine power and work of Christ than on the divine name.

Jesus' entry into our life to judge and bless us is the act by which God lets us know Himself and draws us to Himself. Our keen critics may say as much as they please about our still lacking the most important thing of all—we have through the Man Jesus all that we need, and we know that to long for anything higher is to fall away from the highest, it is to deny Christ, and to harden our hearts against that which is good. We know that in Christ we meet with God, and we know what sort of a meeting this is ; we know that this God gives us comfort and courage to face the world, joy in facing the demands of duty, and with all this eternal life in our hearts. He who has already found the actual fact of this God in Christ, thinks it indeed a strange suggestion that he must start by presupposing God to be in Christ if he would enter correctly on the way of salvation.

But in the second place, we affirm that in the Protestant Church no other conception of Christ's Deity is justifiable except that to which we adhere, and that therefore we alone have a good right to use that expression which our opponents would forbid to us. The general proposition, that God came to us in the historical appearance of Christ, requires various interpretation, just according to the particular view which is taken of the redemption that Christ brought. If we understand by redemption our equipment with certain powers of everlasting life, of whose nature we have, however, no clear conception, and if our entry on possession of these powers is not to be realised in any conscious process of our inner life, then it will be quite sufficient to express

Christ's significance as Redeemer by the statement that
the substance of the Deity was present in Him, and
that this has worked upon human nature to produce its
restoration and enrichment.   In that case such an expression suffices, because the indefinite conception of what
redemption is demands no more definite conception of
the presence of God in Christ.   Athanasius and Gregory
of Nyssa, indeed, following this old Catholic view of
redemption, expressly rejected the idea that redemption
is the inner deliverance of the sinner from the burden
of guilt.   If they thought like that about redemption,
of course they could rest content with an inadequate
confession of a divine nature in Christ.   They defended
from their standpoint the honour of Christ against
Arianism, and the generation in which they lived might
very likely have their faith strengthened by the theological speculations which went on as to how a divine nature
could exist in Christ alongside of His human nature.*

But the Reformers, on the other hand, had gained
another and a clearer view of redemption, and hence
along with this they were necessarily led to another view
of the presence of God in Christ.   They had become

* Nevertheless, even at that early date there were not wanting
some who felt that the necessity of entering into these speculations
was a burden imposed upon the Church by faithless heretics.   *Cf.*
Hilarius Pict., " De Trinitate," ii. 2 : " Compellimur haereticorum et
blasphemantium vitiis, illicita agere, ardua scandere, ineffabilia loqui,
inconcessa praesumere.   Et quum sola fide explorari, quae praecepta
sunt, oporteret, *adorare videlicet patrem et venerari cum eo filium,
sancto spiritu abundare*, cogimur sermonis nostri humilitatem ad ea,
quae inenarrabilia sunt extendere *et in vitium vitio coarctamur alieno*,
ut, quae contineri religione mentium oportuisset nunc in periculum
humani eloquii proferantur."   And again, in vii. 38 : " Non relictus

convinced that only those can live the life of the redeemed who have some measure of certainty of their
redemption.   Now such certainty can never attach itself
to an equipment with supernatural power, which equipment is, moreover, entirely concealed from our consciousness ; but, on the contrary, it does arise from the vision
of a fact, when the understanding of that fact is always
accompanied by a complete change in the inner life,
accompanied, in other words, by a re-arrangement of
our conscious relation towards God.   According to the
teaching of the Reformers, this renovation of the inner
life is faith, *i.e.*, it is the reliance of the repentant sinner
upon God, brought about by his understanding of
Christ.   Certainty of redemption is, of course, connected with faith as thus conceived, for such faith is
redemption itself.   Thus we find it stated in the
" Apology," ii. 62 : " Haec fides in illis pavoribus
erigens et consolans accipit remissionem peccatorum,
justificat et vivificat. *Nom illa consolatio est nova et
spiritualis vita.** This faith has for its correlate, as the

est hominum eloquiis de dei rebus praeterquam dei sermo.   Omnia
reliqua et arcta et conclusa et impedita sunt et obscura.   Siquis aliis
verbis demonstrare hoc, quam quibus a deo dictum est, volet, aut
ipse non intelligit aut legentibus non intelligendum relinquit."   If
our opponents will compare with these passages an utterance of
Augustine's, which is equally candid (" De Trinitate," vii. 4–9), they
must surely doubt their right to denounce our abandonment of that
sort of speculation, as though we were shirking the highest problems
and robbing Christianity of all its meaning, when these very speculations were so condemned by their own classic authorities.

   * *Cf.* Luther, Erlangen edition, vii. 159 : " And Christ redeems
us *through this faith* from all unrighteousness, makes us free once
more, that we may live divinely and heavenly, which we could not
do before in our prison of unrighteousness."

" Apology " explains (ii. 50–52), the *promissio Dei*, and just as the latter counts upon the faith of men, so this faith can stretch out to nothing but the good news of the gracious mind of God. All the various items enumerated in the Reformers' Confession of Faith point to objects of faith only in the sense that they work together to bring about the *finis historiae*, that is, the *remissio peccatorum*. In other words, these must be means of expressing the gracious will of God, who is seeking to awaken in the heart of the sinner the trust that will set him free.

Thus the man who shares that need of redemption which the Reformers felt, will certainly not expound that most important object of faith, namely, the presence of God in Christ, by the mere statement that in Him the divine substance was united with human nature. We might indeed calculate upon its substance, or argue from its existence—that suits the Catholic conception of our need for redemption, which seeks safety, not certainty—but to place confidence in it is impossible. This winning of trust, this peculiar power which works amid the moral intercourse of persons, enters into us only when the will of some person lays hold of our inmost being, and quickens our life by giving us a free intimation of its own intention.* Hence the Protestant Christian, who can stand before God with the confidence of a child, must have found in the Christ, to whom he owes that relation to God, not some mysterious divine substance, but a living power, acting upon him, over-

* On this point compare Kähler in " The Atonement through Christ," 1885, p. 26.

whelming him and announcing to his soul the will of
the Personal God. In Jesus, as His historical work
shows Him to us, we have before us the inmost will of
God, to which everything is subject, and we experience
it to be a power constraining and emancipating our
souls.

Now, of course, our opponents tell us that this is not
confessing the Deity of Christ; for, say they, we admit
that only when we presuppose that in Him there is the
substance of the Deity. Lipsius demands, therefore,
in the work quoted above, that we shall speak only of
a Revelation of God in Christ. But that expression is
liable to misunderstanding; it might be thought we
meant that Jesus mediates to us a doctrine concerning
God. Jesus certainly does that, too, but that is not
the way in which He is the ground of our salvation.
For He is our Redeemer because He Himself compels
us to understand the will which is active in His work to
be the mind and will of God, of that God who comes
near to us in order to draw us into communion with
Himself by the touch of Jesus upon our life. The
question whether we are right in speaking of the Deity
of Christ when we have found God turning towards us
in the disclosure of Jesus' personal life, must be decided
according as we conceive God to be in His nature a
substance on the one hand, or on the other hand a
Personal Spirit who asserts His nature by the energy
of a will directing itself towards certain ends and pre-
serving in itself a certain disposition. If we choose the
former conception of God, then certainly the proposition that there is divine substance in Christ will be

chosen as the proper expression of belief in His Deity ;
but if, on the contrary, the latter conception be
followed, which is clearly the only one represented in
the Sacred Scriptures, and the only one permissible in
the Christian community, then it is self-evident that
the Deity of Christ can only be expressed by saying
that the mind and will of the Everlasting God encounters
us in the historically active will of this man.

The other interpretation of the Deity of Christ is in
any case a departure from the Christian idea of God.
It was excusable in an age when the Christian community had not outgrown that meagre conception of
redemption with which the great fathers of the fourth
century were content.   It is endurable when employed
in discussing the theological question—a superfluous
question, certainly—as to how a union of God with
man is possible ; it is endurable if we unite to it,
as Luther did (see the passage quoted above), the perception that it is not the thought in which the redeemed
have life and which the devil cannot bear.   But when in
the Protestant Church the Lord's people are taught,
by those who are counted their proper leaders, that this
is the only possible expression for the Deity of Christ,
then the way is barred to that knowledge without which
no one ever enters into communion with the Living
God ; and this is done for the sake of a conception
which any one can adopt, without having redeeming
faith at all.

I do not doubt, of course, that many, who, as theologians, are enthusiastic adherents of the barren formula of the " two natures," are yet, as Christians, able

to find the God who is working upon them in the Man
Jesus. If we may try to account for such men's inability to use this their own living utterance of their own
God-awakened faith as the source of their knowledge
and estimate of the Deity of Christ, perhaps the
explanation lies in their giving too little regard to the
fact on which, in every instance, Christian life is based,
the fact, namely, that we are compelled to regard the
entrance of Christ into our life as an act of God upon
us. If only we bear this in mind that faith in Providence, or that "fiducia dei" which alone deserves the
name of faith, arises within us in the way just described,
then it will not be a difficult matter for us to apply the
method of judgment which we follow in that case to
the historical appearance of Christ, and to behold in
Him the Living and Working God. Any theological
opponent, in so far as he is a Christian, will surely admit
that we stand thus towards Christ in a relation of the
greatest conceivable dependence, and that we find in
Him something the possession of which prevents us
from being embittered and wounded by the hatred
and calumny of men.

§ 28. *The Advancement of Christian Piety by Means
of Luther's Thought.*

We by no means deny that our conception of Christ's
Deity differs from that expressed in the dogma. We
rather regard the difference as being of the greatest
value. That difference, to put it briefly, is this: That
conception of the Deity of Christ which is expressed

in the dogma, can only be asserted in the form of a scientific theory. On the other hand, in religious practice, in other words, in the actual uplifting of the heart to God, it is necessarily put aside, and this has always happened. The religious practice which accompanied the undisputed rule of the dogma was mysticism. That worship of the Man Jesus, which went on at the same time, had nothing to do with the reverent bowing of the soul before God ; it was therefore only a mere accompaniment to the religion, and it did away with the Deity of Christ rather than confirmed it. Quite the opposite is the case with our view of the matter, for with it we can have what Luther demands respecting Christ and the Father : " in our heart and faith they must be entirely one." * Our view makes it possible that " the recognition wherein He and the Father are recognised is one recognition." With our attitude towards Jesus it becomes possible to look on God and Christ as one in the Christian religious experience. On the other hand, it is not possible to describe the unity of Christ and God, which we experience in our faith, in terms of any previously established conceptions of divine and human nature. This impossibility arises from the fact that we first know what Divine Nature is when we apprehend it in Christ. For us God is none other than that Personal Spirit, who comes spiritually near us in the existence in this world of the Man Jesus, and who thus compels us to think of Him as the Lord who holds in His grasp both ourselves and that infinite realm by which our life is

* Erlangen edition, xlix. 126.

conditioned.   What do we lose by our inability to support a fact, which we experience in the stirring of faith, by a scientific theory which any one might adopt without any such stirring of his faith ?   Certainly we do lose the ability to make that fact quite accessible to the unbeliever.   But that is not a fault; for we all expect that for the man who turns his back on the Person of Jesus, the marvellous fact in which our confidence rejoices must remain the meaningless cobweb of a dream.   Whoever undertakes that task which we have thus seen to be impossible is desecrating what is divine.

For the very reason, then, that we believe in the Deity of Christ in the full sense of the term, we must reject the dogma concerning it as an utterly inadequate effort at thought.   Luther's attempt to combine the correct idea concerning Christ's Deity with the dogma proved to be an impossible task ; for among those who wish to follow Luther here, that correct idea has been lost sight of, and deductions from the dogma have been developed which reduce it to an impossibility.   For these circles are raising to the dignity of a first and foundation principle the proposition that we must confess Christ's Deity before we can possibly experience the divine work of redemption through Jesus.   Luther, on the other hand, did indeed hold by the Christological dogma, but at the same time always asserted that we find the Living God in Jesus Christ alone.   If Luther was right, and indeed he was right, then that main principle of modern Lutheranism just cited is untenable.   If I am to speak of the Deity of Christ, then God Himself must already have become a reality to me. But He only becomes real to me when He lifts me to Himself. He does this through the man Jesus, and when this act of God revealing Himself gains power over our inner life, we are redeemed. Hence modern Lutherans require men to regard as a condition of redemption that which is really its result. The injury they do in this way is not little, for the men who follow their advice are playing with the Holiest. They speak of God as a reality before their souls have been uplifted to God. In that case their hearts must wither. They hide from themselves the fundamental truth of all religion, namely, that the redemption of a mortal being can mean nothing else than its being lifted up into fellowship with the Everlasting God. This is the fate to which the practice ruling at present in the Church is bringing those who would be devout. Or are we, in saying this, once more doing our opponents an injustice ? They tell us, aye, unceasingly, that we must first know that Christ is very God before we can possibly be redeemed by Him. (C. Luthardt. Zeitschrift fur Kirchl. Wissenschaft und kirchliches Leben. 1886, pp. 632–658.) Nevertheless, we can partly excuse such procedure by the following considerations : In the first place, a man who has been lifted up by Christ to God and received into fellowship with Him, will say ever afterwards to his soul : Thou couldst not have had that experience through Him, had not God appeared to thee in Him. Eternal life is the gift of God alone. How easily may this thought lead to the error of supposing that we must know that Christ is God before we can have eternal life through Him ! In the second place, we say with truth that we are to find in Christ something inexhaustible, which shall be constantly assuming a new significance for our lives. " What I believe is always more and greater than what I have experienced " (Kübel, in the Theol. Litt. Bl., 1891, No. 12). And so, when we say that the inner life of Jesus is itself the power of redemption, it may appear as though we are setting something which our poor experience can compass in the place of that immeasurable magnitude which the Church finds in Christ. Only thus can we understand and excuse the rejection of the correct doctrine and practice on this most important point. But it is easy to show that here is a misunderstanding ; for we are to learn the mysterious and overwhelming power of the Divine Being only in and through the phenomenon of the inner life of Jesus. The man who thinks he can exhaust that fact and become master of it, will never, of course, bow to the sovereignty of Christ. But even though we can thus find excuses for the procedure of our opponents, we none the less regret that procedure. For it hides from men the truth that to come into personal communion with God through the appearance of Jesus is to experience the marvellous fact of redemption.

" Now what I have said means this : that God will not suffer us to rely upon aught else, or to cling at heart to aught that is not Christ in His Word, however sacred and spiritual it may appear." * When we come to understand the historical Christ, and only then, does

* Erlangen edition, xi. 27,

God so touch us that He lifts us above our trouble and our sin, so that we become certain of Him. Hence we come into contact with God only through the Word that makes such understanding possible to us; and so we must receive the Person of Christ Himself as the tidings of God in which He desires to come near us.

§ 29. *Communion with God and Christ through the Imagination.*

At this point we may revert to that objection of our opponents in which they assert that since Christ brings us to God, therefore there must be an *immediate* communion of the soul with God, of which that fact forms the basis.* This assertion is particularly interesting for the reason that it lets us see plainly how far the acknowledgment of a divine substance in Christ is from the true confession of His Deity. If, after a man's experience of Christ, he still feels that he lacks and must obtain an immediate communion of the soul with God, then, evidently, that man is unable to apprehend and feel God to be in Jesus Himself: and he who is unable to do this even if he claim to be an orthodox believer on the ground of some dogmatic formula, however venerable it may be, is not in fact a believer, for he has not found God in Christ, but distinguishes between God and Christ in the way which Luther, in a passage quoted above, ascribes to "the heart void of understanding." If God, in bringing Christ near to the individual soul, gives to that soul the full tidings of

* *See* page 111.

what is in God's heart, and if He thereby gives the soul
clear vision and peace, then He makes that soul feel
His own Almighty power, and deals with such a soul
in the most direct and intimate way possible.   A more
immediate contact of the soul cannot be conceived or
wished for, save by those who do not think of their God
as a Personal Spirit but as an impersonal substance.
The Personal Spirit communes with us through
manifestations of His inner life, and when He consciously and purposely makes us feel what His mind is,
then we feel Himself.

Hence we must utterly reject the idea that God can
in any way come nearer to the individual soul than
when He lets Himself be found in Christ.   Here the
difference between us and our opponents becomes quite
clear.   They conceive of the Deity of Christ in such a
way that they only use Him and His work as a presupposition before their communion with God ; they
think that this presupposition holds good indeed for all
cases alike, but that in addition to the presupposition,
and over and above it, every individual must strive for
himself to come into immediate contact with God.
Such a desire for God is quite justifiable where men
have been accustomed to contemplate the Christological
dogma instead of fixing their attention on Christ
Himself; but of a surety it also leads men into uncertainty.   It is to us incomprehensible how men can
appeal to Luther in support of such a position, for
Luther saw in the historical Christ no mere presupposition fulfilled centuries ago in order that ever
afterwards men may become Christians.   He writes :

" To me it is not simply an old song of an event that happened fifteen hundred years ago; it is something more than an event that happened once—for it is a gift and a bestowing that endures for ever." * And when we read in the same connection : " through this we are so profoundly taught, that we know what God's will is, and what God has in His heart," Luther docs not mean some knowledge concerning God which may be held as a general truth apart from the historical deed of Redemption, but he means that every one whom this deed touches and causes to come to himself experiences therein exactly what God purposes concerning him and is producing in him as an individual soul.† I do not need to remind the reader how very often Luther repeats the assertion that every Christian has this experience of being set free, amid his own particular surroundings, when the figure of Christ comes face to face with him through the preaching of the Gospel. Hence the Reformer can say : " Nothing which takes place in ourselves and of ourselves can make any man a Christian. What then can ? This alone, that we know this Man, and that we receive from Him and expect from Him what He wills that we shall receive at His hands." ‡

When the Christian experiences this at the hands of

---

* Erlangen edition, xx. I. 114 ; l. 241.

† In the Erlangen edition, l. 241, Luther says that the faith that Christ was sent of the Father into the world amounts to this : " That thou shalt esteem and hear without question every word that fell from His lips as though thou heardest now the voice of the Father speaking with thee from heaven."

‡ Erlangen edition, xii. 50.

the historical Christ, and sees that thus God Himself lays hold of him and makes him feel there is a most special divine care over him, then he listens without concern when any one claims that God and Christ have entered the realms of his imagination in forms distinct from that historical event, and that they so commune with him. Luther knew the language of that Roman Catholic piety which can talk of such experiences with the Bridegroom of the soul, and he even used it sometimes; but he gave it a new and Protestant meaning, as we shall see later on. The strength of the man lay herein, that it was in the actual world that he found the God who talked with him, and it was there he sought Him. That other sort of seeking and finding God within the realm of the pious fancy was thoroughly well known to him from his monastic life; but he was aware that in it the soul supports heaven, not heaven the soul. " God made His Son one with human nature in order that we might discern and know in Him God's friendly will towards us;"* the man who knows this will hold by the voice of God only as it speaks to us in this fact, and will not try to make God speak within his soul in any other way. " Therefore, I say: I will hold by His common revelation to all men in the word and works of Christ."† As monk, Luther, like the rest, crept into a corner and thought that God would work for him " something all his own."‡ Later on he came to see that sectaries indeed " claim to hear " a secret voice and a revelation;§ but that the Christian

* Erlangen edition, xiv. 228. † *Ibid.* xx. I. 29.
‡ *Ibid.* xx. I. 414. § *Ibid.* xv. 151.

hears the speech of his God in facts that speak plainly
to all men.*   Luther did indeed give abundant testimony to his faith that Christ lived and worked in
him, and we shall discuss later on, in chap. iii., the
correctness and value of this thought of faith ; but no
one will venture to prove by this that Luther, as a
Protestant Christian, made out of this experience any
peculiar communion between himself and the risen
Christ.   On the contrary, Luther was aware that we
find the true Christ and *experience the direct influence
of our risen Lord* when we come to understand the
Christ of history.   It was not Luther's mind that a
Christian, who has drawn the necessary teaching from
the historical work of Christ, may then turn his back on
those facts and seek to reap from them a harvest
peculiar to himself in a special communion with God or
with the risen Christ within the sacred quiet of his own
inner life.   On the contrary, he would have thought
that in so doing he would be departing from the realm
of real, life-giving power.   " For the man who lets go
of Christ's life and work, and desires now to seek Him
as He sits in heaven in some private way, betrays Him

* Monachi celebrant patrum suorum Benedicti, Bernhardi legendas.
Sed profecto Deus in genere cum quovis Christiano multo copiosius
loquitur et *familiarius conversatur*, quam illi jactant de suis patribus.
Imo si in manu mea res esset, non vellem, Deum mihi loqui de coelo,
aut apparere mihi.   Hoc autem vellem, et tendunt hoc quotidianae
meae preces : ut in digno honore habeam et vere aestimem donum
Baptismi, quod sum baptisatus, quod video et audio fratres, qui
habent gratiam et donum spiritus si, qui consolari, erigere verbo
possunt, exhortari, monere, docere.   Quam enim tu optas meliorem
et utiliorem Dei apparitionem ?—Luther's " Latin Works," iv. 157–162 ;
cf. lvii. 45, 51.

afresh.   He must seek Him as He was and walked on
earth ; then shall he find life ; it was there He came to
be our Life, our Light, and our Blessedness ; it was
there that all took place that we are to believe concerning Him.* Even as it is said in the Mass, ' In Him
was Life ' ;   not that He is not now our life, but that
he does not now do what he then did."

§ 30. *The Mediation of True Communion with God by Means of the Christian Community.*

Nevertheless, there is an element of truth in the
insistence that God must come to each individual soul
in a special manner, even though He comes near to all
through the same fact.   For the appearance of God in
Christ meets each of us in special circumstances of His
own.   Those things and events which open up the
understanding of Christ for any particular individual
must necessarily have special modifications according
to the circumstances of the particular case.   We must
necessarily take into account all the circumstances
connected with the influence of Christ upon the soul in
our observation of the accomplishment of the act
whereby God comes into communion with us.   Hence it
is true to say in this sense—but in this sense only—that
God communes with every individual soul in a special
way ; or, in other words, as men prefer to say nowadays, that God enters into a personal relation with
each individual soul.

The first relation of life to be considered, wherein

* Erlangen edition, x. 189 ; *cf.* xxxv. 170f.

the Christian traces the redeeming act of his God, is our environment by the Church. God cannot disclose Himself to all men without distinction; He holds indeed the guidance of every life in His hand, but He can open His inner Self only to such as are in the Church, *i.e.*, in the fellowship of believers. Our experience that the Gospel helps others gives us also an ability to accept it for ourselves. Hence when Christians interest themselves in us, Christ comes near us. The proposition that the Church is the mother of believers is not understood in its true sense until we think of her, with Luther, as " a Christ-like, holy people," * and not as an institution which possesses within itself certain mysterious redemptive powers. When we live in the midst of Christian people the sense is awakened by which we may see God in Christ, and the germ of understanding is nourished. When we ourselves have found our God, and so have become new men, then we are linked with Christians in fellowship, not only by our joy in that fellowship, but also by the life it gives us. It is this power of bringing our new life into being that gives to the Christian Church its name of " mother." † And since we see that in her alone do we meet with the Creator and the Redeemer, ‡ she becomes to us on this earth an element in that divine act by which we

* *Cf.* the Greater Catechism and the Erlangen edition, xii. 50 ; xxv. 354.

† Erlangen edition, xlvi. 278. Here Luther says, in talking of the new birth : " Christ does this, who, by baptism and the Word of God, lays thee, as a Christian, in the lap of the Christian Church, as of our dear mother."

‡ *Ibid.* xxiii. 238.

know that, in the midst of this world, we have been set within the Kingdom of God. But we can be certain that God turns to us through the Church only in so far as the activity of the Church gives expression in a way that fits our own special circumstances to the Gospel in which God is brought within our reach, and develops in us the ability to receive this Gospel. The Church enables us to do this in so far as it is that fellowship of believers which enables every one of its members to meet with the Word of Christ, through direct preaching in the first place, and, in the second, through Christian life. Without the second the first is of little use. Hence, if we wish to remain in communion with God, we must remain in communion with Christian people, who make us feel their moral severity towards themselves and their love towards others. Through this moral communion with Christians we enter a realm of experiences amidst which we see more and more clearly how forlorn our condition would be if the personal life of Jesus were not a reality in the world, standing there before our eyes. Hence it becomes evident also that a Church which does not direct all its efforts at developing such fellowship of moral intercourse is lifeless and dead. In the events wherein a believer experiences this two-fold influence of the Church, he sees of necessity the special communion God has with him which no other has in exactly the same way. It is certainly highly important that every one should come to the certainty of this special communion of God with himself.

The possibility of all this vanishes just in proportion as we regard the Church, not as the instrument of that

Gospel which saves us when it is understood, but as the shell containing certain mysterious redemptive powers which are to save us when we submit to their operation. The Church, in the former sense of the word, exercises her redeeming power over us when believing Christians give us their sympathy and care ; for these are counted worthy as believers to represent God speaking to us, and thus to open to us the Kingdom of God.* But the Church in the latter sense, on the other hand, is supposed to do all its work by means of indefinite divine powers which are presupposed to belong to the ministerial office, and its acts. In this latter sense the Church necessarily loses all its significance as an expression of the speech of the Living God ; she rather thrusts herself in between Him and us, and leads us to the worship of a dumb idol, to wit, the redemptive power concealed within herself.

But " we have a God who speaks and lives, who gives us His sure Word ; and we know how He is disposed towards us and what we are to expect of Him."† We are surrounded by the Christian Church, which brings the tidings of Christ into our hearts in a thousand ways ;

* *Cf.* Luther's Erlangen edition, xi. 347. " To him who has the Holy Ghost is the power given ; to him, that is, who is a Christian. But who is a Christian ? Whosoever believes has the Holy Ghost. Therefore, every Christian has the power that the Pope, bishops, and monks have in this case to retain or to remit sins," xvi. 495. " Now mark that the Gospel is a common thing and not appointed for the Pope *and the clergy* alone. I have just as much power as the Pope to forgive sins and make absolution, and we must not let this power be taken from us, but must assert and establish it. If we let it go *we lose God, His Gospel and faith*," xxv. 364 ; xxviii. 27ff. ; li. 387, 482, 483.

† Erlangen edition, ix. 203.

and when we understand its tidings, this environment becomes to us an evidence that God desires to assure us of His grace. The man who accepts this testimony of God that is offered him knows hence that he is lifted into a realm where God's grace will continually reveal itself to him, and will remain immovable, even if he fall into sin: "Just as the sun rises daily in the heavens, and does not only drive away the night that is past, but goes ever onward and lights up all the day, even though he be somewhat darkened and hidden by thick clouds."* To see that God communes with him thus is certainly the matter of most personal importance for each Christian. That "peculiar exercise" amid which Luther in his monkish life enjoyed richly what was supposed to be communion with God, did not make him a Christian. For this alone makes a man a Christian, "that his faith lays hold of and knows this point, that he dwells in the kingdom of grace, since Christ has taken him beneath His wing, and gives him the forgiveness of his sins without ceasing."† The fact is, as Luther says in the passage already quoted, that the Christian can never even wish that God should specially appear to him or speak down to him from heaven. He receives the revelation of God in the living relationships of Christian brotherhood, and its essential contents are that personal life of Jesus which is visible in the Gospel, and which is expounded by the lives of the redeemed. If he has really found God thus, he will desire with all his heart that the God who has already appeared to him may come ever nearer to him, and

* Erlangen edition, xi. 320.   † *Ibid* xiv. 211.

that he himself may ever experience more deeply, in his own growing clearness and firmness of moral purpose, that God is redeeming him.

The significance which the Church has for the Christian as a fellowship of believers, must remain unknown if the false claims of church officials deprive believers of the priestly dignity, whereby all of them are the organs of God for their brethren. Hence Luther says, in the passage just quoted, that such hierarchical claims do not simply injure Christians in a matter of privilege which they might conceivably waive, but that they rob them also of God, of the Gospel, and of the faith. For the assurance of God's grace is limited by such claims to a single official act, and so loses its certainty. The forgiveness of sins is not to be interpreted in reference to a single moment, namely, " when the absolution is pronounced ; but it is to be a continuous, eternal treasure and an everlasting grace which works and is mighty always." * Whenever the Church thus makes the divine act of revelation, that is, the Christ of history, an element of our present life, then all the events we pass through begin to utter the speech of God. First among these stands all that directly helps in the preaching of the Gospel. " Therefore God appears thus to me through His Word : item, I apprehend him in baptism ; item, God appears to me through the schoolmaster, through my parents, through preachers, through His Word ; item, in the Absolution." † But the light which thus enters the soul

* Erlangen edition, xi. 319.
† *Ibid.* xx. I. 27 ; xlvii. 222.

throws its radiance necessarily over all life's course.* In all our providences we recognise the pressing in upon us of that earnest love of God, whose reality and meaning are made certainties for us by Jesus Christ in His work for the eternal kingdom of God. The very same events which lead men who have no faith into a pathless desert, shape a way through life for the Christian to his well-known goal, as he sees it growing definite before him amid his various moral responsibilities and experiences.

§ 31. *The Difference between this Christian Religion and Mysticism.*

That experience which, in the light of Christ, we have learnt to count as a work and word of God for us, has the power to make us rejoice in what is eternal, and so brings us actually to live in it.   For God, who of His nature desires the good, gives to us a token of His loving care for us herein, that He makes us feel at home in that which is good, and makes us able for that self-denial which is laid upon us by our sharing in eternal life.   We can know in all experiences, great or small, that we are laid hold of and borne up by a Love that is not to be distinguished from the power of the Eternal which through the moral law claims us for itself. In this inner process we feel ourselves touched by the

* Erlangen edition, xlix. 90, 196.   God sends trial " that He may reveal Himself to us the more, that we may know His love. For such trial and conflict are to teach us (what preaching alone cannot do) how mighty Christ is, and how truly the Father loves us."

Infinite, fed by it and certain of it, as no mystic ever does. For the emotion of the mystic, however sweet and mighty it may be, has nothing to do with the Eternal in its relation to our inner life, or with the moral end. For this reason it is impossible for mystic piety to get assurance of an inward truth that can never be buried and lost amid the alternations of excitement and reaction. But we, on the other hand, are certain of God and of His communion with us, seeing that nothing can ever blot out the historical fact to comprehend which is to feel God's nearness in all the relations of our life, and that the inner use of that historical fact lifts us up into joy in God and so to a share in the Eternal. In our comprehension of Christ, and in the new meaning of all our experiences which that comprehension makes possible, we become certain of the fact that God touches us. It is not to be supposed that the difference between mysticism and our way of experiencing the communion of God is that only the mystic believes that he can feel himself inwardly grasped of God. That experience is obviously the Christian's greatest joy. Indeed, so true is this that it can be said of Christians, in Luther's words, " that even if they knew that there were no heaven, no hell, and no reward, even still would they seek to serve God for His own sake." * We differ from the mystic solely in the way in which we become aware that God is touching us. To the true mystic God is the Eternal as opposed to the temporal, and hence the mystic enjoys his sense of possession by God when he has such an exalted sense of the Eternal

* Erlangen edition, xxii. 133.

as makes him feel the charm of a wonderful calmness
of spirit amidst the unrest of the life that feeds on
this world.   We also have such experiences, and hold
them in no light esteem ; we believe that in them we
are aware of the incomprehensible glory of God.   But
we do not find in them that communion of God with
us which is all-important in our eyes.   For to us God
is not the Eternal itself, which inspires us and humbles
us ; but He is the Power who rules both the eternal
and the temporal, and who brings us, men who live in
time, to a life in the Eternal.   Life in the Eternal is
laid open before us when we understand moral necessity:
and we share that life in the Eternal when we choose
with joy, and so of our own free will, to do what is
morally necessary.   The power that helps us to do this
is our God.

It is not in the Eternal itself that we find the God
who turns to us with abundant help : it is in that
process in time which makes a life in the Eternal possible
to us.   Whether in this case the inner life is richer
than one lived in blind devotion to the Infinite, and
whether it means more to men to live in the Eternal or
to disappear before its presence—these are questions
on which we shall never agree with the advocates of
mysticism.   But *the former is Christian, the latter is not.*
And yet the prevailing theology of our time is compelled
to try to join forces with mysticism, unless it is willing
to appear devoid of all religious content.   For whatever
may be the secret attitude of heart towards God
amongst those theologians, their theological theory
does its utmost to conceal the fact that in the Christ

of history God so touches each one of us that we may apprehend His reality and comprehend His love. Before any mention is made of the Redeemer, without whom for a Christian there is no God, this theology erects altars to a Deity whom we are supposed to know from metaphysics and from detached texts of Scripture. To such an image of Deity, which the reason has constructed, the soul is expected to struggle upwards of itself! From every one who becomes a slave to this kind of worship, the figure of Jesus withdraws into the far distant past. Jesus Christ is God present for us, surrounding us with grace and compassion, only when we give to Him the glory that in His appearance, as it stands before us in the Gospels, we see God's approach to us and God's presence with every one of us. Thus far, unfortunately, in German Christendom, official dignity and esteem are accorded to a theology which tells a people who no longer know their Luther that we deprive Christianity of all its worth if we make the simple confession that the man Jesus is God appearing in history and redeeming us ![33] And at the same time this official theology itself, which evades the confession of the Reformers, which openly gives up the old dogmatic doctrine of Inspiration, and yet will not admit the Person of Jesus Christ the sole authority for our faith, to be counted as such—this official theology nevertheless poses as the defender of the faith because, with skilful art, it laboriously binds together the conflicting elements of tradition. So long as such " scribes " rule, so long will mysticism remain necessary as a substitute for Christian piety. For mysticism is cer-

tainly true religion in this sense that it aims to bring
men into fellowship with God Himself. But the man
who has found Jesus Christ, and God in Him, can
dispense with mysticism, for in the narrow experiences
into which mysticism withdraws there is no room for
the life of Christian faith.

The chief end of every real religion is to secure God's
communion with each individual soul, and every devout
man knows that he himself cannot bring about that
communion, but that God does it for him. This act of
God is the revelation on which the reality of all
religion rests.* In the soul of the man who stands
amid such revelation religion is established ; and that
participation in the divine life, towards which our
religious longing yearns, consists in a man's becoming
conscious that he means something to God, and that
God is entering into communion with him. He who
does not admit these propositions to be true does not
know what religion is. We feel that we have a common
understanding with all who show that they understand
religion thus, whether they are Christians or not. But
these persons can only become Christians when they
learn to lay hold of the inner life of Jesus in the tradition
which has come down to us in the Christian brotherhood.
When they learn to see that, then they are at once set
free from mere dependence on that report, and move
on to the firm ground of their own indubitable experience. For this personal life works upon the man
that is at all able to see it in such a way that by what
it is it confirms for him the tradition. The man who

* *Cf.* my lecture on "The Meaning of Revelation," Giessen, 1887.

feels the strength of Jesus' love, and sees that confidence
of victory which welled up from His peace of soul,
and is thus filled with amazement and humility—
that man will no longer see a historical problem in
Jesus, but a Reality before which he bows. On this
alone it depends whether a man is to become a
Christian. For Jesus would not be the Redeemer if
He could not help the man whom He Himself had so
overwhelmed by the strength of His inner life ; but
He does redeem us by compelling us to see in His
existence in the world the reality of a God whose
Presence made Him, Jesus, glad and confident, even
when He was forsaken of all others.

We can know of ourselves that we stand in the
midst of an incomprehensible infinity, which brings on
suffering that we cannot alter ; but the Person of Jesus
alone can give a man the invincible certainty that it is
the almighty power of His Father in heaven which
rules in the boundless world. And if the Person of
Jesus so works upon us that we cannot think of Him
without God, then inevitably His existence and His
influence over us will appear to be the working of God
upon our own souls. Thus God reveals Himself to us.
In the man with whom God enters thus into communion
there arises a new inner life. He turns to God with
the consciousness that he is doing a thing which was
impossible to him before, and he has the experience
constantly renewed that the God whom He has found
in Christ is making him a new creature. He learns to
grasp thoughts concerning God and Christ, concerning
the world and himself, whose meaning was previously

completely hidden from him, although, perhaps, he had often heard them expressed. And all this new experience is based on the fact that in the Person of Christ that which is truly supernatural has entered the world, and is now lifting us above it. But this knowledge that He alone can loose our bonds and make us out of mere elements in the world into sharers of divine life, would all be simply concealed from us if, instead of looking at Him, we should give ourselves up to the sway of an indefinite conception of an "influence of the supernatural." The vision of the truly supernatural is ours only when we experience Jesus' power to make us certain of God.

THE EXERCISE OF
OUR COMMUNION WITH GOD IN
RELIGIOUS FAITH AND MORAL ACTION

§ 1. *Turning to God is Wrongly Supposed to Begin in Prayer.*

As God comes near our souls by giving us tidings of His love towards us, even so do we, on our part, turn to Him by giving Him tidings of our inner life. These tidings given by man to God are prayer; in the awaking of the voice of Christian prayer God's purpose to draw us to Himself reaches its goal. When prayer dies in us, then the soul closes itself against revelation. Prayer is the expression of human need before God, the expression of satisfied need in the prayer of thanksgiving, and of need still felt in the prayer of supplication. From this we might seem to get the rule that the Christian is to turn towards God by telling Him all trouble and thanking Him for all help received. Yet, self-evident as it may seem that such is to be the Christian's use of prayer and such his experience, we have by no means fully and correctly described the Christian's communion with God by saying this.

If prayer is not to be simply the cry of agony from a helpless man, but a real communion with God, then it must have direct relation to the fact that God turns

towards us. The Christian must know well the fact
that he wanders away into emptiness if he tries to find
and lay hold on God outside of his own actual historical
circumstances,[34] in some realm of fancy. But if this be
true, then supplication is not the · first fact in the
Christian's turning towards God. To quote Luther,
"Before thou callest upon God or seekest Him, God
must have come to thee and found thee." * By
his own efforts a man may become a praying man, but
not a Christian.† The Christian grasps God because
God has grasped him, and it is only in prayer breathed
out of this experience that the Christian can be certain
that God hears him and answers the cry of his soul.
The supplication that is wrung from the heart by
trouble, and the idea, born of the wish of the tortured
soul, that an Almighty God will break the chain of
causes and effects—these are not the elements which
make Christian prayer. The most important feature is
lacking. A prayer that contained nothing more than
these would clearly be no communion with God, since
the utterer would certainly not be in the presence of
God. He would be alone, alone with his fears and
wishes, making simply an uncertain venture if perchance
he may accomplish anything by the inner travail of his
soul and by his concentration on the object of his desire.

On one condition certainly, supplication might
possibly be the first thing in our communion with God.
If we could perceive God with the senses, if we actually
grasped His reality in all its relation to other things,
and knew Him by His ways towards other persons, then

* Erlangen edition, x. 11.   † *Ibid.* xii. 135f. ; xiv. 335.

it would have some meaning to say that our communion with Him might begin in the form of supplication by us. We could then begin relationship with Him with a request, just as we often do thus approach our fellow men. But we do not see God with our bodily eyes : neither does the story of what He has done for others make us acquainted with Him ; hence there can be no meaning in the supposition that the communion of the Christian should begin by supplication. Of course, many Christians take the reality of God as a self-evident fact, and they consider this to be a merit, and a sign of their immovable piety. So it becomes possible for such to begin their prayer with a request ; and to count on a time of thanksgiving in case the prayer be answered. But at the same time they put themselves, with their immovable piety, among those men whose nature Jesus hated from the bottom of His heart, namely, among the hypocrites. Let us consider what would really be implied if the reality of God were a self-evident fact for us. It would mean that every-thing which presses itself upon our consciousness, whether we will or not, impresses upon us the idea of God just as clearly as it impresses upon us the idea of an actual world. Now we are always taking the reality of the world into account ; on it hang our fears and our hopes. How, then, would it fare with us if the reality of God had this same power over our inner life, if that reality determined our feeling and shaped our resolu-tions in exactly the same way ? We only need to put the question before us to see that the assumption that the reality of God is a self-evident fact, even to a

Christian, is a miserable fiction. The man who has become entangled in it cannot come near to God, for we cannot do that in falsehood, but only in the truth. Yet on that assumption rests the view that the Christian can turn to God by first addressing supplication to Him.

§ 2. *The Form of the Personal Life in which a Communion with God can take place.*

The fundamental features of Christian piety must depend on the way in which God appears to us in Christ and works upon us. Now the God whom we feel laying hold of us when the appearance of Jesus becomes an experience of our own, is that power of goodness which, with victorious love, throws down all the barriers which divide us from what is good. Hence Christian piety can only arise in the field of men's moral experience. God and all that He wishes to give us remains afar off and dark unless we abide under the pressure of duty, under the constraint of work, and under the discipline of people of whom we think with reverence.

According to the preaching of Jesus, our life with God takes place in a kingdom of God, which Jesus Himself brings; but this kingdom is presented only where pure love rises up in persons and goes out to persons.[35] For only in such love and such activity does God reign in persons and for persons. This means, however, also that it is only in an inward yearning towards this kingdom of God that there can be any turning towards God Himself, or any enjoyment of His goodness. This thought of Jesus, simple and clear, as it is, has not ruled the teaching of the church as it might claim to do. On the contrary, its force has been materially weakened by the weight of a mystical tradition, according to which a man is supposed to attain to the vision and enjoyment of God by conduct which stands in no necessary relation to moral purpose. To souls smitten with this idea, that thought of Jesus seems to lack the warmth—they mean the imaginative charm—in which for them lies the guarantee of truth. And yet it should not be a difficult matter for any earnest seeker after truth to yield assent, for every Christian knows at heart that moral claims have the right to overrule all others within him. Just here, then, is the sign that we are to seek communion with God, not as something alongside of devotion to what is good, but only in this devotion. Indeed, every other impulse is proved to be a clinging to what is temporal by the fact that it must inevitably give way to the claims made on us by an eternal law. We share therefore in the life of a God who is above the world, and we are actually lifted above the world ourselves only when our inner life is moulded according to this law. Our aim must be to live in that eternal thing which we human beings can understand, namely, in the morally good. Otherwise our desire for God lacks truth, for then we do not seek God Himself at all, but only His help in temporal matters. There is no true search for God without those painful conflicts which the desire to live in the Eternal causes every child of the world, and if we have no joy in the sovereignty of the Eternal over the temporal in the realm of moral conduct and order, there is no true finding Him.

The Reformers advanced these same thoughts in another form in their doctrine of repentance, and in their principle that moral life in our ordinary calling is an essential part of Christian perfection. The Reformers declared in that doctrine that the Christian faith is not understood by those who are without temptation, but only by those who know what agony of conscience means; and herein they imply that only amid the stress of the moral life can we have the sure experience that God helps us. This principle is clear, and we must not let it be clouded by any discussion as to whether repentance, as the experience of moral need, precedes the rise of faith or follows its awakening. In any case, God can only reveal Himself to those to whom He makes clear what is good, and whom He causes to feel the constraint of the truth that the good alone has power, and that they are sinners. From this it follows that the Christian can only turn to God and experience God's help while he is occupied in truly fulfilling his own moral duties. The doctrine of the Reformers that repentance is a necessary element in the Christian life is supplemented by their principle that the calling of a citizen is no hindrance, but a positive necessity, to Christian perfection. Even if this principle were not expressly asserted in the well-known passages in the Confessions, countless utterances by Luther would show how anxious he was to impress it upon men's minds.* He insists unceasingly

* *Cf.* Erlangen edition, xxvi. 8f.; xxvii. 49; also "Augsburg Confession," viii. 25.

that "God will have Himself served in common life and common circumstances not by fleeing from the same." * And the argument for this is that it is just in the work of his calling, whereby the Christian helps and serves others, that he is a consecrated priest and bishop, and therefore communes with his God.† When a man withdraws from his worldly calling he ceases to take part in God's eternal work, and puts a human work in its stead, a human work that is worthless because it is arbitrarily chosen, and lacking in all reverence for what is truly necessary. "For who is the better for it, that thou enterest a cloister, makest of thyself a thing apart, and will not live like other men ? Who is helped by thy cowls, thine austere countenance, or thy hard couch ? Who comes thereby to the knowledge of God, or to comfort of conscience ? Or who is provoked by these things into love for his neighbour ? Nay, how is it possible for thee to serve thy neighbour and show him love, humility, patience, and meekness if thou wilt not live among the people ? " " The Christian life, on the contrary, the life of faith and its fruits, is so ordered that all serves to maintain love and unity, and further men in all virtues." ‡

We do not see the full significance of these assertions of Luther's unless we remember that their purpose was to do away with the Roman Catholic ideal of Christian devotion. Luther's opponents followed the rule that everything which binds a man to the world, and therefore also the work of his calling, separates him from God,

---

* Erlangen edition, ix. 81.   † *Ibid.* xxi. 283.
‡ *Ibid.* ix. 280–9 ; *cf.* x 26, 413–4.

and therefore ought to vanish as far as far as possible
from the life of a perfect Christian. Certainly, when
Luther opposed that view by including in the requirements for Christian perfection that a man must have a
worldly calling as the only possible means of fulfilling
his moral duty, he did not mean that a Christian would
become more perfect if he allowed worldly affairs to
withdraw him for a time from communion with God.
His idea was rather that just in bowing to moral obligations we turn ourselves to the divine. Luther's intuitive
genius, which enabled him to grasp the original meaning
of the Gospel, and the greatness of the work he accomplished, are shown nowhere more clearly than at this
very point, where he certainly had not a clear insight
into the Scriptural ground for his ideas, namely, the
preaching of Jesus concerning the kingdom of God.*

In the Middle Ages the soul's craving for God had
found its nourishment either in thoughts on the Infinite or in fanciful pictures of a self-abasing God which
invited a sensuous communion with Him. In both
these cases piety necessarily forbade as far as possible all
connection of man with the world, and therefore threw
off the moral tasks of life, except where these could be
regarded as ascetic mortifications of the flesh or as
praiseworthy imitations of the poverty of the Christ.
This kind of piety, intense and full of warm feeling, is
able to enchain and intoxicate men ; but it fails to create
any stronger bond of union between them than that of
an accidental similarity of emotions. Consequently its

* *Cf.* Ritschl. "Die Lehre von der Rechtfertigung und Ver-
sohnung." Second edition, iii. 11.

experiences have no absolute validity, and therefore they have none of the nerve of certainty. Continual fanning of the feelings of such thoughts and emotions nurses in quietness this form of piety, but without ever lifting the soul into that realm of the Eternal where it knows itself linked to all men. Ritschl's wonted expression, characterising this Roman Catholic kind of Christianity, is very apt; he says that it strives after an imaginary private relationship with God.* Nevertheless he misses the main point. It must be emphasised that this sort of piety can never be communion with God because it is disjunction from reality. It uses the imagination not to convert what is real into a present experience, but to overleap the bounds of reality. It is, therefore, empty and imaginary piety.

Luther was well acquainted with the charms of this Catholic piety, yet he did not " creep into a corner," but remained, not merely outwardly, but with his whole heart in the calling in which God had placed him. For he knew that God was accessible for him only in that realm of moral necessity where alone all men alike find themselves amid things that are eternal. Thus did Luther remove the veil that hid the truth of Jesus' preaching concerning the kingdom of God, and thus did he prepare the way for a renovation of Christendom in its inmost life. We accordingly hold back from the sensuous charm of that " private relationship with God." In our turning to God we do not feel that we are isolated from

* Of course, in saying this Ritschl laid himself open to the mis-understanding that he did not believe in God's care for the individual, and of this his opponents made abundant use.

all other men, but rather directed towards fellowship with them. We believe indeed that we are to look for God's care for our individual lives, but only for that in our lives which belongs to the moral brotherhood, and not for that which refuses to enter such fellowship, and so is cut off from the Eternal. Neither in what is opposed to morality, nor in what is morally indifferent, are we able to, or do we want to, meet with God. And we take this attitude although we, too, hold with Luther that God means " to care for each soul separately, as though there were only the one soul, and no other on earth besides.* Here then at last is the definition of the form of personal life in which alone a communion with God can take place. As long as we are occupied with a spiritual task which is not, so far as we are concerned, in relation to what is morally necessary, so long do we also keep our souls far from God. For the good, or the morally necessary, is nothing else than the expression of the Eternal claiming our devotion, and calling us to partnership. Thus, of a certainty, it is only in submission to moral obligations that we can turn towards that God who seeks to help us to a life in the Eternal. But this moral attitude on the part of men, this

* Erlangen edition, xxxvi. 42. Luther takes this expression from Augustine (*cf.* p. 49) ; but from this presentation of the love of God the two teachers derive widely differing views of religious practice. Augustine derives from it that mystical communion with God which can only be enjoyed in separation from the world, and it is only later on that a soul is to be allowed to turn to the world in love, bearing the divine secret in its heart. Luther, on the contrary, combines with this idea a doctrine of communion with God, which bids the Christian conceive of and realise all his relations to the world as messages of God to his soul.

recognition that all that is within us ought to yield to
the good, is only the presupposition necessary for the
religious act in which we commune with God, and is not
that act itself. The man who thinks of the good and
wills it, enters by so doing into that inner state wherein
he can see the God who is working upon him ; and yet it
is not in moral activity in itself that we rise to God, for
we may agree in spirit with what is good or morally
necessary, and try to follow it out without at the same
time having God in mind.

§ 3. *Our Turning to God begins in the Use of His Act of Beneficence, that is, in Faith.*

We are accustomed in common to call the lifting of
our heart to God "*Andacht*" or devotion.[36] This
expresses rightly our sense that there should be an
inward bringing of God before us, and a conscious
direction of the thoughts towards Him. But the
question arises as to how we actually bring this to pass.
We turn truly towards God only when we take and
use that beneficent act of His in which we experience
His working upon us. "Thanksgiving and the blessing
of God make our requests bold and strong ; prayer is
cold, listless, and difficult unless the heart be already
kindled by the coals of blessing." * But the blessing
or beneficent act which kindles that fire within us is the
fact that God comes near us in Christ. No other human
act has any place in our communion with God save our
understanding and use of this blessing from God. If

* Erlangen edition, vii. 130.

such religious significance be ascribed to any other
human act whatever, then the most fervent devotion
will become a species of denial of God; for so soon as
we think that we can reach and influence God by what
we ourselves originate, we conceive under the name of
God a Being who belongs to the world, and can therefore be used as any other element therein.

The inner process moreover which makes us joyfully
conscious of this blessing from our God lifting us into
communion with Himself, and which extends the power
of that blessing to every relationship of our life, is
faith. "It is not needful for thee to do this or that.
Only give our Lord God the glory, take what He gives
thee, and believe what He tells thee." *   "Thou mayest
do no good thing for God, but only seek to obtain, to
pray for, and to receive good from Him through faith."†
"By no other work can we reach God or lose Him, save
by faith or by unbelief, by trust or by doubt. Of other
works no one reaches up to God."‡ All attempts on
our part to establish in us a meritorious piety prove
worthless when we come to know the real God who is
above the world. "Faith must do all that is to find
place between us and God." § All other human doing
will be taken up with the fulfilment of that law of duty
which points a man to his fellow men and says: Thou
shalt love thy neighbour as thyself. Faith alone applies
to God, love to our neighbours. Hardly any other

* Erlangen edition, xviii. 20.

† *Ibid.* x. 25; xlix. 343: "Here we are always wanting to turn
the tables and do good to that poor man, our Lord God, from whom
we are rather to receive it."

‡ *Ibid.* xvi. 142.   § *Ibid.* x. 26; xv. 163, 349.

principle is so often emphasised in Luther's writings as this terse description of the Christian life.*

As soon as we have once grasped the idea of the God who is above the world, whom we cannot force into our service, but by whose grace we live, it cannot be hard for us to see that to commune with Him can be nothing else than to receive and make use of what he gives us when he comes inwardly near us. Fear of the Holy One, indeed, forbids us that other kind of piety that would strive to press upward to God by human endeavour, but much more are we kept from such a course by our joy at the gift of God, that is something incomparably different from all that any human struggles could work out. Nevertheless the proposition that faith is the Christian's communion with God needs explanation. For faith, wherein arises our knowledge of divine things, might seem rather to constitute the pre-supposition on which communion with God is based ; and then, when the Christian follows the knowledge he has gained and turns actively towards the God who has laid hold of him his action might seem to belong to another kind of activity, which we distinguish from " faith " as " prayer." Luther's understanding of faith gives us all we need to help us to a decision on this question.

§ 4. *Faith is not Experienced by the Renewed Man as a Work of his Own.*

We must first do away with the claim that faith, like every other means whereby men seek to come to God,

* *Cf.* Erlangen edition, xv. 547f. ; xlvii. 254 ; li. 403 ; ix. 273 ; xi. 55, 350 ; xiii. 90 ; xvi. 332. In xv. 48, Luther reminds his

is a human work. Had we to admit the unqualified truth of this claim with regard to the faith of which we speak, then even our faith would be an effort to lay hold on God by human means. But it is just this that we ought expressly to exclude from the communion of the Christian with God. It is well known that in their opponents the Reformers encountered the view that faith is one among many human efforts all equally necessary to union with God. "They think that faith is a thing which it is in their power to have or not to have, like any other natural human work; so when in their heart they arrive at a conclusion and say, " Verily, the doctrine is right, and therefore I believe it," then they think that this is faith. Now when they see and feel that no change has thereby taken place in themselves and others, and that works do not follow, and they remain as before in the old nature—then they think that the faith is not enough, but that there must be something more and greater." * Thus Luther knew a kind of faith which a man himself begets by bringing himself to assent to doctrines of some sort. Luther calls such a faith worthless, because it gives us nothing.† The same holds goods of acceptance of narratives of sacred Scripture as true. This also is to Luther a " natural work without grace " ;‡ even Turks and

hearers that they have often heard him say the same before ; and in xi. 349, he insists : " See thou to it that the works thou doest shall not be for God, but for thy neighbour."

* Erlangen edition, xiii. 301.

† *Ibid.* xi. 201 ; xv. 539. In xlviii. 5, we read as follows : " If thou holdest faith to be simply a thought concerning God, then that thought is as little able to give me eternal life as a monk's cowl is."

‡ *Ibid.* x. 142.

heathens may accomplish it.* He loves to show how easy such a faith is. He says, indeed, concerning the presence of the body and blood of Christ in the sacrament, "Men are easily persuaded to believe this article."†

§ 5. *Luther rises Superior to this Error.*

We might be tempted to think that although this opinion of Luther's may have been justified in his own day, it will not apply to our present situation, since it is now far more difficult than it was then to accept such things. But even if we make such a distinction between our own age and that of Luther, yet his judgment still holds good. For without doubt it is still possible, with the aid of human art and science, to set about attaining and to fight out a belief in the possibility and reality of such things as the presence of the body and blood of Christ in the elements of the Lord's Supper. Compared with such sort of convictions, which it always remains possible to reach, the faith of Luther is incomparably harder; not then alone was it hard. For it is simply unattainable by any human power. No insight, however deep, can found it; no will, however strong, can build it. "The true faith of which we speak cannot be made by our thoughts, but is purely a work of God in us, without any aid of ours." ‡ Indeed, Luther is speaking of a faith which

---

* Erlangen edition, xvi. 483 ; vii. 253. † *Ibid.* xi. 198.

‡ *Ibid.* xiii. 302; l. 341 : "But simple dependence on Christ through faith is not man's work but God's"; lxiii. 126 : "For as no one can give himself faith, so no one can remove his own unbelief."

makes man a new being ;[37] which certainly therefore
cannot be experienced as the work of the man himself
who has not been made new. *   If it be asked now
what kind of faith it is which a man must regard as
produced in him by God, we get Luther's answer
in passage after passage, but his answer has the
tendency to lead men back to the standpoint from
which he wishes to set them free.

Luther tells us very often† that true faith is not the
mere acceptance of the truth of any doctrines or
historical narratives, but that it is bound up with the
firm conviction that all these things have happened for
our salvation and are availing.   It is clear that, viewed
in this way, another effort seems to be expected in
addition to the effort to hold these things as true, and
that the new effort is to produce the conviction just
named.   It is in this perverted form that Luther's
doctrine has been handed down in Lutheran orthodoxy.
The orthodox theology holds firmly that faith consists
in *notitia, assensus,* and *fiducia,*‡ and so treats " assent,"
or " the acceptance of certain things as true," as a work
that may be accomplished before "*fiducia* " is reached,
and having its origin, either in a pure decision of the
will, or in considerations of some kind which appeal to
the reason.§   But if we imagine that faith can so grasp

* Erlangen edition, viii. 226, 284 ; x. 173–4, 216.   † *Cf. e.g.*, x. 142.
‡ Knowledge, assent, and confidence.
§ Hence Quenstedt declares that the first element of faith is to be
found even in heretics, the second only in the orthodox, and the
third only in those who are born again.   He says also that each suc-
ceeding step in the process always implies the preceding one, but
that the reverse does not hold good.   Clearly, then, it is conceived

its object, then the "confidence" which make faith
complete must also take the character of a work
accomplished by man; for the effort of the "*assensus*"
is continued all through this peculiar "confidence."
And even if it be added that the whole process is really
based on God's working upon men, this assertion has
nevertheless no value for the inner life of faith, for
according to the requirements of the doctrine, this life
is to reach its perfection in human efforts. And so
faith is experienced and counted none the less a product
of human effort: just as Roman Catholics regard their
good works, in spite of the doctrine of "*Gratia
operans*."

Luther's real view was certainly different, as we see
from his sharp distinction between the faith which God
awakens and that produced by men. He is not
content to assert that faith has its origin in the working
of God upon men, but he describes the inner processes
which also the believer is to regard as a work of God
within him. In the following he describes, more fully

as necessary to faith to have an "assensus" which is not inseparable
from "fiducia," and therefore not produced by God's revelation of
Himself. Baier's definition sounds better : "Assensus cum fiducia,
seu fiducia cum assensu conjuncta ; ex quibus actibus velut unitus
constat, et nunc illius, nunc hujus nomine appellatur, altero semper
connotato " (assent is bound up with confidence, or confidence with
assent ; of these acts, united as it were (faith) consists ; now called
by the one name and now by the other, both being always connoted).
Cf. H. Schmidt, " The Dogmatic Theology of the Protestant Lutheran
Church." Sixth edition, 1876, p. 303f. But here also the main point
is lacking, namely, that the "assensus" in faith can only be regarded
as an element in the "fiducia" which God awakens by the fact in
which He reveals Himself, unless it is to become simply a fruitless
human endeavour that hinders faith.

than his custom was, the difference between the faith
which makes men blessed and that which is worthless.
He says : " For when faith is of the kind that God
awakens and creates in the heart, then a man trusts in
Christ ; yea, he is then so firmly founded upon Christ
that he bids defiance to sin, death, hell, the devil, and
all God's adversaries ; and he fears no misfortune,
however hard and cruel it may prove.   And that is the
nature of true faith, which is utterly unlike the faith of
sophists, Jews, and Turks ; for their faith simply lights
upon a thing with human thoughts, *accepts it*, and
believes that it is thus or so.   But God has no dealings
with such delusion ; it is the work of man, and such
delusion comes from nature, from the free will of man,
so that, possessing it, they can say and repeat after
others : I believe that there is a God, that Christ was
born, died, and rose again *for me*.   But what such a
faith is, and how powerful it is, of this they know
nothing." *

It is noteworthy that Luther includes even those
words, " for me," in the possible contents of a false
faith.   Above all, however, we must observe how far he
is from prizing that assent to doctrines and narratives
to which men force themselves, as if it were the
beginning or first step towards the true faith, for, says
he, " God has no dealings with such delusion."   He by
no means calls us to such a work as to a necessary
preliminary to further progress, but he warns against
such a course with earnest cry, saying, " Wherefore

* Erlangen edition, xv. 540 ; *cf.* xvi. 442 ; and the " Latin Works,"
xxiii. 522.

beware of that faith which is made and imagined, for
the true faith is not a work of man, and, therefore,
faith which is made and imagined will not avail in
death, but will be overcome and utterly upset by sin,
by the devil, and by the pains of hell. But the true
faith is the heart's utter trust in Christ, and God alone
awakens this in us. He who has it is blessed; he who
has it not is condemned."* Luther was no doubt at
times overpowered by the weight of the tradition
which ascribed to "faith on authority," or, in other
words, to submission to doctrines not understood, the
power to open the kingdom of heaven to men. But
when he speaks out of his own faith, that faith in which
he knows that he has been lifted by God to God, then
he testifies with his whole soul that we do not come to
the true faith through works and doctrines,† and that
a "faith on authority," which our own resolve creates,
cannot help us one whit, since the revelation of God
which creates true faith works only upon the man who
understands it.‡

Luther would not allow that a "work" of reasoned
and determined assent to doctrines and narratives is
real faith. Did he mean by this that the Christian
faith has nothing to do with any objective fact distinct from itself, and that it is simply a free motion
of the divine in the human soul? Most certainly he
neither meant that nor anything like it. "But faith
cannot be fed by aught save by the Word of God
alone." "For where there is no promise of God there

* Erlangen edition, xv. 542.
† *Ibid.* xiv. 46.   ‡ *Ibid.* xi. 176.

is no faith." *   It is Luther's view of the matter that is
laid down in the " Apology " (II., §50–52), where the
promissio dei and the *fides* of man are said to be
correlata and intimately related one to another.†
Luther's great and only aim was to keep faith free
from the " delusion of works "; but all the more closely
on that account did he connect faith with the fact
through which the creative power of the Almighty, the
Maker of all things out of nothing, lays hold on the
man who is lost to the world, in order to make him His
own child and supreme over the world.   That fact, for
Luther as for us, was the historical figure[38] of Jesus,
which makes clear to us our forlorn condition, and yet
works upon us as the *promissio dei*, the emancipating
revelation of God.

§ 6. *The Reappearance of the Catholic Idea in Protestant Christianity.*

But now if faith is so bound up with an objective
fact, it seems impossible to deny that if we are to have
faith at all, we must enter into a relation to this same
fact which shall express not rejection but acceptance.
In that case we should be once more on the standpoint
of that orthodox doctrine which plainly inserts between
the *notitia*, or acquaintance with the historical
report, and the *fidutia*, or religious realisation of the
fact reported, the *assensus* as the requisite acknowledgment of the reported facts.

* Erlangen edition, xxvii. 154f.

† *Cf.* Erlangen edition, xii. 178, " Therefore on our side is nothing
save faith alone, and on His side only the Word and Sign."

Undoubtedly, among us all at the present time, this course of thought is so universally followed that the most widely different theological schools find themselves at one on this point.* If we compare, however, the discussion concerning faith in the "Apology" (as already quoted), we cannot overlook an essential difference. The "Apology" speaks only of a becoming acquainted with the fact by which faith is kindled, and of that appreciation of its contents in which faith consists; that is, it speaks only of *notitia* and *fiducia*. No mention is made of the necessity of a special assent to the fact as such, apart from its significance for the faith which it awakens. Clearly the Reformers looked upon the ground of their faith as an unquestionable fact, which had *by its very content* the power to awaken the new life of faith in any man who became aware of it. It is quite true that the notion of the *assensus* as an act which must be accomplished before the experience of faith, has not been received into Protestant theology without Luther's sanction; for Luther preserved many of the ideas of the old dogmatic without showing how such ideas arise within the life of faith as that is created of God. And ideas which are made the object of faith without such understanding of them, certainly do, of course, require the so-called act of *assensus*, for their acceptance. All the same, Luther did not hark back to the scholastic doctrine that *assensus* is the funda-

* *Cf.* E. König, in "The Christian's Act of Faith," 1891. In this book the proposition is defended, that the Reformers had no other notion of faith than that of the Roman Catholic Church. Yet Frank ("Neue Kirchliche Zeitschrift," 1891, p. 555) praises "the true Protestant tone and aim" of this treatise.

mental act to which the *fiducia* or *spes* must be attached. A stronger impulse in the direction was given by Melancthon, whose followers enlarged their Protestant theology by openly going back to the schoolmen. J. Gerhard had no suspicion of the significance of the step he was taking when he set out by laying down the definition of Thomas Aquinas : *—" ad fidem duo requiruntur : 1. *ut homine credibilia proponantur* ; 2. *assensus credentis ad ea, quae proponuntur*." † Certainly, when he did so, he was working with a conception of the object of faith which necessarily led on to the scholastic conception of faith. He says, namely, that the object of faith is, *the coelestis doctrina*, the heavenly doctrine, which we must not only know, but assent to, in order to attain to *fides*. In this he is undoubtedly right from his point of view as to what is the object of faith ; for if the *fiducia* of faith is to apply to *doctrine*, then that *fiducia* can only arise when the doctrine has received assent.

The so-called Lutheran finds this notion of an *assensus* preceding *fiducia* to be necessary, because he has no longer in view the same object of faith as Luther had. The fancy, of which people to-day can scarcely get rid, that there must be an *assensus* before *fiducia* in order that faith may exist, arises from the same deeply rooted presupposition that the object of faith is a *teaching* concerning divine things. How

* *Cf.* Erlangen edition, xlviii. 5 : " We say that this is faith ; when *I see* what faith has to lay hold on and grasp." *See* also xii. 249.

† " For faith two things are necessary : (1) That things be propounded which a man can believe ; (2) The assent of the believer to what is propounded."

powerfully this overlaying of the notion of faith operated in Melancthon's constitution of the Lutheran
church has been shown by Ritschl.* Even Luther,
who knew faith to be the work and gift of God, and
who found his freedom in that knowledge, did not
always assert it, but could continue to present the idea
that faith is an acceptance of prescribed doctrines.†
Already in the "Formula Concordiae" we find a contradiction of Luther's characteristic idea laid down as a
self-evident truth. It is there stated (*Solida declaratio*,
v. 20),‡ that the Gospel is a doctrine, which teaches
what men are to believe that (*i.e.*, in order that) they
may obtain the forgiveness of sins. Thus faith is here
looked upon, not as a confidence awakened in human
hearts by God's revelation, but as assent given to
doctrines to which a man must bring himself, and for
which he is to be rewarded by forgiveness. And however strongly it may be insisted alongside of this, that
faith is a work of the Holy Spirit, such a faith inevitably becomes a work which the believer regards as an
achievement of his own.

§ 7. *We get Free from it by Personal Forces.*

We must break away altogether from this idea. And
to do so is no innovation of ours. We simply set aside

* *Cf.* Briegers "Zeitschrift für Kirchengeschichte," I., 89ff. ; also
Gottschick "Die Kirchlichkeit der sogen. Kirchlichen Theologie"
(The churchliness of the so-called churchly theology).

† *Cf.*, *e.g.*, Erlangen edition, xiii. 190 ff. ; xi. 268 ; xix. 9. "Because
of such sayings, which cannot be attributed to man or angel, I must
believe that He was very God " ; xxix. 340 ; li. 122.

‡ The Completer edition of the "Formula."

an idea which the Reformer's idea of faith has always contradicted. Christian faith looks, in the first instance, not to any doctrine, but to a fact which stands firm and sure in the life of the man who is summoned to believe. In accordance with this, *notitia* is certainly a necessary condition for faith. The fact to which faith looks, and on which it may be founded, must somehow or other have come within our circle of vision. But it would be no confession of that fact's saving power, but rather a confession of its impotence, if we should say that, given the perceived fact, a human effort is then needed which shall master the fact and make it the basis of faith. They who do not know the divine power of this fact, that is, they who do not believe in it, will certainly judge in such wise as to the origin of faith ; but the believer is necessarily certain that he himself has been overpowered by it. Only when he has this certainty does he actually see the reality of that power of God which is the object of faith. And so that judgment as to the origin of his faith is nothing else than the faith itself ; that judgment is simply the expression of the faith which cannot declare the reality of its object in any other way. When a fact exercises such power over our soul that it becomes for us the witness to the reality of the God who is saving us, then we say that fact wins our confidence. All Christian faith is thus really a confidence in an event which has taken place in the Christian's own life. No discussions concerning the credibility of a report or inquiries into the truth of a doctrine can supply faith with its real object, at least not that faith which regards itself as an experience of divine help, and not as simply the work of man.

Now the event whose occurrence in our life is fraught with such importance, is the fact that the portrait of Christ is brought before us by the New Testament and expounded to us by life in Christian fellowship. It would be absurd to speak of some effort supposed to be necessary to establish that fact. But since this event is different from everything else in our experience by its power to give us the courage of a trust that there is a God caring for us, all uncertainty as to whether the figure of Jesus, which works thus upon us, belongs to legend or to history, is in the nature of the case impossible. The proof of the historical reality of Jesus for a believer rests always on the significance which the story of Jesus has gained for his life. It is only when the Christian has taken this story to heart as an unquestionable fact in his own life that all that testifies to the historical reality of Jesus stands out before him and is clearly and easily grasped. Thus the *assensus* to what is historically reported, so far as such *assensus* has any place in faith at all, does not precede the *fiducia* as a work of human effort, but is bound up with it as a result brought about by the fact on which faith is based. An assent produced in any other way to the judgment that the Person of Jesus belongs to human history, could not be so organically bound up with religious faith as to form a unity; for a judgment reached by a process of historical inquiry could not lay claim to anything more than probability. But to Christian faith it is a *certainty* that Jesus lived as the

Man who opened up the possibility of an eternal life for
men by His Gospel of the Kingdom of God, and who
was at the same time conscious that the existence of
His Person in life and death would make that kingdom
real for all who did not pass Him by. The certainty
that these are not the features of an ideal adorning a
mythical figure, but the real claims of a man full of
peace and power, does not result from historical inquiry.
Rather is it true that a view of history which shares
certainty springs up only in those who have felt, under
the influence of the story of this Man, what a significance that story has for them and for all men.

Again, it is just as impossible to combine with faith
such an assent to the historical reality of Jesus as would
come of a simple resolve on man's part to believe it.
For such an achievement of defiant will-power would be
the exact opposite of that submission to God which is
characteristic of true faith. If we are to avoid both
these by-paths, we must grasp and hold fast these two
things following : first, faith is trust in an event which
moves us so that we interpret it to mean that God is
seeking to admit us to His favour by this event; and
secondly, for us this event is first and foremost the fact
that we are brought under the influence of the Christian
brotherhood, its life and preaching. We receive from
every side about us evidences of Christian faith and
Christian love, and so we are pointed to Christ Himself
and prepared to understand His Person. Thus, in spite
of all the darkness which sin causes amid our human
intercourse, we gain a vision of inward riches which
reveals to the maturest intellect as well as to the child-

like mind what is the perfect life of the spirit. Of course, these experiences alone do not make any man a Christian, but the condition of need into which they bring us places us in a position where we can apprehend the Person of Jesus to be, not a problem which perplexes us, but the fact in our own life that sets us free. Through the historical influences gathered around that personage which reach even to us through the continuous life and activity of the Christian brotherhood there is awakened in us a longing for the perfect life of the Spirit. When a man is burdened by this longing for what seems impossible, then arises before him the figure of Jesus, which appears to him no longer as an ideal picture all unreal, but as the historical fact, which marvellously and incomprehensibly justifies his longing. The ideals of untrammelled love for what is good, and of inward peace over against the world, which beam down as the sunshine upon the life of the Christian brotherhood, do not actually cause our faith in God, but they do lift us into an inward condition where the figure of Jesus, as history records it, touches us with such power that it draws our confidence to itself as a revelation of God. In its commencement and in all its development alike, Christian faith is nothing else than trust in persons and in the powers of personal life. We begin to understand God's gift and God's help in our religious intercourse with Christians, and through our reverence for them; then, when we have received such a training, the picture of that wonderful personal life which the Gospels set before us, becomes an earnest plea that we shall put our trust in it as testimony concerning a Man whose existence in our world makes us certain of God. When our eyes have once opened to perceive what it means to us that Jesus is there for us, and what we should be without Him, then we see also the living naturalness of the historical portrait of Jesus, and the impotence of any doubt as to its historical truth. Only for one whose soul has not been so placed that this historical phenomenon could awaken his confidence has this doubt any power. And there is no method, either of art or science, that can dispense with that personal trust, or in any other way make it possible to acknowledge that Christ is the revelation of God. Possibly some sort of faith might be *manufactured* by such means, but we can become conscious of a faith born within us as the work of God only if the root of that faith be the confidence by which we feel ourselves swayed through the appearance of Jesus. In such trust our own free will breathes and acts, and yet we experience it as the doing and gift of One who is stronger than we.* Hence, when Luther is seeking an expression for faith as no work of man, but as that wherein we know that we are being lifted up by God to God, he can find none better than these words of child-like simplicity : " a heartfelt trust in Christ." †

* *Cf.* Erlangen edition, xxxv. 239₁: " We honour God only by our faith, and God rules in us by faith."

† *Cf.*, for instance, Erlangen edition, xlvii. 12.

§ 8. *The Relapse into the Old View Accounted for by the*
Force of Criticism Inherent in Faith, Especially
in Regard to Miracles.

When we ask, why then have Luther's followers fallen
away from this emancipating knowledge, and burdened
themselves again with a piece of human workmanship
under the name of faith ? the answer is easy when we remember, in the first place, that even Luther himself did
not altogether give up the old traditional conception of
faith as a human act (see above, p. 224). The answer
is easy, again, when we remember, in the second place,
the fearless critical power which must come along with
this new understanding of what true faith is. When
faith insists on being nothing else save confidence in
Christ, then any element in the story of Jesus necessarily becomes a matter of indifference, if, from its very
nature, it cannot satisfy the desire for a salvation which
means forgiveness of sins and life in spiritual freedom
as over against the world. In face of the seriousness of
such a desire for salvation, then the miracles reported
in the New Testament necessarily become of minor
importance, for in no case can we say of them that they
must be there in order that we may get help to this
sort of salvation to-day. All such things retire into
obscurity, but so much the clearer grows the one ground
of salvation, the Person of Jesus Himself, who lives
altogether for the Kingdom of God, and dies in the
certainty that He has brought sinners to God. It is
not a doubting intellect that makes this distinction ; it

is faith. He who has found Jesus Himself to be the ground of his salvation has no need of those miracles. It is well known that Luther did not hesitate to say this. Here are his words: " Even if there were no miracles of Christ, and we knew nothing of them, we should still have enough in the Word, without which we could not have life." * Again: " Those visible works are simply signs for the ignorant, *unbelieving* crowd, and for their sakes that are yet to be attracted; but as for us who know already all we do know, and believe the Gospel, *what do we want them for?* " And again: " Wherefore it is no wonder that they have now ceased, since the Gospel has sounded abroad everywhere, and has been preached to those who had not known of God before, whom He had to attract with outward miracles, just as we throw apples and pears to children." † And yet again: " And what does it signify if He made a score or two to see and hear, or even if He raised them from the dead? For such signs happened only to the end that the Christian Church might be founded, instituted, and received, along with that baptism and preaching with which it was to be established." ‡ No one could declare more plainly that the miracles were intended for the age in which they happened and were meant for *unbelievers* then, in order to direct them to Christ; but that they no longer possess the same significance for believers and for us, who do not see them, but only hear about them. It cannot be denied that the story of Christ's miracles does not give us now

---

* Erlangen edition, li. 327.
† *Ibid.* xii. 236 f.　　　　　‡ *Ibid.* xix. 169.

the comfort that His words afford ;* or to quote Luther
again : "For I am not so sure of the grace that was in
the miracles and that was shown *to others*, as when I
have clear plain words for myself; and it comforts me
more to hear such friendly admonitions and persuasions,
than to hear preaching concerning miracles." †

In Luther's faith, the Person of Christ as being the
one miracle that can be grasped in personal experience
pressed aside the miracles reported by others, and a
clear example of this may be seen in his discussion of
the miracle of Christ's birth, where he writes : " Hence
we see that the dear apostles, Paul, John and Peter,
together with Christ Himself, do not say even one
single word concerning the mother, the Virgin, for the
greatest power does not lie in the fact that she was a
Virgin ; but *everything depends on this*, and for this
end everything else took place, that we should know
that the Child came for our sakes, that for us He
walked and stood, that He is our Lord and God, who
will receive and protect us." ‡ Moreover, Luther's
faith did not find its interest in the fact that the Child
was born, but in the Person of Christ in his life-work,
or in that which Christ did as Man : " The Scripture
does not make much of the birth and childhood of
Christ.   Therefore the Evangelists write little concerning His childhood, but hasten to His thirtieth year, to
describe His office whereto He came "; "and there
(*i.e.*, at Christ's baptism) begins the New Testament,
and not with the childhood of Christ "; "and, to sum

* Erlangen edition, xv. 289.
† *Ibid.* xv. 290.   ‡ *Ibid.* xv. 155.

up all, with His baptism begins His office—*it is then that He becomes our Christ, our Saviour,* which He came to be." * Luther will not have these miracles despised, and he makes the customary allegorical use of them ;† but it is clear to him that they cannot be the basis and object of that faith wherein he knows himself redeemed. It is simply inevitable that when we have found redemption in confidence in Christ Himself, this element of the tradition about Christ should be put on one side; for whether Jesus healed few or many sick persons or none at all, whether or not He raised any from the dead—all this can neither strengthen nor weaken our trust in that Man who makes sinners certain of God's grace, and who takes away from a soul all fear of fate.

Now, however, one who quite rightly remarks that many of the most vivid features of the historical portrait of Jesus depend on narratives of His miracles, will naturally be inclined to link together as the object of faith all that is linked together in the traditional record, and so to regard the miracles as the objects of faith equally with His Person, since they are recorded of Him. It needs a very serious recollection of what is the real basis of faith to enable one at such a point to assert the truth as opposed to the claims of instinctive piety. If this be considered, it will help to explain how the notion of faith as awakened of God which Luther had formed, has vanished again from Protestant theology, though not indeed from the Protestant Church. Of course, a conviction of the historical truth

* Erlangen edition, xv. 238 f. ; xxxv. 208.
† *Ibid.* xv. 290.

of these stories of miracles may be appended to a real faith without doing any detriment to the purity and strength of the latter. Although the inner process of actual faith is in no way dependent upon that conviction, yet most of those for whom the Person of Jesus has become the basis of a new life, would count it a disturbance of their faith if one were to assail that confidence in the stories which has grown in them with their growth in sound religion. Nevertheless this attitude, which is quite natural to many, and worthy of every Christian's regard, is not without great danger to clearness of faith and purity of conscience. For if the inner life of the Christian never reaches such seriousness and depth that faith on the one hand, and the acceptance of those narratives as true on the other, are seen to be quite distinct things, then even the faith "which God awakens in the heart" is contaminated and made impure by impotent human efforts. As soon as acceptance of those narratives as true is honoured as the most important element, or beginning, of faith, then at once there will also appear the injurious consequences of founding faith thus on human endeavour. A faith in which there lurks an element so utterly different from confidence is God is not felt to be a work of God, however strongly it be asserted that He brings it about.

The objection has been raised that in order to get a true portrait of Jesus we simply must believe previously in the miracles, since the disposition of Jesus is manifested precisely by the way in which He performed the miracles.* If this were true, then Christ

* A. Oppenrieder, in the "Neue Kirchliche Zeitschrift," 1891, p. 312ff.

would not be our Redeemer, but we should have to
redeem ourselves by our own resolve. No miracle of
which others tell us has of itself the power to influence
us so that it shall appear unquestionably real in our
eyes. For us everything depends on this, that something shall come before us which has not first to be
made a fact by our desiring to believe it, but which
simply is a fact. Such a thing alone can be to us the
ground of a faith wherein we shall be really redeemed,
that is to say, lifted away above all that we were before
or could make of ourselves ; and the Person of Jesus
can do this for us, because a clear vision of Him, and a
vision which commands our conscience, can rise up
before us from the records even though we hold the
miracles to be legendary. Indeed, I can conceive a
man getting a most vivid impression of Jesus' power,
just when he thinks he sees that His historical appearance has been swathed in a thick mist of legends, and
that, nevertheless, the glory of His inner life breaks
through all these veils. A man who thinks he sees this
has, at any rate, a firmer ground for his faith than
another who *determines* to believe in the resurrection of
Jesus in order that he may have his feet planted on a
fact that overcomes the world. The objection named
above misconceives the true ground and proper nature
of faith, for it supposes that we neither can nor may
come near to Jesus Himself before we are in a position
to hold as true such a matter as the resurrection of
Jesus. The traditional record may appear doubtful ;
but the essential content of that record, namely, the
inner life of Jesus, has the power to manifest itself to

the conscience as an undeniable fact. That means everything.

§ 9. *Worldly Religion Hardens the Orthodox Notion of Faith.*

The orthodox notion of faith will always return where men who appear to cling to religion are really taken up with its outward advantages. For then selfishness is sorely tempted to take part in religion on the easiest terms possible. The recipe for the process is always the same. You take part in it outwardly, but put it far from your heart. The kind of thought and conduct which springs out of such a procedure supplies all the forms of enjoyment of worldly mastery and all the devices for making religion into worldliness. The richer development of these forms is to be found in Roman Catholicism. Protestantism has really only one workshop for the skilful production of them, namely, systematic theology. Even among Protestants this study has, as a rule, been employed, not to serve religion, but to secularise it. It weaves the broad cloak under which all may creep who either do not know the terrors of religion, or who want to avoid them, but would like to live in a religion of the human sort. That semblance of scientific character which systematic theology knows well how to assume is disappearing now that even in theology a scientific work is beginning which follows seriously those laws of investigation of the truth which have been reasoned out in other spheres. Even attempts to preserve that semblance of scientific character by using the most dignified terminology possible will make but little difference. But all the while the disposition prevalent in this worldly procedure has been blossoming into a giant flower within the Church itself. The desire has been to participate in religion by merely getting one's religious ideas from the sacred Scriptures, or from the traditional story of Christianity in general ; and so participation in religion is made easy in Protestantism.

But in order really to take part in religion we must become certain of the Everlasting God, and that He is communing with us. This comes to no one *sine magna concussione animae.* In order to this we must take to heart the particular situation in which we stand, and live that out in seriousness and truthfulness. If this be true, then, the business of theology is to show that the business of Christianity is to come to an understanding and realisation of our present existence, and then to show how that understanding becomes possible for us if we take into account the appearance of Jesus as the most important element of our existence. That is the task of a systematic theology which will really serve religion. In that way the truth is established that we become Christians, not by an acceptance of thoughts which are strange to us, but by the revelation of God to ourselves ; and that revelation alone, being something that we experience for ourselves, can change our whole inner life. Our hearts shrink when we see that the matter affects us so closely, and this shrinking is rather encouraged by the systems of theology, for the claim they raise that the thoughts of other men who have been lifted into communion with God may be worked together into a system of divine truth, opens a loophole by which we may escape from real religion while we still preserve its appearance.

Of course, it is always insisted that a man must be already renewed by the Spirit of God in order to be able to grasp such ideas of other saints. But then the systematic theologian proceeds to deny this admission by the course he usually follows. It is admitted that these thoughts stand in the closest union conceivable with the personality in which they rise; they are supposed to be movements of a new personal life which receives from divine revelation the power to think such thoughts. But then the very attempt to make a system out of them is wrong. From the nature of the way in which they are revealed to the new and growing personality of the Christian, they are fragmentary; hence they must be disfigured by any theological attempts to form them into a system. The name, systematic theology, is, nevertheless, appropriate, for there certainly ought to be a system clearly mapped out which should show the connection between revelation and faith, and the rise of those Christian ideas. But if we try to make a system, whose relationships of part to part we thoroughly grasp, out of the thoughts which the man renewed by the revelation of God finds himself free to think, then we drag those thoughts down into the very region from which they are to raise us. This one consideration alone shows how in systematic theology the tendency prevails to make a share in Christianity easier in a way pleasing to the sinner but destructive of the truth.

But that tendency has still stronger support in another practice, one which is held to be worthy of the highest esteem, namely, the way in which loyalty to Scripture is misconceived and practised by Protestant dogmatics. Some individual and pleasing changes have taken place in this respect, and in these the advances made in exegesis have been taken in account. But the chief point remains unaltered, namely, that loyalty to Scripture is taken to mean that the thoughts recorded in the sacred Scripture as possessed by its writers are to be fitted into the system of dogmatics with the utmost possible completeness. At this point Ritschl and his opponents would fully agree. Nevertheless it cannot be ignored that such an undertaking will always lead to the legitimation of a faith which is nothing more than a ready acceptance of unaccustomed thoughts. For where lives the Christian who could with truth presume to say that he treasures the thoughts of a Paul as his very own? Surely all of us read the apostle with the feeling that he has a different measure and a different energy of faith from ours. If that be so, then the dogmatic which undertakes to fit together and give us as its own the apostle's thoughts with the utmost completeness, serves corruption. If we adopt such a view of the task of theology, we are proposing for the sake of so-called loyalty to Scripture, to call our own even those thoughts which still remain strange to us ; and in that case we countenance the belief that Christian character is to be established precisely by accustoming oneself to use the thoughts of other Christians. Wherever this belief is established, longing

for true life dies out. He who thinks to gain help
in religion by a mere access of strange thoughts, will
soon forget that he needs above all things to have
thoughts of his own. It has so fine a sound to say
decidedly that the task of theology is to include, as far
as possible, all Scriptural thoughts. But the inevitable
consequence of so doing is that we learn to be content
with a mere outward relation to such thoughts. True
loyalty to Scripture is quite another thing. We are
really on the path which the apostles trod when we in
our position become certain of God and of His grace in
the same way in which they in their position gained
that certainty, namely, through the Person of Jesus.
Thus we have the same faith that they had, and can
rise to the level of their thoughts. The thoughts amid
which their faith moves become, in such a case, no
longer a prescription which we are to try to follow outwardly, but a means whereby we may gain inward enlightenment. They are to be a help to us in that task
which is really incumbent upon us, namely, that we are
to live with a faith of our own; they are not to be a law
which prevents us from seeing the one thing needful.

Still, it will always be the case that many who would
like to share in Christianity, will seek to attain
Christianity by a faith which follows this direction :
" Put thyself in accord with the thoughts of Christians,
and so shalt thou be a Christian." That is an easy
thing for them to do, and gives them that outward
appearance on which they put a value. It is uncommonly
hard to help such persons to real Christianity. You
may tell them as often as you can, and the Protestant

theology does indeed tell them this faithfully, that a man must become another being in order to become a Christian. They can do nothing with such a counsel. For they have robbed themselves beforehand by the falsehood of their faith of that in which the new birth should manifest itself, namely, the power of living in the thoughts of all who are holy. Theology can, and it should, at least avoid the error of leading such persons on by its own conduct to a faith that seeks to make Christianity easy for itself, but avoids the actual experience of religion.

We asked the question how it is that, in spite of Luther's mighty struggle, the ready acceptance of the thoughts of others is regarded even in the Protestant Church as the beginning of faith and of Christianity. The chief explanation is to be found in the fact that such a conception of faith makes it possible for men to pass for Christians who will not be at the trouble to seek God Himself in their religion.

§ 10. *True Faith in Itself Communion with God, and not merely a Preliminary Condition for Communion.*

Only when we reserve the name of faith exclusively for the trust which the picture of Christ awakens in us, and the new purpose and courage which are born of that trust, is the notion of the faith given us by God made quite definite and clear. For we experience all that confidence and its fruits to be the work of Christ, and we understand it to be a gift of that God who turns to us through Christ. If, then, it be correct to say that the communion of the

Christian with God can only be realised in a process in which we know that we are raised by God to God, then faith, when rightly understood, fulfils that condition. It is not true that faith in this sense either can be or needs to be supplemented by mystical excitements of any sort whatever, in which the devout soul shall feel himself in the very grasp of God. But we shall, of course, fall into such a fancy if we lose sight of the faith which God awakens, and put in its place a humanly wrought acceptance of doctrines and narratives. Hence it is easy to understand why such a lively sympathy with mysticism is frequently met with in the Protestant Church. The healthy religious instinct there, the longing for life with God, runs in this direction precisely because the faith which is consciously cultivated is usually an impotent human struggle, and therefore is anything but a life with God. Those who are fond of mysticism furnish, on a smaller scale, the same spectacle as the great schoolmen did; they seek to rest from the work of their faith in mystic piety. We get away from this evil only by learning again to value faith in Christ as Luther valued it, that is by finding in Him, not merely a necessary condition for our communion with God, but that very communion itself. Having thus described faith as arising as a confidence in the historical phenomenon of Jesus, we have now to point out the inner nature of such faith, by which we recognise it to be actual communion with God.

§ 11. *Submission to God only in Pure Trust.*[39]

Only in entire submission to God can the Christian
commune with Him. Every act of the soul wherein we
think of offering God anything other than this acknowledgment of His honour, and every sort of self-exalta-
tion to equality with God, must be regarded by the
Christian as a departure from his God. We have truly
reached God's presence only when, in the very depths of
our life, we are conscious of our dependence upon Him.
Therefore our communion with God can consist in
nothing else than the experience of dependence, for
every attempt to develop any other communion with
God must turn into an attempt to establish our own
independence as over against God, in such a way that we
really deny Him. Hence we may start with the proposition, as with an axiom, that the ideal of Christian
piety is an inward condition of soul in which everything
is blotted out from us that tends to hold aloof from this
dependence on God ; a condition, therefore, in which our
inextinguishable desire for life has found rest through
our experience of God's power over us. This proposition,
though not foreign to mysticism, is nevertheless inseparably connected with the Christian conception of God's
nature : for that idea of the nature of piety can be
maintained only when we conceive of a God who is, as
Luther says, " nothing but pure love," * or whose nature
is pure beneficence.†   Indeed, the task of entire devotion

* *Cf. e.g.,* Erlangen edition, xviii. 311–316.
† *Ibid.* vii. 168 ; xii. 354 ; xv. 532, 543, 545, 546.

to God plainly presupposes the certainty that joy in personal life, *i.e.*, love, forms no subordinate element in God's life, but is rather the controlling and unifying element in His whole life and activity.   It is only when possessing this certainty that a personal spirit could, from its very inmost living source, submit itself to God ; whereas, if we felt compelled to think of some other definite element or some hidden and nameless power as the ruling feature in God, then the task of utter self-surrender to Him would become an idle phrase.   There is only *one* way in which that surrender is possible, and therefore only *one* way to God, and that is the experience that the overwhelming impression of His love and faithfulness lifts us into a confidence that we are safe with Him.*   When our confidence is established in such a way, then we are dependent upon God from our inmost soul. We are brought to God, not by fear and terror, but by a beneficence which takes us entirely captive, because it increases wonderfully our desire for life, and at the same time wonderfully gratifies it.   Hence, to enter into communion with God is possible only when such confidence becomes powerful within us.   " *Now to come to the Father* is not to run afoot towards Rome, nor yet to soar with wings towards heaven ; but it is to lean on Him with heartfelt confidence, as on a gracious Father, as the Lord's Prayer says at the outset.   *The more such*

* *Cf.* Luther, Opp. var. Arg. IV. 299 : 'Cum Deus coli non possit, nisi tribuatur ei veritas et universae bonitatis gloria, sicut vere tribuenda est."   (" Since God cannot be worshipped, unless truth be ascribed to Him, and the glory of universal kindness as is indeed His due.")

confidence thrives in the heart the nearer do we come to the Father." *

If we are to commune with God we must learn to know Him in His creative power ; and this is disclosed in the effect which the revelation of God has upon us.   We find by living experience that that revelation awakens a wonderful desire for life in the hearts of men whose life is steadily passing away ; and the power of His word turns our despair into confidence, and converts the self-contempt of the sinner into a courageous joy in what is good.   But to see this is to recognise God's creative omnipotence bringing into being something entirely new, to wit, the inner life of the redeemed man.   Such a new creation of God is not the work of a moment, it occupies the Christian's whole life ; and we lay firm hold of its reality only when we add to our *experience* of faith a judgment of faith regarding itself, a judgment that is based on Christ.

Thus a communion with no imaginary picture of God, but with God Himself in reality, takes place only when we allow Him to make us new men with the deepest need of our life satisfied.   The stirring of this new life, a life that is bound up with the consciousness of its own divine origin, is communion with God : and the life of the Christian, as it comes from God, is just his faith, wherein, with new purpose and courage, he remembers his sin and learns to love his cross.†   The

* Erlangen edition, vii. 71 f.

† *Cf.* Apol. for Conf. II. 62 and 63 : "Haec fides in illis pavoribus erigens et consolans accipit remissionem peccatorum, iustificat et vivificat, nam illa consolatio est *nova et spiritualis vita*.   Adversarii nusquam possunt dicere, quomodo detur spiritus sanctus." ("This

reason why Luther says with unceasing repetition that
God wants nothing from us except trust and faith,*
can only be that he knows that the living exercise of
faith is the actual communion of man with God. But
faith can have this significance only when, in the first
place, it is called forth by the impression made by the
revelation of God, and not by a human resolve, and
when, secondly, it is not an acceptance of doctrines as
true, but a trust in God Himself which He Himself has
awakened. The Reformers' expressions for the content
of this faith are often incomplete, since they emphasise
only the certainty of the forgiveness of sins, as. *e.g.*, in
the passage in the " Apology " above quoted. But they
believed that the life of faith, which is a life with God,
contains more than this, as may be seen in the " Augsburg
Confession," where it is said that the knowledge of the
gracious God who forgives our sins is continued in confidence in His care and providence, and therefore in
confidence in His help when confronted by the world.

§ 12. *The Place of Forgiveness of Sins in the Life of Faith.*

It is a great merit of Ritschl's that he drew attention again to this declaration, for it follows that the
faith arising amid those fears, and giving comfort, receives forgiveness of sins, justifies and makes alive. For that consolation is a new
and spiritual life. Our opponents can never say in what way the
Holy Spirit is given.") *Ibid.* 68 : Haec diximus hactenus ut modum
regenerationis ostenderemus." (" We have said these things so far, in
order to set forth the manner of regeneration.")

* *Cf. e.g.*, Erlangen edition, x. 26, 108 ; xiii. 205 ; xvi. 12, 16 ;
xvii. 358 ; xix. 12, 51, 362 ; lii. 307.

Reformers held that we are certain that God forgives our sins only when we submit ourselves to the operations of the gracious God with confidence in His help for every situation in life. Certainty of forgiveness is no doubt the first thing in Christian faith, in this sense, that any Christian who is morally mature, will regard it, and ought to regard it, as the clear pre-supposition for all other experiences of God's grace; but it is not necessary that the certainty of forgiveness should always come first *in point of time* in the life of faith. Still less is it right to regard it as a thing apart from the rest of that life. The network of facts which constitutes our environment in the Christian brotherhood is all of it certainly a declaration to us that God desires to forgive us our sins; but in that case it cannot be our business to strive after a certainty of forgiveness as something quite distinct from the other blessings of faith. The facts which are all summed up in our environment by the Christian brotherhood are indeed the ground of our certainty of forgiveness; but they are this because of that peculiar significance they have, which gives us all our certainty of the reality of God and of His grace. This significance of the facts whereby God lifts us to Himself is of such a nature that if it has given us a heartfelt confidence in God's love and care, it will also in due time give us experience of God's forgiveness. Indeed, it is self-evident that the same facts which convince us in any way of God's love must also set forth His willingness to forgive our sins. Through the objective forces which work upon the Christian he finds himself in such a position that he has access to the Father. Necessarily he will see that his very understanding that this is his actual position implies the further fact that God is ready to forgive him his sins. If therefore our faith means that we understand the God who is speaking to us through those forces, then the forgiveness of sins is implied in the very foundation of faith, and is as sure and real to faith as faith is itself.

This is denied in effect when it is said to be man's task, through a special agony of penitence to reach the certainty of the forgiveness of sins. Rather is it the case that in the way the Christian obtains it this certainty can arise only by our taking to heart what God has already done for us. Luther taught this connection of forgiveness with the very foundation of faith after he had as a monk learnt to know how fruitless is the longing for a forgiveness which should show itself by signs in the soul that has wrestled in penitence and prayer. For the Christian the only source of forgiveness is the comprehension of the revelation of God. " If thou dost not seek forgiveness in the Word it is in vain that thou shalt sigh to heaven for grace, or, as they say, for inward forgiveness."* This Word comes to us through the factors of redemption, which are all included in the Christian community. It must make the Christian realise with fear his sin and its consequences, but not so that he may be kept for a longer or shorter time in remorse and doubt, but so that he may see clearly in all its reality the grace of God that constrains him even in spite of his

* Erlangen edition, xxxi. 171.

sin.* For a man who stands within the Christian community is by virtue of that fact under the forgiveness of sins.† The unbeliever may certainly deny what the Christian community brings to him, but ' he will in time experience how certainly his sin has been forgiven him even before he was willing to believe it.' " ‡

When a Christian becomes inwardly aware of the forgiveness which is bestowed upon him, this forgiveness is not conceived by him as a single act wrought by church officials ; Luther warns us to beware " of thinking that the act of forgiveness refers only to a single moment, when the absolution is pronounced." § Luther sees the forgiveness of sins in the whole Kingdom of Christ, " which lasts for ever without ceasing. For just as the sun shines and illuminates none the less brightly when I close my eyes, so this throne of grace, or this forgiveness of sins, is always there, even although I fall. And just as I see the sun again when I re-open my eyes, so also I have forgiveness of sins once more when I look up and come back to Christ. Wherefore we are not to measure forgiveness so narrowly as fools dream." ‖ We belong, by baptism and Christian

* *Cf.* Erlangen edition, xxxi. 182, 183 (1530 A.D.)

† *Ibid.* xxii. 21. I believe that in that community, and nowhere else, is there forgiveness of sins, and that outside of it nothing, no good works, however many or great, can bring about forgiveness. And within it, it does not matter how much, how greatly, how often a man may sin, the forgiveness of sins *stands sure whenever and so long as this community endures.*

‡ *Ibid.* xxxi. 172.

§ *Ibid.* xi. 319.

‖ *Ibid.* xiv. 294 ; the same simile occurs in xi. 320 f., and in xl. 312 f.

training, to the brotherhood which Christ adorns with His love ; herein, then, we have before us the fact that God desires to forgive us.

Of course, it is essential that we do not regard our connection with the Christian brotherhood merely as a course in life that has valuable consequences, but that we understand it as a message of God to us. When we do so understand it, then we necessarily place ourselves in that relation of dependence upon the Christian brotherhood which Luther describes by the well-known expression in the Greater Catechism, where he says that the Church is our mother. Ritschl adopted this idea as the principle which every churchly theology must maintain against separatist endeavours ; but for doing so he frequently had to endure the reproach, even from " churchly " theologians of our time, that this was a relapse into Roman Catholic ways of thinking. But in spite of this, it should not be difficult to see the difference between the doctrine inherited from Luther and upheld by Ritschl on the one hand and the Roman Catholic doctrine on the other. According to the Catholic conception, the essential thing is to suffer or have *imposed* on us a state of dependence on the Church, and to submit to her summons to obedience to her laws. According to the conception followed by Ritschl, the essential point is that in the light of our knowledge of Christ we should understand our dependence on the Christian brotherhood to be *the expression of the grace of God that is turned towards us.* If our souls have attained this attitude towards the Christian brotherhood, then we can indeed regard the forgiveness of sins as an unchanging blessing that is given to us as the sun that shines above us, as the firmament that is vaulted broad and far above us, or the covering that enwraps us.* Luther used all these pictures to express the fact that the forgiveness bestowed upon us is continuous, that it is implied in the basis of faith, and that, therefore, it is an indwelling element in every phase of faith.

God's way of turning to us in Christ lifts us into communion with Him because the perception of this fact enables us to set the certainty of reconciliation over against the feeling of our guilt. Therefore we are not to behave as though that had not happened for us, but we are to open our eyes to see what God has done for us. We are to ask daily forgiveness from God, as the Father "who does not deal with us in severity, but can indeed bear with us somewhat, and can overlook much that we do." † And yet in such case it might seem as if forgiveness were a mere matter of course in a Christian's eyes. The fact is rather that to every one who really experiences it, forgiveness comes as an astounding revelation of love. This reflection, correct as it undeniably is, has caused much confusion. For it may easily seem that in such case the Christian, in seeking forgiveness, must first forget all the evidences of God's love that he presently possesses. But is it really so, in personal intercourse, that all the bonds of confidence between two persons must be broken before the one can experience forgive-

* _Cf._ Erlangen edition, xiv. 213 ; l. 249 ; "Latin Works, iv. 143."
† Erlangen edition xii. 186.

ness from the other ? It is certainly quite otherwise.
So also in our communion with God, the convincing
power of His revelation may abide with us, even
although we sin, and may prevent the trouble caused
by our sense of guilt. And yet in each case we only
find anew how God is stronger than our heart. The
impression, indeed, that God's love seeks us out in spite
of our sinning will not cease ; it will never grow old,
but will constantly open afresh to us the gates of a new
life. So we are not by any means to push away from
our hearts all belief that God is gracious to us, and
deliberately try to work up a deep sense of God's anger
against us, with the idea that only so do we treat our
guilt seriously, and only so can we receive forgiveness.
Rather must we sincerely live our life in the reality
amid which God has placed us, and obey the obligations
in which this reality is realised. It may be the case
that a Christian does believe that he feels all the awful
anger of God, because he feels deeply the burden of
his guilt, and looks forward to a desolate life in the
unavertable consequences of his sin. If he remains in
that condition and so perishes inwardly, he does indeed
fall before the judgment of God, who is a God, not of
the dead, but of the living. But when, on the other
hand, in this state of mind the grace of God in Christ
wins power over his heart he undergoes the miraculous
experience of redemption, of rescue from the anger of
God. It can never be the duty of a Christian to work
himself violently into a feeling that he has been rejected
by God.[40]

§ 13. *Repentance as an Element in the Life of Faith.*

Certainly all experience teaches that on the other hand no Christian is able to maintain himself unwaveringly at the purest altitude of childlike trust in God. Even he who is preserved from grosser sins will nevertheless feel within him that self-condemnation which his moral short-coming keeps before his eyes, and he will feel it more and more keenly just as he grows more and more sensitive to the weight of moral obligations. It is inevitable also that the difficulties of life will at times overmaster feeling so seriously that the weary soul will let go all that it has hitherto gained of Christian joy in life. Luther's words hold good, therefore, of the most advanced of Christians : " It is not necessary that he should be altogether without fear. For nature always remains within us, which is weak, and cannot stand without fear of death and Christ's judgment." * Luther does not indeed mean for a moment that every one must fight the same inner battles as himself. " God holds the measures here, so that He will lay upon each one his cross according to his own person, according as he is strong and able to carry it." † Thus he says that God sometimes tries His great saints, and exercises them with the *desertio gratiae* (deprivation of grace), " and then a man feels in his heart just as though God and His grace had deserted it, and would no more of him, and wherever he turns he sees naught but anger and terror only. But not

* Erlangen edition, x. 77.　　　† *Ibid.* ix. 87.

every one suffers such great trial, nor does any one understand it save he who experiences it." * Luther admits to himself, too, that such inner battles may have their cause in imperfect Christian knowledge ; they were experienced " especially in the blindness and darkness of the Papacy, where they had little true consolation." † But, above all things, Luther saw in these circumstances only a suffering which the Christian cannot avoid, and not an achievement which he is to accomplish. It is only in lives of thoughtless pleasure that such suffering can possibly be entirely absent. " Therefore such fearsome persons are indeed nearer their salvation than the reckless and wilful who have neither fear nor care for comfort all day long." ‡

But as we ought not to pray for trial but to be kept from it,§ so also it is folly to count it a duty to have trials, wherein we lose sight of God's grace. Whenever Christians search earnestly what is the basis of the assurance of faith, or whenever they come to serious knowledge of duty, they are met by the contrast between their own unworthiness and God's unhesitating love. But the Christian is not to aim with conscious purpose at having this experience of remorse. He is rather to aim always and only to do the positive duties of the Christian life. Only amid the light of that life does a true repentance arise out of and instead of the languid discomfort of the sinner. The sinful will never brings forth such regret by any process of its own.‖ Hence repentance does not mean purposed self-chastise-

* Erlangen edition, xi. 21.   † *Ibid*. ix. 87.
‡ *Ibid*. x. 76.   § *Ibid*. ix. 88.   ‖ *Ibid*. xxvii. 392.

ment, but, as Luther says, "a real bettering and change of the entire life.* Similarly, "if thou wilt confess sin, then have a care that thou lookest and thinkest far more on thy future than on thy past life." "For it is easy to forgive that wherein thou hast sinned already. Therefore must thou see to it how thou mayest begin another life, and that thou feelest in thy soul that thy former life irks thee, and that thou hast had enough of it."† Amid such endeavours the Christian will and ought to find that he cannot help himself by any mere straining of his own will, but that he draws strength from his experience of God's love. "This despairing and seeking of grace is not to be something that lasts for an hour or a time and then leaves off; but all our work, words, and thoughts, while we live here on earth, tend to nought save increase of distrust of self, of abiding rest in God's grace, and of desire and yearning for Him."‡ On the other hand, Luther says that a wish to stay in the despair of remorse and in fear because of sin is an abuse of that fear. The longer a man thus keeps looking at his sins "the worse things become, and the man lives in constant doubt." § That carefully purposed regret which the sinner seeks to bring about of his own direct resolve needs to be unmasked, says Luther, for it is the mistaken effort of man to set himself right again

---

* Erlangen edition, xi. 290.   † *Ibid.* xi, 211.   ‡ *Ibid.* xv. 442.
§ *Ibid.* xvii. 434 ; *cf.* xlix. 12 : "It would be well indeed for us if we could only learn and take well to heart how Christ says and testifies with His own mouth that it is against His will, and hurts Him when any Christian's heart is sad or fearful."

in the eyes of God.* He says that the man who uses
fear and repentance unwisely " only increases them and
remains in them, as though he would purify himself
from his sins by doing so ; but nothing comes of it." †
On the contrary, the Christian should set it clearly
before himself what God has given him. For it is
God's doing that he finds himself within the sphere of
the Christian brotherhood, where he meets with Christ,
and where he is trained to understand Him by innumerable influences of Christian ways of thought and
Christian conduct. These facts are to be to the
Christian God's declaration of His gracious intention
towards him, and when he reflects upon them he is not
to think, if he falls into sin, that " therefore God has
forsaken him and cast him away as a worthless tool " ;
but he is to take comfort in the thought " that he is
in the Kingdom of Christ, the kingdom of that grace
which is mightier far than sin." ‡

§ 14. *The Element of Contemplation in Faith.*

In this faith we are lifted up to God, and because
of its objective basis this faith is essentially a faith
in reconciliation, although it may not from the
beginning, or at every moment, take on the form
of certainty of forgiveness. Now it would be a
strange proceeding for a Christian who had grasped
that fact to aim nevertheless at devising for himself
some additional special communion with God, and

* *Cf.* my essay, "Repentance in the Protestant Christian."
"Zeitschrift für Theologie und Kirche," 1891, p. 37 ff.

† Erlangen edition, x. 76.   ‡ *Ibid.* xii. 318 ; *cf.* xvi. 139.

at bringing about the same by some special effort. The real man of faith does not creep into the corner of lonely contemplation in order to gaze on divine things as on a quiet picture; * he rather seeks experience of God, and to be aware of Him in His activity as the almighty and life-creating Spirit. Hence the Christian who has any care to remain in that union with God which God Himself has begun with him, will turn his attention to those experiences in which this faith affects all relationships of life, and proves itself to be the power of God making a new man of him. " *Through faith* shalt thou experience the might and mercy of the Father, and experience Him to be a Comforter and Life-giver." †   " To name God outwardly with thy mouth, or to pray to Him with kneelings and postures, all this is not having God; but it is when thou trustest Him heartily, and when thou lookest to him for all goodness, grace, and favour, whether in doing or suffering, in life or death, in love or sorrow." ‡ " To have a God at all means to trust God." § " And to

* Erlangen edition, xv. 186 : "The clergy, especially those who stick in the monasteries, boast that they live a life of contemplation ; they know just as much of a contemplative life as a goose knows of the Psalter. Wherefore let that go ; our Lord God has not commanded thee to *sit and gaze luxuriously up into heaven as they do who fancy that such is a contemplative life*." " Faith is a thing of such a sort that it sets one right everywhere and in all affairs. This is the truly contemplative life." " Therefore all this sort of faith comes to pass without any work of ours, and it is not my work but God's ; nothing is necessary to make it save the Word which creates faith in the heart." "That is a truly contemplative life ; it consists not in fleeting thoughts, but in a certain knowledge." *Cf.* xliii. 41f.

† *Ibid.* xv. 329.   ‡ *Ibid.* xvi. 131 ; *cf.* xi. 337.
§ *Ibid.* lii. 301.

hang upon Him with the heart is nothing else than to trust one's self utterly to Him." *

What else, then, can communion with God mean if it be not to have Him, to feel His power, to hang upon Him with the heart, " since He is the one eternal Good, the eternal well-spring running over with pure goodness and flowing with everything that is or is called good " ? † Instead of giving ourselves up to a luxurious contemplation, in which, after all, one only busies himself with his own fancies, we are to live the life of faith which arises within us by our contact with God through that almighty fact, His own word. ‡ As we apply this faith to every kind of situation in life, and win from it our view of the Whole of things, we receive gifts from God, and we answer Him by joy in that power of His which renews us marvellously, and makes us free men as over against the world. The right contemplation is life in the " freedom of a Christian man." §

§ 15. *Faith Fleeing the World.*

A coming to God which did not include at the same time a new valuation of what we experience and of what we are in the world, would not be a coming to the God revealed in Jesus Christ, but to the hidden God of mysticism. It would therefore be a kind of piety which no Protestant need feel it his duty to possess. It belongs to the Roman Catholic way of thinking, which resists the view of the world which

---

* "Greater Catechism," I. 15 ; *cf.* section 28.   † *Ibid.* section 25.
‡ Erlangen edition, xv. 432.   § *Ibid.* viii. 141.

God desires to see in His own children. " Now if a man have a wife, or a wife is occupied with her child and tends it, the Roman Catholic teachers say that these have not pure hearts because all this cannot happen without thoughts that attach to such things. For it is necessary to think, yea, daily, of food, of money, of work, of other things ; yet these are things from which, as they say, we ought to be quite free, so that we may have no thought but to sit and speculate on heaven, and meditate on nothing else than God." " Thus have the blind guides led us, and they have written countless books full of such speculation as to how men are to become free from things." * If Christ Himself were measured by the standard of this kind of piety, even He, as Luther properly remarks, would appear to have no perfect communion with God ; for His calling bound Him to the world, and " where then did His heart remain the while and his thoughts, that ought, forsooth, to be absorbed with God alone ? " " To have nothing to do with outward, worldly matters and things, but to live, cut off from all these, a life of spiritual contemplation ; this is not a guiding and a teaching according to faith." † Thus such sort of flight from the world seems to Luther not only an abandonment of moral duties, but also a hindrance to faith or the right communion with God.

The Christian certainly does know one kind of flight from the world, without which he could not come to God ; if Christianity did not share the tendency of all

* Erlangen edition, li. 290.
† *Ibid.* xii. 150 ; *cf.* ix. 81, 280–81 ; x. 416.

genuine piety to flee from the world, then the spread of mysticism in the Church would be quite inexplicable. But Luther felt that he had really found a deeper significance and a more powerful method for Christian denial of the world than the older Church had done. The tendency of the religious nature to forsake the world reaches its perfect satisfaction exactly when the Gospel, as Luther understands it, lets us find our God in the midst of our relations to the world and our energetic action therein, and lets us enjoy communion with God as Him who thus makes us blessed. Hence Luther demands, first of all, faithful work in a worldly calling as a part of the priestly duty of the Christian, and therefore as necessary to his communion with God.

From this follows Luther's opposition to the Catholic idea of fleeing from the world. " They do not forsake or flee from the world (as they dream). Thou mayest be in whatever position, life, and existence thou choosest (for thou must indeed be somewhere, since thou livest on earth) ; in none of these does God sever thee from the people, but rather places these among them ; for every human being is created and born for the sake of others. Where thou art now (say I), and in whatever position thou mayest be found, there art thou to flee from the world."* Here Luther expounds the true flight from the world in this sense, that while the Christian lives amid the arrangements of the world

* Erlangen edition, viii. 272 ; *cf.* l. 248. To become holy is said to mean to be withdrawn from the world. But "the holiest rank or life on earth is nothing else than the ordinary Christian rank." *Cf.* xxix. 327.

and enjoys its good things, he does not pin his heart to
it,* but uses it as a means for eternal bliss.

In another passage he writes : " See, this is to die to
the world and to be without fear, namely, to be troubled
about nothing save what God wills, to speak nothing
save what pleases Him, and what I know are His words ;
in short, that I so live and so do, that I know the works
are His works, and that I *am certain that my whole life,
inward and outward alike, is His ;* then I am cut off
from the world and still am in the world." † Thus
Luther recognises the world-flight in the longing of the
Christian for an eternal good which is not to be found
in the world, and in the fact that in spite of this he
seeks and finds God in all that he does and suffers here
" in his ordinary life and rank." The former makes us
strangers in the world, but the latter sets us free from
that inner bondage to the world which is rendered all
the heavier by our longing for a bliss that is above the

* *Cf.* Erlangen edition, xxxv. 220 : "Hence the world is to the
Christian sheer night and darkness which faith makes since it clings
to the blood of Christ alone, and neither regards nor pays heed to
aught else." Thus, when the Christian asks what is the ground of
his hope of life, the world fades away for him in darkness. That is
the world-flight of faith, in which we recognise and seek for Christ
alone as our Helper. *Cf.* the description of the Christian's independence of the world, xxxv. 247.

† Erlangen edition, xv. 412. We read in this passage also : "No
one is less in the world than a Christian, and no one is more worldly
than a Christian." This sentence would make an admirable summary
of all those thoughts of Luther's which we have just expounded ; but
just at this point, in the second half of the sentence, Luther lets the
main point escape him. For he goes on to say : "That is, the world
observes him more, and the devil fights harder against him than
against the heathen."

world. The first is in a sense the natural instinct of all genuine religions to flee the world, the second is that inner deliverance from the world which our faith effects by letting the Christian find his God amid his earthly life. We are truly cut off from the world only when we learn to " use it " aright, *i.e.*, when we rule it through faith.

Of course, since the Christian breaks loose from the world in this way, he misses the reputation for piety which those who forsake the world in the usual way take to themselves and easily gain from people around them, who say : This man does not live like a common man, wherefore he must be a saint." *   " For the truth does not so shine and glitter, because she does not make herself plain to calculation. For example, when an ordinary Christian hears the Gospel along with others, believes, uses the sacrament, lives spiritually at home in his house with wife and children, that does not shine like the fair and clever lies of a holy Carthusian or hermit, who lives apart from the people and claims to be a holy servant of God."†   Yet without doubt there is a greater depth and strength of world-abnegation in that achievement of faith which makes us feel free from the mastery of the world even when actually in its power, and which makes us feel the limits and sufferings laid on us by the world to be a very help and a blessing. For we could not be more deeply separated than this from what the world is to the natural man, the basis of his hopes of life, the sovereign before whom he bows, the blind force before which he trembles. But again this overcoming of the world which Christian faith works is

* Erlangen edition, xx. I. 18.   † *Ibid.* ix. 81 ; *cf.* xlix. 303–306.

certainly much harder than that contempt for the world
" which makes itself plain to calculation," or, in other
words, follows nothing but the very illuminating principle that God is something other than the world. A
man can accomplish this latter of himself, but not the
former. " Only try it with earnestness, and with true
wrestling of conscience, then shalt thou surely know
it." * It is only by stern fight that we can secure this
inner freedom from the world, and this peace " that can
still the heart, not when there is no misfortune, but in
the very midst of it." † So Luther had to say concerning
himself : " At times I believe, at times I do not believe ;
at times I am joyous, at times I am sad." ‡ And yet he
can say of this mood of freedom from the world that
faith brings : It is a true and continual peace, which
abides for ever and is invincible," § because the inner
state is no product of human reflection, but comes only
of the revelation of God which continues in imperishable
power. "As the joy of the godless never rightly reaches
the heart, so also the sorrow of the Christian never goes
to the bottom of his heart." ‖ All the sum of that which
the world can give or take away could never, taken
altogether, suffice for a foundation for a joy that should
so outweigh all our sorrow. We do not create this
foundation for ourselves ; but we receive it when we find
God in Christ.

Thus we may put away from our thoughts all temptation to seek, in utmost disregard of the world, for

* Erlangen edition, xii. 153 ; cf. xvi. 165 ; xviii. 300 ; xix. 17, 18.
† Ibid. xi. 352.   ‡ Ibid. xix. 76.   § Ibid. xi. 353 ; l. 231.
‖ Ibid. xv. 108 ; cf. vii. 116.

fellowship with a God whose revelations come only to solitary souls, and that within the realm of their imagination. For inward freedom from the world is indeed sought for in this way, but never found. We have communion with God—He works on us, and we turn to Him—when we receive from Him the strength in which we overcome the world, and when with joy and gratitude we use the same. If we are in contact with the living God, we must necessarily experience His creative power; hence our communion with Him comes to perfection only when, face to face with the world, we experience that God is making something different of us. Were our God something inert, then we might be able to enjoy the bliss of communion with Him in a world-forgetting contemplation. But since He is the Living Power which presses in upon us through all the complexity of our lives, we must let Him lift us in and by means of that complexity if we would enjoy the bliss of a real communion with Him. Our turning towards God comes to its perfect fulness in our grateful joy at what God makes of us. This normal attitude of Christian piety is classically described in Luther's treatise, " On the freedom of a Christian man," * and it is Ritschl's great merit to have brought this ideal of Christian piety once more to the front as the practical principle of the Reformation, and to have taken up once more the corresponding renovation of theology which the Reformers left incomplete.

* *Cf.* Ritschl's "Doctrine of Justification and Atonement." Second edition, i. 181 f.

§ 16. *Luther's Idea of the Freedom of a Christian Man.*

In that treatise Luther describes the inner life of the Christian which springs from redemption. It is in essence nothing other than Christian freedom, *i.e.*, faith.* From this faith are excluded all *speculationes, meditationes, et quidquid per animae studia geri potest ;*† it is nothing but the *cognitio Christi Jesu,* that understanding of Christ with which the *sacrosanctum Dei verbum* (the most sacred word of God), the gospel of Christ, makes us rich and blessed. ‡ Through *this* faith we enter into that wonderful fellowship with Christ through which our sin becomes something that belongs to His Person, and His relation towards God and towards the world becomes our own. The taking and giving in which this fellowship consists is realised in our understanding of the Person of Christ that is in the faith which He awakens in us and which we base on Him.§ And the riches we thus receive constitute the whole inner condition of the believer, in which he finds himself brought into the same attitude towards God and towards the world as Christ. When we recognise in Christ the God who desires to reconcile us to Himself, we are

* *Cf.* Luther, Opp. var. arg. iv. 266 : "Haec est christiana illa libertas, fides nostra."

† Speculations, meditations, and whatsoever can be carried on by effort of the soul itself.

‡ *Ibid.* 221–223.

§ Hence marriage is but a poor copy of that fellowship ; *cf.* the same, p. 227.

ourselves raised to the priestly dignity of Christ. *Per spiritum fidei*, by the spirit of faith, that is amid those inward experiences that the comprehension of Christ awakens in us, we gain courage to come so near to God that we see in Him really a Father who clasps us to His heart.* In proportion as God is present to us in Christ, and we can lay hold on Him there, we have this priestly freedom of communion with Him. But while Luther declares this priestly power of the believer to be the greatest good we have through Christ, † yet he prefaces his exposition of this by a description of the believer's *kingly* power, and returns to this latter idea at the end of it. He does so for this reason, that the same understanding of Christ, the same *fides* which makes us priests before God makes us kings over the world. For the believer who has come to understand that God turns to him in Christ cannot enjoy that communion with God *without being conscious that therewith a change has come over his whole being*. The exercise of his priesthood necessarily implies that in his communion with God he is spiritually lord over those very things which have caused him suffering in the realm of worldly things, for although he still feels their bitterness, he nevertheless understands them and uses them as God's gift to bring him blessedness. This spiritual kingship enjoyed amid subjection, free and powerful amid overwhelming trouble, is unattainable by the man who has not been brought near God through faith, and just as impossible is it for a man to enjoy that nearness to God without feeling

---

* Hence marriage is but a poor copy of that fellowship ; *cf.* the same, p. 232.   † *Ibid.* 231.

and acting as a new creature over against the world, as the wonderful impulses of this great power beat within him. Any other supposed communion with God and Christ but this experience of what God means to make of us in Christ, lacks that humility in which the soul really yields to God. If, then, we turn to the Redeemer only in the sense that our human sympathy is stirred for Him, in love and sorrow, then Luther did not speak one whit too strongly when he said that such ways are *puerilia et muliebria deliramenta* * (childish and effeminate hysterics). Instead of such feeble artifices, which are always a practical denial of the Deity of Christ, we are to recognise God in Christ and to become free men by utter submission to Him.†

§ 17. *Christian Humility.*

The Christian's submission and his freedom are both inseparably included in his communion with God, yet at any given moment we may prefer to call the whole by either name. Our communion with God is, first of all, utter submission to His majesty. But submission is possible only when God makes us certain of Himself and of His grace, or, in other words, when He is present

* Luther, Opp. var. arg. iv. 233 ; *cf.* "Kritische Gesamtausg," I. 341. Erlangen edition, x. 155 ; xi. 154f.

† This topic, handled in "De Libertate Christiana," is also fully discussed in Erla gen edition, xv. 262 ff.; xxxv. 246 f.; li. 398. The idea of the believer's spiritual lordship over the world is very often taken up. *Cf. e.g.*, x. 257 ; viii. 141 ; xi. 207 ; xii. 282 ; xiv. 338 ; xxxv. 130 ff. On the other hand, Luther speaks of "the priestly power of believers," generally in the sense that they have received power to open the kingdom of heaven to others.

to us and comprehensible to us in the historical figure of Christ. It is only when our surrender is joyful that we do fully submit ourselves. The attitude of the heart which finds compensation for all life's burdens in a conscious submission to God's guidance has been pointed out by Ritschl as the same as that gladsome lowliness manifested by Jesus Himself.*

This religious lowliness, or humility, as Luther translates it, is experienced in the first place as a condition in which God places us, although there is bound up with it the consciousness of the freest self-determination. For that joy in God which is essential to a true submission to what He may ordain is awakened in our hearts only when God becomes an *objectum amabile* (a lovable object) to us by some actual proof of His love.† The heart does not become " a quiet, humble dwelling-place of God " until we are able to recognise Him as our Father ; " for when I come to know that, then I let Him rule as He will, and take Him alone as all in all." ‡ The man who tries to submit to or to humble himself before God in any other way than under this touch of God Himself achieves only a hypocritical humility, and remains inwardly far from God.§ For the more and the worse a man tortures himself to obtain eternal life,

* *Cf.* Ritschl. "Lehre von der Rechtfertigung und Versöhnung." Second edition, iii. 587.

† *Cf.* "Apologie der C.A." iii. 8.   ‡ Erlangen edition, xii. 288.

§ Hence it is that only the mistaken, "manufactured" humility is self-conscious. "True humility never knows that it is humble." "Humility is so tender and exquisite that it cannot bear the sight of itself." Erlangen edition, xlv. 236 ff. "It is a secret of God's," viii. 78.

the less He attains to it. He must be humbled, and must crave the Spirit of God alone. The man who means to make himself blessed by works is the devil's own for ever.*

Secondly, that humility through which we stand in the right relation to God is always likewise a corresponding behaviour towards the world in which the salvation God has given is enjoyed.† For joyful self-surrender to the living God means willing submission to those laws and arrangements by which He works on us on every side and actively influences our life to its very depths. That man alone is humble who finds in prosperity God's great claim upon Him, who sees in the boundlessness of things God's almighty wisdom, and who finds in incomprehensible suffering God's love : for then only is the man submissive to God in respect of the actual facts of his existence. But when this is the case, the man does indeed possess that spiritual sovereignty over the world which gives him a share in the Kingdom of God and makes him blessed. Hence Luther, in the passage quoted above, ‡ after describing humility as a heart that is quiet and contented before God, straightway goes on to say : " It must come to pass that the heart recognises God's glory, God's power, God's wisdom. *For then it lets God rule all things;* it knows that all things are works of God, and therefore it can be terrified at nothing." " Thus there grows in us undaunted defiance against all that exists on earth,

---

* Erlangen edition, xvi. 468.

† *Cf.* Ritschl, in the volume quoted above, 592.

‡ Erlangen edition, xii. 288,

for we have God, and all that is God's ; we do all that
we are to do, and we are not afraid." *   It is the same
power that works for us, although in another direction,
when humility guards a man who has reached the
pinnacle of success and is enjoying earthly riches, from
losing the inner freedom of the children of God, and
setting up a mistaken independence.   Humility then
overcomes that pressure of the world which threatens
to drive men into a narrow trust in self, and so it
proves itself to be a real communion with the life-
giving and liberating God.

§ 18. *The Fear of God.*

Another expression for that inward submission in
which we commune with God is " the fear of God." To
the Christian this fear is not a momentary horror at the
mysterious power that is over his life.†   It is always
possible for the creature moved by its love of life to
escape from this emotion into renewed calm forget-
fulness of God.   But the Christian fear of God is rather
that deep and joyful acknowledgment of God as the
only mighty and living One, which we may and ought
always to feel.   " It is thus we must understand the
fear mentioned in the Scriptures ; it does not denote a
fear or a terror lasting for an instant, but it is our whole

* Similarly he describes (Erlangen edition, xi. 337) the thoroughly
humble heart which God desires by saying that it is nothing other
than trust and confidence in God, without whose sole help and
deliverance man can do nothing.

† With this fear is combined the "optare non esse deum " (the
wish that God did not exist), var. arg. i. 69.

life and being, walking in reverence and awe before God.* "What we, following the Scriptures, call the fear of God, is not terror or dread, but an awe that holds God in reverence, and that is to remain in a Christian, just as a good child fears its father."† Thus the Christian's fear of God is the reverence of the child for that Father within whose mighty care it feels itself still sheltered.‡ The Christian fears the Father whom he recognises in Christ, "not on account of the pain and punishment, as unchristian men and the devil fear Him," but because he sees before his eyes the actual power of God giving him blessing; and he fears to take one step beyond the sphere of that blessed power "as a good child fears, and will not arouse its father's anger, or do anything that might not please him."§ Here again we see that the communion of man with God can take place only as an experience caused in the man by God Himself. For any one can work up for himself those feelings of horror that arise from a sense of inevitable dependence on a power we dread; and such feelings are to be found, too, in any Christian life, for no Christian is perfect; ‖ but, on the other hand, that fear of God which looks at God Himself, and is therefore

* Erlangen edition, xxxiv. 174. † *Ibid.* xviii. 349.
‡ *Ibid.* lvii. 56. § *Ibid.* li. 365; *cf.* xvi. 187.
‖ But "Sine timore inferni nullus est nec esse debet nisi sit perfectissimus. Ideo justorum timor semper est mixtus sancto et servili, sed proficiunt de servili magis magisque ad sanctum, donec nihil nisi deum timeant." Var. arg. i. 73. ("No one is free from fear of the infernal one, nor ought we to be so, unless we be utterly perfected. So the fear of the just is always a mingling of the devout and servile. But they go on from the servile more and more to the devout, until they fear nothing except God.")

true communion with Him, arises only in the soul that experiences the emancipating power of the Gospel amid contact with the Christian brotherhood, through Christian training, custom, and preaching. But it is only complete when we have found in Christ the God that draws back to Himself even those who feel deeply estranged from Him by the sense of their own guilt.* Inward trembling before the holy power of the Good can never cease to be part of man's communion with God. If we cease to fear God, we have lost our inward relation to Him. The communion of the Christian with God never succeeds in overcoming the inner opposition between fear and love.

§ 19. *Love to God or to Christ.*

In Jesus' combination of the two sublimest commandments of the Old Testament, He described the normal attitude of the human soul towards God as love to Him. Nevertheless, He and the apostles rarely used that expression in their testimony concerning their own communion with God; and this makes us see that its use may easily lead to error.† It is

* There can be no communion with God without awe under the sense of the holy power of goodness; when that awe ceases, communion with God ceases also. (*Cf.* Luther, Erlangen edition, xi. 248): "We have prophets in this country, up and down, who teach the people a courage that is all too free, and bid them talk with the High Majesty as with a cobbler's lad. These impudent and haughty souls no man should follow, if he love himself." (*Cf.* the same volume, p. 194).

† *Cf.* Ritschl. "Lehre von der Rechtfertigung und Versöhnung." Second edition, vol. ii. 99f.

especially instructive in this connection to note how seldom the Epistles of the New Testament speak of a love to Christ. The reason why the expression is thus avoided is explained by Ritschl in the following passage : "That formula does not indicate whether, in our love for Christ, we set ourselves on equality with Him or subject ourselves to Him. But the expression, 'faith in Christ,' implies confession of His Deity and of His sovereignty, and therefore excludes the possibility of equality with Him." * The expression for communion with God most frequently used in the New Testament is that of " reverent trust in Him," and the reason, doubtless, is that just such reverent trust fulfils the command to love God. If we are not merely speculating in general concerning love to Him, but thinking of that particular form of it which is prescribed by the nature of the God that Christ reveals, then it is not difficult to see that to have faith in the true sense is to have love to God. We may by no means lose sight of the high command, "Love God," but, at the same time, this is not to be abused by reading into it an arbitrary meaning, and calling the play of human imagination with its own dreams a holy thing.

Luther once casually defined love thus : "To love means to carry a good heart, and to favour all that is good ; to be heartily kind, helpful, and sweet to every man, and not to laugh at his sorrow or misfortune." †

* *Cf.* Ritschl. " Lehre von der Rechtfertigung und Versöhnung." Second edition, vol. iii, 552. It is remarkable that in spite of this true observation, Ritschl wished to understand by the Godhead of Christ only what might also be predicated of the Christian community.

† Erlangen edition, xliii. 152.

It is clear that we can love men in this way; but we cannot so love God. If this were all of love, then we could love God only indirectly, namely, by making God's purpose and work our own through willingness to help our neighbours. In that case love to God could be carried out only in the form of love to our neighbours, as Luther frequently declares. He puts the question: "How may love of a neighbour be the fulfilling of the law, when we ought to love God above all things, even above our neighbours? Answer: Christ Himself solved this, for He says, in Matthew xxii., 'The second commandment is like unto the first,' and He *makes of love to God and love to one's neighbour an equal love.* And this for the reason, first, that God does not need our work and kindness, but thus points us to our neighbours that we may do for these what we desired to do for Him. He wants nothing more than that we trust Him and hold Him to be God. *For even the preaching of His glory and our praising and thanking Him take place on earth in order that our neighbours may be converted and brought to God thereby.* And yet all this is called love to God, and is done from love to God, yet really to the use and profit of our neighbours only." "It is thus we are to find and love God, thus are we to serve Him and do Him good if we wish to serve Him and do good to Him : and so the command of love to God is brought down altogether into love for our neighbours." * And Luther says in paradoxical fashion that God would

* Erlangen edition, viii. 65f ; *cf.* x. 109 ; xv. 40f ; xxii. 332 ; xvii. 260–3.

rather forego our service of Himself than our service of
our neighbours,* and he insists earnestly that when we
find some work that we wish to do for benefit to God
and not for our neighbours alone, then are we to count
that work an evil thing.† And starting from this
argument, too, he went on to utter his disapproval of
misleading ideals set up in the mystics' theory of love
to God; he says: " Here now is a check given to those
slippery and high-flying souls who seek God only in
great and glorious things, who thirst after His greatness, who bore through heaven, and think that they are
serving and loving God by such noble ways, while all
the time they are betraying Him and pass by Him in
their neighbours here on earth in whom He desires to
be loved and honoured." "For therefore did He put
from Him the form of God and put on the form of a
servant, that He might draw our love for Him down
and fasten it on our neighbours, whom we leave lying
here, and gaze the while into heaven thinking to show
God great love and service." ‡

Yet Luther knows also of a love to God which is
rendered directly to Himself, and this is joy in God.§
All love is joy in personal life; joy in our neighbour's
claim upon us is love for our neighbours; joy in God's
claim upon us is love to God. And as we are to show
the former when our neighbour is in trouble, so the
latter is manifested amid troubles of our own. Joy in
God, the " tasting and seeing how gracious the Lord

* Erlangen edition, xiii. 168 ; cf. xiv. 155.
† Ibid. xiv. 59 ; x. 25, 146 ; xvii. 152.   ‡ Ibid. viii. 66.
§ Ibid. xvii. 257-60 ; v. 205 (heartfelt contentment, pleasure, and
love to Him).

is, " all this does faith that is tried bring to us at the
end of our travail. For so long as the strife and trial
last faith is in travail, and all is hard and bitter : we
neither taste nor see any sweetness in God. But as
soon as the evil hour is past, if we endure it and abide,
then comes God's sweetness, and God becomes so dear,
so pleasant, and so sweet to the heart that we desire
nothing more than more strife and more trial and
travail." * Thus love to God springs from the experience that He comes personally near to us, that He lifts
us inwardly above our trouble, and lets us find peace and
blessedness amid conflict and suffering.† This assistance in life is never ending, for it helps us not simply
in this particular or in that, but makes entirely new
men of us, and in our joy over this we love God as He
would have us love Him.

The love for God thus awakened may be required of
us by a commandment, because necessarily it is a kind
of regulative of our behaviour, so that we willingly
acquiesce in what God commands and enjoins. " A
true love to God says from the heart, ' Lord God, I am
Thy creature ; do with me what Thou wilt, it is all
the same to me ; I am indeed Thine, and I know that." ‡
But these two things, the love God awakens and the
love He claims, are together clearly nothing other than
that true faith which is an actual communion with the
Living God. Luther says, after discussing at some

* Erlangen edition, xiv. 77.

† *Ibid.* ix. 38. " Love to God is nothing else than gratitude for
unspeakable kindness received."

‡ *Ibid.* xiv. 172 ; xvi. 426.

length the impossibility of our fulfilling this chief commandment if we love God only as a thief could love
the hangman : "Just as God is satisfied *with my faith*,
with my love for Him as a gentle God and a merciful
Father of whom I love to hear, so He desires also that
I aim all my works earthward and toward my neighbour only."* This view of the identity of love to God
and faith is expressed in the countless passages in which
Luther says God wants nothing of us save trust and
faith ; or, that faith is to be exercised towards God,
and love towards our neighbours. And so, seeing that
love to God is the joy caused by His coming near to us,
Luther is able to say that love does not exactly result
from faith, but it is the chief element in faith itself.
"Now we have said above that such confidence and faith
bring with them love and hope ; *but if we rightly consider
it*, love comes first, or at the same moment with faith.
For I could not trust God if I did not think He desired
to be favourable and gracious towards me, whereby I
may become gracious towards Him, and may be moved
to trust Him heartily and to expect from him every
good thing.† Thus the Christian's love to God does
not move in an atmosphere of contemplation of inactive
beauty. It arises when we actually experience the
Living and Working God, manifesting His love and
making us understand it, and so turning the rebellion

* Erlangen edition, xvii. 260.

† *Ibid.* xvi. 131. The same connection of thought occurs in
v. 204 : "For no one can love Christ unless he trusts Him and
takes comfort in Him." "Thus does the Lord desire us to think
of Him, *that we love Him, and set our hearts upon Him*."

and despair of our hearts into humility and consolation. The blessedness which grows up out of this spiritual and true contact with God is that joy in Him, which we call love for him. Hence true love to God is widely different from the tenderness we are wont to manifest when some peculiarity of a stranger awakens in us a natural inclination towards him. Our spiritual personality has to be rescued and kept free from the fetters of such natural love. Love to God is quite different, and arises as we feel the freedom into which God's own act emancipates us.

It may now seem that what we have said is contradicted by Luther's use of the features of natural love as illustrations of the Christian's love for God. And even if his doing so had meant that he had relapsed into the practice of Papists and sectaries who " talked and dreamed of trafficking with God," * it would not be strange to find even in Luther such a sign of the powers of the past. We find him saying concerning the prophet of the Roman Catholic love for Christ : " Saint Bernard I hold very dear as the man among all those writers who preaches of Christ most sweetly ; I follow him when he preaches Christ, and in the faith wherein Saint Bernard prayed, do I also pray to Christ." † But it cannot in the least be affirmed that with all this attachment to Bernard, Luther ever allowed himself to be won by him to that love for God and Christ which

* Erlangen edition, li. 290.

† *Ibid.* xlvi. 243 ; *cf.* on the other hand, xliv. 73 ; xlvii. 23, where he directly reproaches Bernard for having fled from God in Christ and for having resorted to a communion with the Virgin, which was simply human tenderness.

only a monk can show. Indeed, in the very passage quoted, he adds immediately that he does not follow that revered man in anything which would make it appear that persons engaged in their worldly callings could not be perfect Christians.* But it is still more important to note how Luther developed his comparison of love to God and Christ with bridal love; for then we may see plainly that Bernard's heartfelt yet effeminate piety acted only as an occasion for setting in motion thoughts of Luther's own which he derived from his own correct understanding of the Revelation of God.

Luther refused to know anything of any sort of contemplation save that which is incumbent upon every Christian without exception. Faith is to him the true life of contemplation.† He does indeed compare faith's love towards God with the love of a child for its mother, and even with that of the bride for the bridegroom; but by these pictures he illustrates simply the strength of the love,‡ and the confidence with which the believer can turn to Christ his Redeemer, who makes the believer owner even of His own great Kingdom.§ When Luther speaks of love to Christ as the Bridegroom, he is thinking of the believer's endowment with the riches which Christ has bestowed upon the brotherhood, and not at all of an interchange of sensuous tenderness between Christ and the individual soul; and so he says *it is the Christian brotherhood that is the Bride of Christ:* " In this faith we are all one Bride, one

---

* *Cf.* also Erlangen edition, xliii. 43.   † *Ibid.* xv. 187.
‡ *Ibid.* xv. 189 ; xiv. 15.   § *Ibid.* xv. 543.

Christian church of this Bridegroom Christ." * That bridal love to Christ which Luther means is nothing else than the faith which relies upon Him utterly, and joyfully acquiesces in His will. " He will have me say from the depths of my heart ' I am thine.' *But this union and this marriage come about through the faith where I rely upon Him freely that He is mine."* † However tender our love for Christ might be, if it claimed to be anything else than thankful trust in the God who turns towards us in the Redeemer,‡ Luther would regard it as a devotion invented of men and savouring of the flesh.§ He knows indeed a love to God and Christ which God Himself awakens in us by making us happy and blessed through Christ. But the very earnestness of this experience makes him repudiate what is called the contemplative love of God in bitterest language : he says: " It is sheer hypocrisy for a man to creep into a corner and think ' Oh, I will love God. Oh, how dearly I love God, He is my Father. Oh, how affectionate I am to God,' and so forth." || Ritschl has shown how

* Enlangen edition, xv. 547. Luther closes these discussions concerning love to Christ the Bridegroom with the characteristic turn : " The whole of the Christian life consists in these two things : Believe in God and Christ His Son ; help thy neighbour ; the whole Gospel teaches this." *Cf.* xlvi. 154 ; l. 253 ; xxxv. 209.

† *Ibid.* xiv. 229 ; *cf.* Ritschl, " Geschichte des Pietismus," II. 32, and III. 212.

‡ *Cf.* a passage quoted above, ix. 38.

§ Erlangen edition, xlvi. 247.

|| *Ibid.* xiv. 172 ; *cf.* xxxv. 334. "No one shall taste Deity save as He wills to be tasted ; and thus He wills : to wit, that he shall be looked upon in the humanity of Christ. If thou dost not find the Deity thus thou shalt never rest. Hence, let them go on speculating and talking about contemplation, how everything is a wooing of God,

soon the tendency arose among the imitative followers
of Luther to find the Reformer lacking in this respect,
and to turn back to the pseudo-Augustinian writings
of the Middle Ages for more satisfying food.   Ritschl
has proved this so thoroughly that his opponents contradict him in general, but they do not try to confute
him in detail.*

§ 20. *The Historical and the Exalted Christ in the Life of Faith.*

It is clear that Luther knew the error of misusing
what was really the strongest possible expression for the
act of faith, namely, love to God and Christ, by making
it an expression for something that was utterly worthless.
This utterly worthless thing was the so-called "contemplative life," which Luther had found to be the
highest spiritual enjoyment which monastic life knows.
It is not of course difficult for an imaginative person so
to conjure up the Person of Christ before himself that
the picture shall take a kind of sensuous distinctness,
and then the ground is ready for the contemplative
love to Christ.   Some one thinks he sees Jesus Himself,
and *consequently* begins to commune with Him.   But
what such a person communes with in this fashion is
not Christ Himself, but a picture that the man's own
imagination has put together.   It is of no use to object

and how we are always having a foretaste of eternal life, and how
spiritual souls set about their life of contemplation.   But do not thou
learn to know God thus, I charge thee."

* *Cf.* Ritschl, " Geschichte des Pietismus," II. 1 ; IV. passim.

that the imagination itself is led and is made fertile by
what has been given to the soul by the Christ of history.
No doubt this is often the case with those who cultivate
this contemplative love.   And indeed it is quite true
that every Christian who is united with Christ through
experience of God's love does find such a picture arising
in his mind; and the picture is also something truly
sacred to him as a fruit of the new life which Christ
has created within him.   But such a picture does not
bring us the possibility of communion with Christ.

For, first, life is not in this picture, but in the
historical Christ.   It is in this latter that we trace the
power which makes us certain of God and shows itself
to be the working of God upon us.   Even if there
arises a picture of Christ in our minds in consequence
of this experience, we are not to detach the picture
from its foundations and look to it independently for
the bestowal of divine life.   Such an undertaking would
be nothing else than man's flight from God's presence.
It is not the product of our imagination that has power
over us, but that portrait of Jesus the form of which
He Himself has fixed in the faith created by Him and
handed down to us in the New Testament.   From
that alone does the Redeemer's power proceed, laying
hold upon us, so that we are compelled to recognise in
Him the God full of love and faithfulness, who is thus
seeking us out in our earthly abandonment.   Of course
I can also say concerning my dead father that God
sought me out and blessed me richly in all that He gave
me through my father; and yet of a surety I should
not have seen the hand of God in that if my Christian

training had not shown me the historical Christ, and set free my innermost life. Of this Christ that tradition hands down to us, we can say "In Thy light do we see light." His appearance is for us the fact which makes this world God's world, and we can say that of nothing else. In Him alone does that God come to meet us, in the knowledge of whom we can understand for the first time the divine significance which all other facts have for our life.

But all this of course appears but a poor affair to those who follow the monastic sort of worship of imaginative pictures of Christ. They desire, they say, a personal relation with the Christ who is personally present to them now. So they object that the historical Christ is separated from us by many centuries, and that we come into immediate contact only with the after influences that He has left; hence towards Him we can only feel that quiet gratitude which we feel towards all human greatness in the past. To this we reply that this is simply the plea of unbelief, whose dim vision sees only the natural in history, and not the God who is now laying hold of us in that history. At the moment when our understanding of the historical Christ makes us see the Living God, we certainly do not think of the centuries that intervene between ourselves and the earthly life of Christ. That is the true presence of God in our hearts when we experience how the tidings He gives us through Christ place the world and our sin beneath our feet. And this is the presence of Christ which we can *experience* in true communion with God, when His appearance in history comes home to our hearts as the most important thing in all the world. We Christians cannot experience any other presence of God and Christ, and we desire no other.

Of course, we may be reminded of those hymns which tell of the " sweetness of Jesus," and which certainly seem to point to a presence of Jesus in quite another sense, and to a much closer communion with Him ; and Luther himself spoke of what it is " to taste the sweetness of God." But Luther by no means understood by this some quite peculiar enjoyment which we are to get by sore striving after it in addition to that inner redemption which the understanding of God's revelation gives us in our troubles ; he meant rather just this experience of struggling faith.* God becomes sweet to him ; that means that the Christian trusting in Him has no more fear, and so knows that he has been delivered by Him from all his trouble.† In the same way, then, must we expound the expression " the sweetness of Jesus," whenever the Reformer uses it ; he means by it joy in Christ *the Redeemer*. At the foundation of all this lies the experience that our recognition of what His actual appearance in history means to us makes us new men. Luther can never have meant by that expression any tender communion of mere imagination with the " most beauteous of the children of men." If we seek God or Christ in our imagination, then we deliberately withdraw ourselves from that reality in which God desires to meet us. Such flight from the Living God was no worship of

---

* *Cf*. Erlangen edition, xiv. 77 f.
† *Cf*. xiv. 85 ; also xv. 107.

God in Luther's opinion.   It is a mistake to suppose
that Luther sought to have such a personal relationship
to the exalted Christ.   So far as I know, there is
no single sentence where Luther says anything of the
sort.   On the contrary, there are numerous passages in
which Luther discusses the lordship of the exalted
Christ within His own people as something removed
far above the sphere of mere emotion, and where he
describes it as the object of the reflective thought of
faith.*

* To give a small selection, we draw the reader's attention to a few
of Luther's discussions on the following subjects: Seeking Christ:
Erlangen edition, xlviii. 316, 321 ; x. 189.   Receiving Christ: vii.
156 f. ; xii. 73 f. ; xv. 155 ; xvi. 432.   Putting on Christ: vii. 39–42,
316 ; l. 136.   Having Christ: xvi. 494 ; x. 256 ; xiv. 335.   Christ's
life in us : viii. 39 ; xi. 5 ; xvi. 435.   Christ's dwelling in the heart :
ix. 272 ff. ; xii. 162, 288, 313 ; xlix. 313.   Christ's rule within us : xvi.
470 ; viii. 193 ; x. 12 ; xii. 179, 203 ; xv. 25–32, 188, 230 ; xxii. 66 ;
xviii. 39 ; xi. 80 ; xii. 47 ; xvi. 318.   A feast with Christ and Christ's
bride : x. 145 ; xi. 204 ff., 231 ; xiv. 257 ; xv. 135 f., 155, 374, 490, 494,
543 f., 554.   Fellowship with Christ : x. 256 ; li. 361, 474.

In these discussions it is clear enough that Luther was very far
from thinking of what men nowadays say they prize as a personal
relationship with Christ.   And Luther recognises the presence of the
Christian brotherhood only, " where there are such people as hold it
for truth that Christ is so near to us that He talks and deals with us
through the Word and the sacraments without my seeing it, and yet
while I see clearly the manner of life that is learned there " (Erlangen
edition, xx. 1, 510).   But such "holding as true" follows for Luther
from the significance which the historical appearance grasped in faith
had gained for him.   None of the expressions which Luther uses to
show how near Christ is to His own, mean that the Christian perceives His nearness as he perceives that of a man who is present to
his senses.   They are not expressions used to describe an experience
coming to us with sensuous evidence ; but they express rather a
thought which arises as we reflect accurately concerning faith ; and
the particular thought here concerned arises from the experience we
have as we come into relation with the Christ of history.

Of course, it may be said that surely a man's inner life belongs as much as anything else to the reality by which he is affected, and that it is, indeed, the most important element in that reality; that consequently we may regard a meeting of the soul with God which takes place entirely within the inner life as the most important experience of a pious soul. But our inner life consists in working out and realising the value of our relationships to the actual world, and, above all, of our relationships to other men and to that historical course of events to which our own existence is due. Our consciousness is real in any case only as a power which orders the various circumstances around itself. In the same way the inner life of the personal spirit, founded as it is upon the idea of an unconditioned value, is real only when it has spiritual sovereignty over the existing worldly situation. It is in that kind of life that we must find God; and Christians find Him first of all in the appearance of Christ, and then in all events which help to build up our inner life. The man who seeks for an inner life of some other sort is seeking to withdraw himself from reality into the realm of imagination. This may be permissible to other devout persons, but to the Christian it is forbidden. For him the power which decides his fate is and acts in the real world. The unbeliever, indeed, may talk slightingly of our historical relation to Christ, but the believer sees therein the Almighty arms with which God lifts him to His heart. If there be any Protestant Christian who is inclined to seek the joys of so-called contemplative love to Christ, even he will hardly

deny, on a little reflection, that he has an incomparably
higher experience when he sees God coming to save us
in the historical event of Christ's life in the real world,
than when he cherishes nothing more than an indefinite
feeling of God's nearness, or has his emotion roused by
a picture of Christ created by the imagination. The
life-creating power which we need daily does not come
from a picture in our imagination, but forces itself
upon us from the real world in which God has placed
us, and which we are to understand and take to heart.

We find, then, that such sensuous contemplation turns
its back on the real Christ. But, in the second place,
that contemplative love to Christ which is supposed to
gaze on Him as something alive and present, takes away
from the Christian hope of a future perfection. The
Christian lives by faith and not by sight. He may have
a strong desire to depart and be with Christ ; hence he
is aware that Christ is not visibly present to him now.
The picture which we are able to make of Christ now,
exhibits only faint traces of that glory which we shall
some time see in Him. Therefore we will not cling to
that picture, but hold fast by the power which the Christ
of history has to set free our souls, so that we become
aware of God. That work of Christ upon us fills with
the longing to come some day nearer to Him. If any
assert that they have already this sort of communion
with Christ, and that they cling with all their love to a
Christ whom they can already see as with bodily vision,
then we cannot but have the impression that these good
people are injuring their Christian hope for the future.
What the Christian can see at present points always to

something away beyond itself, The Christian's life of
faith does not culminate in a sensuous vision, but in
thoughts which point to a future of immeasurable glory.

Thirdly, this contemplative love to Christ refuses to
find in Him that very blessing by which alone He
becomes our Redeemer, namely, the way to the Father.
It is true that all who fasten such "contemplative"
affection upon such a picture as they have made of
Christ, may also at the same time preserve a proper
attitude towards Christ Himself. But as far as the
production of that contemplative love is concerned, it is
not Christ whom they allow to lead and redeem them.
That sort of love to Christ has nothing to do with what
He Himself desires to work in us. Instead of being
lifted up by Christ to the God who at once humbles us,
and makes us free by reliance on His love, we remain
clinging, with tender feelings, natural and easy to us,
to something which was given us only in order to lead
us forward. We may deck our picture of Jesus with
the predicate of deity, but that makes no difference; for
whenever we seek in Him something other than that
Almighty Will and Love which actually makes us free,
then we cling to the human in Jesus and do not come
to God. " Although Christ Himself is truly God, and
is enough for the man who relies on Him, *yet He always
leads us to the Father;* so that no one may *remain
clinging to the humanity,* as the disciples did before His
Passion, or be unmindful of the deity above the humanity.
For we must let *Christ in His humanity be to us a way,
a sign, a work of God, through which we come to God."**

* Erlangen edition, vii. 73.

Do we not then believe that Christ lives and rules?
And if we do believe this in real earnest, must we not
then suppose that we can commune with Him? And if
we may have this communion, who would forbid a Christian aspiring to attain the same? When now we come
to discuss this simple and yet most pressing question,
we must first of all be careful that we be loyal and that
we hold to the way of faith. We must not be troubled
by hearing it often said in the Church and by Christians
whom we cordially esteem, that the most important
.hing is that every man come into personal relationship
with the living Saviour and so commune with Him. If
we were to follow such teachers implicitly, we should be
the slaves of men. We have rather to ask how it is
that our own faith comes to conceive of Jesus Christ as
living and present with us.

Our faith combines the certainty that God touches
us in the Christ of history with inward surrender to the
God who thus reveals Himself to us. The exercise of
this fait. implies, then, that God is communing with
us, and we with Him. But God is present to us only
for this reason, that we see in Him the Father of Jesus
Christ. As soon as we try to find our way in the world
without Christ, we have no clear conception of God's
nature and become uncertain of His reality. Only when
we are in the grasp of Christ are we powerfully impressed
with the sense that God is working upon us. Of course
we may be aware, even apart from Christ, that we are
dependent upon an infinite Power; but without Christ
we should not be lifted to the certainty that within this
force dominating all things there dwells the will of One

who is a God who makes strong man's feeble craving
for the riches of personal life and leads it to its goal.
We reach that certainty only when we discover the inner
life of Jesus and find therein that Power which inwardly
overwhelms us, making us despair of all our old gods,
but making us trust Him instead. We find ourselves
in the presence of God, because we cannot think of the
personal life of Jesus as something that could ever be
given over to annihilation. God is to us the Will
which lives in and moves all that is real; and that
Will shields the person of Jesus and His hopes of life
with a Father's love. But now, if the true work of
God be to bring the Person of Jesus to perfection, then
the same faith which sees that God is present, must
also grasp the thought that Jesus lives now, perfected
and freed from all earthly limits. He is now in perfection all that He desired to be, namely, our Redeemer
by the power of His personal life over ours. On this
thought rests the Christian's belief that he sees the
hand of Christ in everything which this Power causes
him to experience; and hence also springs his conviction that the exalted Lord knows how near we have
come to Him, or how far we are from Him.

But Christ, even as the exalted Lord, still remains
our Mediator. Hence the thought that Christ lives
and rules now is based indeed on our faith, but it must
be controlled and regulated by consideration of those
means by which we are led to God. If any man does
not so use the thought of Christ's presence, then it is
certainly not a thought born of his own faith, but
something that has been borrowed from others and

that he is using improperly. But if, on the contrary, this idea is simply the legitimate outcome and completion of our faith in God as the Father of Jesus Christ, then our confidence grows all the stronger in the Power that came into history with the life of Jesus. That saving Power stands in continual conflict with all that tends to injure or oppress our personal life. And even when, at times, we see no victories or no results from this conflict, we are able to endure because we remember that the Lord, who has overcome, is still with us with all His human sympathies. When once the thought has taken root in us that He makes our affairs His own, and that we belong to Him, as the members of the body to the head, then that thought opens up in us a channel for all the true power of redemption ; it suffers the personal life of Jesus to have free course in us. Nevertheless all is subordinate to the great end, namely, that we come to God ; in whose presence we receive power to overcome the world and to live in the eternal. We desire to commune with God ; the way to that communion is to hold to the Christ of history and live in the confidence that the exalted One is with us.

A second consideration, however, must be added. We cannot speak of a communion with the exalted Christ. Nor do we find such communion spoken of in the New Testament, apart from the visions therein recorded. We can commune with God because He touches us and reveals Himself to us in definite facts whose contents have the power of creating faith in us. God is revealed to us ; the risen Christ is hidden from us. We do think of Him, indeed, as taking part in our

battles and victories with all His human sympathy and
power, but this is strictly only a thought of faith.
There is no actual fact known to us which could produce this faith by its undoubted reality and its power to
convince even one who had as yet no faith.[41] It is not
right or wise to say that the resurrection of Jesus is
such a fact for us who live to-day. It comes to us
altogether from the report of others. It is just as useless to appeal to the power which the spirit of Christ
exercises in history. For the purpose of our present
discussion that is a poor staff on which to lean. For
what we observe in the great process of the world's
working, or at the death-bed of a Christian, are things
which do indeed quicken a believer, but certainly they
have not power to disclose to a man the exalted Christ.
Those who see in these things manifestations of the
exalted Christ, must be already in possession of the
faith which gives birth to the thought that Christ lives
and rules. Thus we can grasp the thought that the
exalted Christ is working upon us only when our faith
is already fully matured.

Quite otherwise do we think of God Himself, the
God who reveals Himself through the Christ of history.
For the personal life of Jesus can be grasped as a real
fact in history by a man who has no faith, or even after
the power of faith has been extinguished in such a man.
And it is because the invisible God uses this fact to
make men certain of Himself, that we can say, He
communes with us. In this fact of self-revelation He
reaches down into the realm of our earthly experience.
But we cannot say that of the exalted Christ. Hence

the believer must not try to fly beyond those limits
which are drawn around him while as yet his faith has
to conflict with earthly experiences. He must admit
that the risen Christ is still hidden from him. He may,
indeed, express a thought of his faith by saying that
Christ lives in him; but unless, like Paul, he can appeal
to visions, he may not say that he *experiences* the communion of the exalted Christ with himself.*

It is right for the believer to say of his ordinary conscious life within the limits of earthly experience: " So
far, however, as I still live in the flesh, I live in *faith* in
the Son of God." And it is just when we admit these
limits to our present experience, that our hopes for the
future become so strong that they hold the sovereignty
over our hearts in spite of the attractions of all earthly
comforts. The personal life of Jesus has then so worked
upon us that it has made us see the love of God in the
power of the real : and this makes of all that seemed
before to be utterly controlling us a means for our
eternal life. But if the personal life of Jesus has had this
influence upon us, then the thought that He lives and
rules in perfect bliss fills us with the longing to see Him
some time otherwise than as we see Him in the mirror
of history, and with other eyes than we see with to-day,
while the spirit still struggles to rise above the earth.

* No commentator worthy of mention has ever ventured to say
that the words "Your life is hid with Christ in God" (Col. iii. 3)
were written by their author concerning a communion with the
exalted Lord. These words express the idea born of faith, that the
life of the Christian, in consequence of his union with Christ, has its
hidden roots in God, and rests all its expectation of future glory on
Him.

This is the meaning of the Christian's hope in the future so far as we can understand it now. If we have felt how it fills us with a sense of freedom to see clearly the divinely marvellous character of the person of Jesus, then the prospect that some time we shall experience His power in unrestrained and immediate personal communion with Him will release us from our bondage to all earthly troubles and pleasures. It makes no difference in this respect, whether the Christian expects the second coming of the Lord as the primitive Christian brotherhood expected it, or whether his hope is, as ours must be, the prospect of being taken up to Him. Every Christian needs, for the sake of his inner life, that his hope in the future shall be rich and clear : in this good hope, which we can understand although it concerns life beyond this life, and which comes close to our hearts, there lies a power which we cannot do without while we stray and sorrow in our Christian life here on earth. What God gives us in Christ is meant to render us so peaceful and glad that we get free from all anxiety about our life, and hence can live in true righteousness ; and part of this gift is the fact that our faith assures us of the prospect of future enjoyment of personal fellowship with Jesus. And when the Christian experiences the elevating influence of this desire for the risen Lord and finds how he is relieved from his burdens, and yet pledged to duty by this confidence in future fellowship with Him, then he understands how Christ has risen for our justification.

Such then is the relation with the risen Christ into which we are actually brought by our faith. The

relation comes to us through faith, not through experience. We shall never share in the emancipating
power of the thought that we are united with Christ in
this way, if we try to get it simply by deduction of the
idea from particular passages of Scripture, and by then
deliberately asserting that it is an actual objective
experience, and that we really feel something which all
the time can as yet be only a belief. And yet the prevailing theology of our time seeks to lead us to practice
both these evils. Most men, indeed, only get as far as
using the phrases of this cultus, while their imagination
is not strong enough to realise its fancies. Unfortunately, it is certain that there is also another and an
appalling result : truthfulness is blunted, and men are
learning to forget that the most important matter,
and the hardest, is to become certain of communion
with the living God. On the other hand, it is also
perilous for theologians to try to describe very exactly
the exalted life of Christ for the sake of checking
mere sensuous sharpness of conception. However ten-
derly this may be done,* it leads us aside from the
main point, namely, that we must hold fast to the
clearest possible representation of the personal life of
Jesus which we have got by study of the Christ of
history, for that is the power which redeems us.
There is no need for toiling to define how Jesus
rules as the exalted One with almighty power; a
thing that can be attempted only by negative statements, for it is beyond our grasp; the all-important

* *Cf.* especially A. Schweizer's " Christian Doctrine of Faith "
(" Christliche Glaubenslehre ") ii. 1, 226.

point is that the vision of His person shall lift us up
to God.

§ 21. *Communion with God as an Experience and as an Act.*

All these forms of piety already considered first gain a
Christian meaning when they become an exercise of the
faith awakened in us by God, through His revelation, by which we are made new men ; and it is clear,
from every point of view, that we cannot commune
with God in what we ourselves initiate, but only in
receiving and enjoying what God gives to us. Indeed,
He draws us to Himself just by giving us the mastery
over those things which, without His help, would de-
press and destroy us. We receive from Him our
strength for such sovereignty by coming to understand
His revelation, *i.e.*, His turning towards us. Our act of
receiving this gift takes place when we consciously turn
towards God, and when we understand the tidings He
gives us ; and then we remain in fellowship with Him
by making use of the gift we have received. The receiving is utterly inseparable from the use of what is
received. If the divine gift were a power we did not
know, which worked upon us with some concealed power
of nature, then, in the first place, our reception of it
would certainly be no communion with God. We should
rather have to distinguish that communion with God
in which our own personal will takes its share from this
strange process wherein we should thus be supposed to
undergo unconsciously something we could not comprehend. And, secondly, the use of such a divine gift

would certainly be quite distinct from its reception. But, in reality, since we come into a right state of dependence upon God by our understanding of His act of self-revelation, we receive a gift that we possess only when we make use of it. Such an attitude towards God implies that purifying and freeing of the inner life, that new purpose and courage, which Luther calls faith. But this gift of faith is always also the life and activity of the man who receives it. We cannot stand in the inner attitude of God-given faith without setting to work at once to get for ourselves a clear conception as to how the love of God is seeking to bless us by the very condition in which we are situated at the moment. Clearly, in this case, no line can be drawn between our reception of the divine gift and our use of it. Faith, then, is of a truth ours only when it concerns the realities amid which we live, and, of course, as soon as it thus becomes ours, we have evidently already begun to work out the faith, and to reap its fruits. Our communion with God, then, gains in intensity, according as he makes us richer, and we receive more from Him ; and this is illustrated in the fact that if we will apply our faith to all the various relationships of life, and let it establish us more and more firmly in the world, then all the more closely does it bring us into fellowship with God. If our trust in God's Fatherly Providence helps us to find our way through the world, then the fact that we are in the world does not separate us from God, but just this fact brings us into His Presence. If we regard the cares which befall us as the cross He lays upon us, and so bear them patiently, then surely this conduct cannot be called renunciation of the joy of communion with God, but we are rather led by those very cares into His very Presence, to find Him the source of a peace which passeth all understanding. We are only too apt to imagine that in order to commune with God we must become ghosts, as it were, half withdrawn from the world. But God's way to lead us to Himself rather leads us right into the reality in which for His own ends He has placed us, and in which He desires to make us free and blessed.

§ 22. *Moral Activity in Communion with God.*

If, then, joy in God's gift and the thankful exercise of the inner freedom it furnishes us lead us into the presence of God, then the moral activity of the Christian forms part of his communion with God. For the Christian such occupation is not a foreign service, to which God sends him out and away from His Presence; it is, itself, worship. We must make clear to ourselves this characteristic of Christian morality which Luther was never tired of dwelling upon. We have already seen (pp. 205–212) why the Christian can commune with God only when he desires what is good. He must seek to live in the Eternal, or he does not turn sincerely to the God who desires to bring men to eternal life. But we also observed that simply to desire the good cannot of itself be counted communion with God. But if the Christian's active interest in his duties puts him only in the attitude where it is possible for him to find God, this very activity, especially as related to the world, being not itself communion with God, seems therefore to interrupt this communion; and so Christian morality seems to be a special sphere of life alongside of Christian piety, but not identical with it. So it comes to this, that in his communion with God the Christian is supposed to experience dependence upon God, while when he faces the duties of his calling he is brought rather to the consciousness of his own freedom. We are warned, however, against such a separation when we bear in mind that we are united to God in inward submission to Him only when our will lives in His will. For only in the inward attitude, whereby he seeks to fulfil the command to love his neighbour as himself, does a man live under the Fatherly rule of God or commune with Him. In such activity the Christian must lose the impression that the law is a burden, and feel that duties are rather a gift from God which makes his heart rejoice. The preaching of Jesus concerning the Kingdom of God results directly in the propositions of the First Epistle of John, namely, that he who has true love stands in conscious communion with God through that very fact, and knows Him and abides in Him. But we use these testimonies to the unity of Christian life aright only when we seek to understand them in their truth. Now although Luther so often referred to these truths, and came back upon them, yet he never attained such an understanding of them as would have enabled him to make a clear theological statement concerning them.*

* Luther himself frequently admitted this to be the case. *Cf.* Erlangen edition, xv. 392, 417ff; xlix. 327; xiii. 198; xviii. 58ff.

But he set down many vigorous thoughts on the matter, which may put us in the right way of solving the question.

§ 23. *Faith as the Power to Will the Good.*

In the treatise "On the Freedom of a Christian Man," the discussions in part second, concerning the moral activity of the Christian, are far less clear and sure than the magnificent description of the riches of faith in the first part. Indeed at the beginning he even infers the necessity of good works for the Christian from consideration of his earthly imperfection.* Still he has much to say on the thought that good works are the fruits of faith ; † and later on he constantly repeats this. This gives a satisfactory answer to the question as to what significance the moral activity of the Christian has for his faith, or for his communion with God. Only we must beware of the remarkable one-

---

* *Cf.* Opp. var. arg. IV. 235 : " Si fides omnia facit, et sola ad justitiam satis est, cur ergo praecepta sunt bona opera ? Otiabimur ergo et nihil operabimur fide contenti ? " Respondeo : " Vere quidem sic haberet res ista, si penitus et perfecte interni et spirituales essemus, quod non fiet nisi in novissimo die ; donec in corpore vivimus, non nisi incipimus et proficimus, quod in futura vita perficietur. Ad hanc partem pertinet, Christianum esse omnium servum et omnibus subjectum." (If faith does all, and alone is sufficient for justification, why then are good works required ? Shall we be at ease and do nothing, content with faith ? I reply, so should it be, indeed, if we were deeply and perfectly spiritual at heart, as we shall not be until the Last Day ; while we live in the body, we only begin and carry out that which shall be perfected in the future life. Hence, it is our Christian task to-day to be servant of all and subject to all.)

† *Ibid.* 241ff.

sidedness to which Luther let himself be kept subject in his discussion of the thought.

If perfect moral conduct, or actual desire for what is good, is a fruit of faith, then faith must give men the power to submit with joy to the claims of duty. On this point Luther was quite clear. He not only asserts that true love is impossible to the natural man,* but he is also able to tell us what separates men from what is morally good. "Now this is the sum of the law, thou shalt be friendly, sweet and kind in heart, words, and works ; and if one should even take thy life, suffer it nevertheless with goodness, and thank thy Lord." † But a man fulfils this law only when he does his work for the sake of the pleasure he has in it.‡ Otherwise his heart is not in it. But the law desires to have the heart, and where it is not fulfilled heartily, such fulfilment does not hold good before God. § The law is to be fulfilled freely ; but freely here means, "without any expectation of obtaining anything thereby." ‖ We are to desire only the realisation of the good itself or the manifestation of love. The man who turns good work to his own profit does no good work at all.¶ All this shows clearly that the law demands from man what is impossible. For however sincerely a man may acknowledge that the moral law has a right to unreserved obedience, yet in his secret desires he follows that vital instinct which compels him to take circumstances into account and to estimate the

---

* *Cf.* Erlangen edition, xiii. 176 ; xlvi. 262.   † *Ibid.* xiii. 177.
‡ *Ibid.* x. 94 ; xii. 285.   § *Ibid.* xiv. 174.   ‖ *Ibid.* xii. 348.
¶ *Ibid.* vii. 176, 295f.

profit and loss of his conduct. And seeing that he is always trying to gain satisfaction for this vital instinct amid the world with all its power over his fears and hopes, he learns to look on love as a duty that he cannot understand, for he is told it is to be shown to his neighbour free and for naught. We see what a man makes of the command to love under such circumstances, when we observe how he endeavours to purchase God's love by fulfilling his commandments. Luther ruthlessly lays bare the moral deadliness of such an endeavour. A fulfilment of the law in this sense is sheer hypocrisy. By the good works we do as a service to God, and therefore as a foundation for our own blessedness, we turn our backs on all that is good and destroy the life of the soul. " Dost thou find in thee some task, whereof thou thinkest thou needest it for the soul's salvation, then tread thou that underfoot. Be glad you do this as if you were treading down all devils, and rest thou not until thou dost get free from all such nature and work. Strive that thy life may be of comfort, profit, and service, not to thyself but to thy neighbour alone. *Accursed be the man who lives and works for himself ;* for Christ Himself would not do His own will, or live to Himself." *

But how are we to get free from the power of that natural instinct which compels a man to live for himself ? Were there no such deliverance, then we could indeed see what was morally necessary, but we should find it to be a power which only repelled us. In Luther's view the man who has found Jesus Christ and under-

* Erlangen edition, xiv. 59.

stood Him as the message of God to morally impotent creatures is lifted above such a fate. For the redemption which follows from the understanding of Christ is able also to do away our natural opposition to what is good. The thought that man must be redeemed and restored to pure love by the grace of God was an element, perverted indeed, yet present, in the tradition of the Church in which Luther grew up. But up to that time this thought had been developed only in the direction of inquiries as to the relation between renewing grace and the free will of man. It had not yet been perceived that all such inquiries are necessarily profitless. Even Luther himself did not see this; but he was saved from troubling about such necessarily fruitless questions by the simple fact that his eyes were always open to the real need of earnest men, and he saw clearly what sort of powers could give a man deliverance in such cases. He had no time to discuss the simple question how renewal of grace is possible without injury to the freedom of the human will, because he had to show, as he was able to do, how this renovation actually takes place. He was the first to describe this, and thus he led the way for Protestant theology to knowledge which it is certainly a harder task to gain than it is to thread the riddles of that other old scholastic question.

We know that the ordinary instinctive way in which men seek the satisfaction of all the needs of life makes it impossible to submit honestly to the demands of duty, and we see also the falsity of the childish idea of the mystics that this instinct should be extirpated; it follows, then, that we can only seek moral deliverance in a true and perfect satisfaction of our craving for life. If we do good only when we do it " without fear of punishment and without seeking regard," * then the man who is to be morally free must have his heart so placed that he shall be beyond all fear or desire, and especially that he neither fear the world,† nor depend upon it.‡ For so long as we remained in such bondage to the world we should necessarily seek our own advantage. But we must thus become rich and strong, if we are to be able to love our neighbours.§ And it is only a quiet and peaceful heart that has the true power to work.‖ Now if a man can learn to rejoice in God and to be satisfied in His grace,¶ then that will be a receiving of just that inner treasure through which he can live freely for others. " Thou must first have heaven and be thyself already richly blessed, ere thou canst do good works." ** Works that are really good are done " free and for naught, as by those that are already blessed and possess already for themselves the inheritance of God through faith." †† Now such a feeling of perfect inner contentment is possible to the Christian, only in so far as he understands that God turns to him in Christ. The hour when we enter into such communion with God gives us an inner freedom wherein we desire nothing more than what we already have.‡‡

* Erlangen edition, x. 96.   † *Ibid.* xvi. 216.
‡ *Ibid.* viii. 266 ; xlvii. 24.   § *Ibid.* xi. 181.
‖ *Ibid.* ix. 72f.   ¶ *Ibid.* vii. 169.
** *Ibid.* vii. 174.   †† *Ibid.* x. 213.
‡‡ *Ibid.* xv. 42. "If thou knowest how thou hast through Christ a kind and gracious God, who desires to forgive thy sins, and to

Here then the Christian faith proves itself to be the power necessary for moral conduct. Being real communion with God, it brings such a joy in life that we can feel ourselves to be redeemed. For we have in it a realm of peace wherein we can take refuge from every disquietude ; and in whatever circumstances we may be we enter this realm whenever the fact that Christ is there for us rises in our mind and comes home to our hearts. We comprehend that in this fact the Power which is over all things touches and blesses us ; and at this touch there flies away that ban of the world against which the natural man struggles in vain, the necessity, namely, of looking on the world's gifts as the only means to life. This is redemption, that Christ creates within us a living joy, whose brightness shines even in the eye of sorrow, and tells the world of a power it cannot comprehend. And the power that works redemption is the fact that in our world there is a Man whose appearance can at every moment be to us the mighty Word of God, snatching us out of our troubles and making us feel that God desires to have us for His own, and so setting us free from the world and from our own natural impulses. Then, when we have been made so rich and strong, we may afford to forget all about that " sought-for love " which likes to recline amid the sweetness of things, and may busy ourselves with that outflowing love that shares its inner wealth with the needy and undeserving.*   The

remember them never more : and if thou knowest how thou art now a child of eternal bliss, a Lord with Christ over heaven and earth, then has thou nothing more to do but to go on and serve thy neighbour."

* Erlangen edition, xviii. 282-6.

redemption given in Christian faith can bring a man even so far that "divine love begins to well up and out from within him." * The "Augsburg Confession " (Art. xx. 36) does not say too much when, replying to the objection that the Protestants hinder good works, it says that Protestant teaching shows how we are able to do them ; for the command to love can only be fulfilled in a moment of religious exaltation ; in other words, in the state of faith. The old Church used to say that the grace of God renews a man by filling him with divine strength, and this is not untrue ; but it is too indefinite. It is now replaced by this full expression of the Christian's actual experience : "The divine birth is nothing other than faith." †

§ 24. *Faith as the Impulse to Will the Good.*

Luther is able to show, then, that faith gives us the *power* to will the good, and he shows us how it does so. But with this declaration he has not yet shown us all that is implied in the thought that good works are the fruit of faith ; for if this thought be true, then there must lie in Christian faith, *not only the power to will what is good, but also the impulse to do so.* The real interests of faith find satisfaction only in moral activity ; otherwise, indeed, good works would not be the fruit in which the proper instincts of faith reach their goal. Now the highest interests of faith are expressed in the words : " Whom have I in heaven but Thee, and there is none upon earth that I desire beside Thee " ; that is,

* Erlangen edition, xi. 339.   ‡ *Ibid.* x. 216 ; vii. 178 ; xlvii. 375.

faith seeks simply communion with God. But if it could not be shown that this longing, when rightly understood, impels us to moral effort,[2] it would be an admission that the moral activity of the Christian actually interrupts his communion with God, just because it does not arise out of faith.

Has Luther also *made clear such an impulse to moral action?* Usually he traces back the joy which the believer has in the fulfilment of the Divine commands to thankfulness to God and Christ. This can be interpreted as if the content of His commands had no significance for faith, but only the fact that that content is ordained by God. But Luther did not fix himself to this perverted conception. According to that view good works which were foreign to the Christian in his natural condition are a divinely pointed out way of paying God back. This idea is just what Luther warns men against. We are not to do this or that work in order to pay God back for His love, "but only by believing on Christ does man step out of his lost condition." * God desires nothing further for Himself than that we trust Him and accepts what He gives. † "Thou durst do God no good, only take good from Him." ‡ Yet he does say, too, that thanksgiving is the sacrifice and only work that we can and ought to do towards God.§ Thus everything depends on a right understanding of thanksgiving. The ideas of Luther which have just been cited raised this question. But in this connection so

---

* Erlangen edition, xlvii. 19.
† *Ibid.* x. 108 ; xiii. 205 ; xviii. 20 ; xix. 12 ; li. 362 ; ii. 307.
‡ *Ibid.* x. 25.   § *Ibid.* viii. 90.

far as I know Luther has not done what was needful. I know no discussion in Luther in which he guards the impulse to thanksgiving against the conception that it signifies the desire to requite God, to do Him good. Nor has this point been treated in later Protestant ethics in connection with the customary use of the thanksgiving *motif*. But we only thank God aright when once we have let ourselves be united to Him through what He offers us in Christ. The proper thanksgiving is joyful turning to God. Even in respect of other men, we do not thank them by trying to pay them back for their kindness. Such requital can always look like wishing to be quits with them, to be under no obligation. We are really thanking them only when we begin to kindle with desire for that thing which their love was seeking, namely, personal fellowship between us and them. We show them real thanks only when we put ourselves to trouble and self-sacrifice in order to come into inward communion with them.

Thus the whole moral activity of the Christian must proceed under the form of thanksgiving such as that. In it the Christian must seek God Himself; in his loving intercourse with his neighbour he must be constantly filled with the thought that he is thus coming near to God. Then only has it a meaning to call his action a thanksgiving to God. And at the same time it is clear that a moral activity that has this origin is truly a fruit of faith. It springs from the natural impulse of faith and has its place within the life of religion or the communion of the Christian with God. It is, however, a vital question for Protestant Christianity whether or not this is the actual character of the moral activity of the Christian. For the fundamental proposition of Protestanism is that faith, this new attitude of man towards God, itself signifies redemption. This assertion obviously can be maintained only if the moral strength and freedom into which we are said to be redeemed, grows out of faith or is to be understood as the development of that religious experience. If that is not so, then one cannot say of redemption that it consists in God through His revelation bringing the sinner to deny himself and to trust Him. If such faith is really to make us new creatures, to make us redeemed men instead of men lost in the world, the natural impulse of faith must culminate in a Will in which is overcome the old powerlessness against the world and the law. Religious experience must come to its natural completion in the moral will. This connection between religion and morality is at least asserted by Protestant Christianity when moral conduct is called thanksgiving for the grace that has been experienced. Apart from this idea redemption has always to be conceived again in the manner of the Romish church. The two ideas that stand side by side there, then inevitably come to the front. In the first place, the Divine power that gives the Christian a tender heart and a strong will is looked for not in religious experience but in indefinable forces which remain something external to the inner life of the spirit that is set free by God's revelation. Redemption is then a magical process, and not the new purpose and courage that is born in the Christian when he meets with God in Christ. In the

second place, when the moral will cannot be comprehended as an expression of religious desire, there is
always a return to the idea that after the help of God's
grace has been received a man is, of himself, as a being
independent of God, to bring to pass what is good.
Protestant Christianity has found its safeguard against
these two representations, the one magical, the other
co-operative, in so far as it sees in the longing of faith
to thank God the fulfilment of the law, and the will
that produces the miracle of self-denial.

§ 25. *Luther is Defective as Regards this Point.*

But here there lies yet another task, in carrying out
which Protestant theology has perhaps been hampered
by the enduring impression of Luther's personality.
The thanksgiving with which we turn to God would be
ingratitude if it expressed anything else than desire
for fellowship with Him. If, therefore, the moral conduct of the Christian is to take the form of thanksgiving to God, the question arises whether we can make
it clear that the religious desire for God expresses itself
in the moral conduct of the Christian. Luther certainly
described the religious meaning of Christian morality in
its various colours with all the variety that he knew
from the experiences of his own rich inner life.* But
he did so casually. He did not make a special theo-

---

* *Cf.* K. Thieme. " Die Sittliche Triebkraft des Glaubens," an
investigation of Luther's theology. Leipzig, 1895. This book has
done the great service of showing for the first time with what a wealth
of imagination Luther has grasped this inner process of moral
liberation.

logical problem of the matter. On the contrary, his casual allusions to that important fact are cast entirely into the shade by the energy with which he opposed his own view to the former conception of Christian morality.

" Just as a living man cannot keep himself alive without moving, eating and drinking, and doing things, and because he is living it is impossible that such acts cease so that he has not to be ordered or driven to do such works, but does them just because he is alive ; so also nothing more is required for the performance of good works except to be told ' Only believe and thou wilt do all naturally of thyself.'   Therefore, it is not to be asked whether or not good works are to be performed, they are done spontaneously." *   This is the most important of Luther's ethical ideas. To this he was fondest of coming back when he touched on the problem of good works. What is in itself impossible to man, the fulfilling of the law, follows naturally when he has received in faith a new inner life, a new nature with impulses that are divine. It is therefore not at all needful to inquire how it happens that the heartfelt turning of the Christian to God passes over into will and action directed towards the world and towards men. A reflective theory of the inter-relation of spiritual experiences seems to be unnecessary when moral action is springing by a natural necessity from the inner life of a redeemed man. If faith gives the power to do good works it gives the impulse too. So

* Erlangen edition, xii. 175–6 ; other references in Thieme, " Die Sittliche Triebkraft des Glaubens," pp. 88, 243–5, 262–3.

that to distinguish between the power and the impulse, as we have done, has no meaning to the Christian. Both are one in the blessedness which faith brings with itself.[43]

Is this, however, really an adequate description of the inward connection between Christian faith and Christian morality? It would be were the moral activity of the Christian the effortless expression of his inward insight and strength. But in truth, so far as it springs from conscious will, that activity is a struggle with the constantly expanding moral task. Only when, as a whole, the life of the Christian is a struggle, do there come moments of effortless accomplishment. But these moments remain hidden from himself. Others rejoice in the involuntary expression of his sincerity and love. He himself can perceive such a revelation of God's spirit only in others. Without doubt Luther is right in regarding the good act that proceeds involuntarily from the believer as his highest and most effective moral achievement. But this strength of moral beauty will only be his whose life is an effort, who is oppressed by his duties. The good that comes freely from the heart is possible only as a fruit of faith. But this fruit ripens only in a faith that drives the whole conscious life into the channel of earnest moral endeavour. Thus when a special kind of moral conduct grows out of faith it is nevertheless something quite different from a process of Nature. The fruit of faith results from spiritual experiences and spiritual endeavour, so that it must be possible to make clear how the religious wealth of the Christian passes over into the soul-constraining knowledge of moral duty and the heartfelt desire to play one's part in life and minister to the needy. It must be possible to show to what extent the moral will of the Christian is sincere thanksgiving, that is, a desire for God that He Himself awakens, and therefore an element of religious experience.

§ 26. *The Inner Connection between Love to God and Love to our Neighbour.*

If, however, we wish to show how the moral will and achievements of the Christian lie within the sphere of his communion with God we must be able to set aside one weighty consideration. Is the Christian, then, to quench in his soul his inward sympathy for his work, for the object of his work, for the neighbour whom he serves? That certainly was not Luther's meaning. He called Christians who so understood the all-embracing command of love to God foolish saints, and held up to them the example of Christ who went about among men with love in His heart, who rejoiced in God's creatures, and shrank with horror from death.* Luther sees in the indifference to the world, cultivated by monks and nuns, a woeful perversion of human nature, which is the very opposite of the perfection to what God desires to lead us.† K. Thieme ‡ has rightly found fault with the discussion in the former edition of this

* Erlangen edition, xxxiv. 259–261 ; li. 290.
† *Ibid*. li. 438–9.
‡ " Die Sittliche Triebkraft des Glaubens," 1895, pp. 20, 298.

book for not guarding sufficiently against this distortion of the moral ideal. But the method of doing so which he suggests I consider to be a theological blunder, one which is often made, and always with the result of producing the reaction of mysticism in the Christian community.

" If the Christian is to love his neighbour then there must be inward and outward activities in which he thinks not of God but of his neighbour."* This is Thieme's leading idea. He wishes to show " that the command to love God with all the heart and with all the soul and with all the mind is compatible with love to one's neighbour." We may rest assured that we are agreed on this, that as Christians we are convinced that love to God and love to our neighbour go together. But the question is how ? Thieme holds that it is only the case if there are moments in which it is not love to God that fills the inner life of the Christian but the thought of our neighbour, sympathy with his need, delight in his existence and prosperity. Love to God and to our neighbour are to alternate in the heart. Communion with God cannot be continuous. It is inevitably interrupted by the claims our earthly environment makes upon our sympathies. God does not grudge us our joy in the world, least of all our delight in our neighbour. But, on the other hand, the Christian interrupts his communion with the world as regularly as possible by moments of religious reflection in which he experiences anew his relation to God and brings this expressly into consciousness. The experience of Pro-

* Thieme, *op. cit.* p. 26.

testant and Catholic Christians alike proves, as Thieme
rightly says, that God desires two kinds of conduct
from us which are not to be confused one with another,
and the interchange of which constitutes the rhythm of
the Christian life.

But is it possible that this rhythm should be
constituted by the succession in the waking life of consciousness of moments of conscious communion with God
by moments devoid of all conscious relation to God?
This is Thieme's view, and in support of it he appeals
to those words of Luther directed against the Romish
kind of devotion.   But as it seems to me, in this point
Thieme rather runs into danger of siding with Luther's
opponents.   What Luther contends against in these
words is nothing else than an artificial kind of devotion,
a piety which thinks it necessary to dislocate Nature in
order to win access to God.   The religious contemplation of which he speaks in the most disparaging terms
is not for this reason distasteful to him, because in it the
Christian sets aside times of quiet in order to call his
thoughts together in the presence of God.   For he himself would not have been able to live without getting
free in his inner chamber from the weight of his burdens
and receiving continually new power to overcome.   That
contemplation is an abomination to him because it is
an invention of men, and a product of the human heart,
because in it God and His creation are not recognised;
that is to say, the reality amid which God has set men
is despised and denied.*   The piety of the imagination
which thinks to fly to heaven by casting the world out

* Erlangen edition, xliii. 38-47.

of the heart, is, according to his harsh expression, sitting in the dirt. But this kind of piety is nevertheless simply to carry out with full religious energy the idea that Thieme considers true and thinks he finds in Luther. For if moral endeavour really interrupts the communion with God, it will become something distasteful to one who has discovered that it is worth while to sacrifice everything for the sake of having God. Even if he is bound by fetters of law to such endeavour, his heart will not be in it. In short, if the religious longing is strong within him, it will draw him to the habits of monasticism. He is bound to feel in the claims of the world upon his sympathies a power that seeks to keep him apart from God. This was not felt by Luther. And so he was entirely out of sympathy with the saying of the monk : " To him who goes about with men the angels cannot come." Luther's heartfelt joy in the world was however, possible, only because he felt it to be *religiously* justified. And the pious man can feel that joy in the world is religiously justified only if he realises that even communion with the world has a religious significance.

It is therefore false, and certainly not according to Luther's meaning, when Thieme asserts that the Christian must have his communion with God interrupted by moments of moral endeavour or of communion with the world, in which there is no seeking or finding of God, but only surrender to the world. Whenever Protestant piety is so understood, mysticism—that is, Catholic piety—is in the right in its opposition to it. For it is a defect to be willing for the sake of the world to restrict the impulses of religion. Assuredly that is not the intention. Hence the Protestant attitude to the world must be that the morally ordained communion with things visible is to be lived in as a necessary movement in the process of communion with the invisible God. God certainly demands two kinds of conduct from us which are not to be confused. We are first to turn towards the revelation we have received. We are secondly to stretch out for the revelation of God that waits beyond the goal of moral self-denial. The moral conduct of the Christian is not something else alongside of his religion, but is a particular form of his religious conduct.

§ 27. *The Foundation of a Christian System of Ethics.*

To make this clear is a most necessary task. Not to have carried it out is a theological defect in Luther, one we have no desire to reproach him with, but one which, nevertheless, we must not, like Thieme, ignore. It is not enough to say that love to our neighbour springs up naturally from the blessedness which the Christian has won by his faith. It has rather to be shown how truly faith itself gathers together all its own impulses into one energetic desire to love its neighbour. He who is truly blessed in his faith never wishes to get away from God. Conduct that is not a seeking for God would not be capable of being understood as an expression of his inmost motive, but only as an unaccountable lapse from his true ideal. Thus it must be clearly shown how far the natural impulse of one who is blessed in communion with God, is following the tendency towards that which makes him blessed when he gives himself in hearty surrender to his neighbour. This, as it appears to me, will let us see for the first time the characteristic meaning of Christian morality. Then at last a Christian system of ethics, to which the Reformation opened up the way, will come within the bounds of possibility.

But it is not sufficient to bring together a series of motives coloured by religion which are present and and active in Christian action. That has indeed its own worth and importance, and Thieme has rendered good service in showing us so clearly in what profusion such motives were present in Luther. If a person through faith takes up the right attitude to reality, then there presses in on his heart the fulness of all that God is desirous of saying to him through that reality. But these motives become non-religious if they are isolated, instead of being continuously referred back to the one fundamental motive, namely, the Christian's desire to be with God and to receive at His hands. For if the inward process is not regarded as having this form, the Christian is setting himself up as independent of God in so far as he keeps himself apart from Him. This is the case even in the simplest of all these motives, one in which the religious sense seems to be most secure, namely, in the impulse to thank God for His benefits that we have received. If that is anything else than an expression of longing after God Himself, it makes God a Being on an equal footing with ourselves against whom we desire to assert our own independence. The irreligious nature of this attitude is increased when in such circumstances the further idea enters that we will do good to other men because they belong to God. "For God's sake" expresses a religious motive only when it means that I see in the need of my neighbour the nearness of the God whose holy power sets me a-tremble, and in whom I seek satisfaction for my hunger after strength and life. On the other hand, "for God's sake" is a phrase leading to godlessness if it does not glow through and through with the feeling that here I have to do with my inmost self and with that power over my life that I cannot escape. If this sense is lacking, the idea takes the form that I will be careful to give God due consideration. But this means to think of God without realising what He is for me, the highest good, and the power upon which I altogether depend. When I reflect on that, and so take up a religious attitude, it will not occur to me to want to pay God His due regard, but rather with my whole heart I will seek Him alone and bow in submission to Him. Thus it is clear how easily an apparently religious motive of conduct can become a denial of God. Here, as elsewhere, there is a danger lest in the use of means to religion, religion itself may find its grave.

We must break completely with the idea that in his moral conduct the Christian is forced to an activity which is something different from the expression of that impulse that controls faith and presses on to its own goal. That erroneous conception yields the formula faith and love. But the true formula is faith working through love. The former is the Catholic thought, and it has had a great past. The latter is the truly Christian thought, before which there lies a limitless future. It died out soon after Paul.[44] It was revived by the Reformers. To-day it is the pressing duty of Christendom to work out more distinctly and clearly the peculiar character of the moral conduct which is Christian.

If we endeavour now to answer the question how it is that moral conduct proceeds from faith, we are now in the position to see how this is to be understood. Moral conduct must be capable of interpretation as an activity which is not merely a consequence and a suspension of religious experience, but which itself belongs to the communion of the Christian with God.

§ 28. *Eternal Life in Bearing the Cross and in One's Moral Calling.*

How then was it impossible for Christians like Paul and Luther to see the consummation of religious experience in the enjoyment of emotions and moods of the moment. They must have observed that it did not correspond to the truth when a man who had nothing more than these inner experiences thought that he was having communion with God. They did not seek to supplement communion with God with something else as if a man might be too pious. Rather was it their only care to reach true communion with God Himself. Their conviction is this: A man has found God Himself only when, through the influence of what he has laid hold of as God's revelation, his own existence in the world has become serious and important to him, and his neighbour has drawn close to his heart. Only when these impulses to take the world seriously and to serve our neighbour arise within us do we receive from God the highest good, elevation into a Divine life—a life in and with God— By turning in this manner to the world and to other men, we turn to God Himself, and come to a life common to ourselves and Him. Thus, through the heartfelt desire for God that is kindled by His revelation, the Christian is driven to commune with the world in work and in service of his fellows. The Christian learns to know how strong joy in the world can be, and how tender love to other men, when everything else in him has been swallowed up by the longing after God.

But why can it not be true that one communes with God Himself unless the experience which is given this interpretation is the beginning of a hearty turning towards the world, and of energetic action. If a man is really happy in God, he has the blessing of hope. We can never measure by the present what God is to us. The revival, the higher life that He bestows on us, always leads to the impression that we are at the threshold of happiness still hidden from us. Thus to our life's hopes there is opened a limitless horizon. God gives us a future. But at the same time we feel Him to be the Power which rules the facts of life and surrounds us in the actual relations in which we exist. Thus the reality amid which we stand becomes for us rich and full of promise. The state of strain into which we are transferred lets us look with earnestness and deep desire into the depths of things and their relations. The meaning of God's purpose with us presses in upon our soul. Thus, to revel in emotions and to fly away beyond reality into a purely imaginative communion with God is contrary to the instinct of the truly pious man. The genuine religious desire clothes itself in the less magnificent guise of exploiting, with earnestness and sincerity, the reality in which we are placed. One who is seeking God will not merely endure the compulsion of the relations that he sees clearly controlling him ; he will understand them as God's summons to him. He hears in them his vocation. The consciousness of this God-given vocation is true communion with God. The same holds true of work in the regular course of one's calling. For such work is supported by the confidence that God is to be found in it, and it is therefore a turning of the soul to God.

" The contrast between the mastery over all things that we exercise through faith in God's fatherly guidance, and the bondage to all things which we gladly, and in love, take upon ourselves, Luther explains by showing that in its freedom and joy, in its independence from considerations of merit, thanksgiving, results, deserts, that is in its universality and its abounding nature, Christian love bears the stamp of liberty and of likeness to God's love, and means therefore, in spite of its formal contrast to faith, an abiding in God and in His love. And in the same way he goes on to show that just through love we show ourselves to be God's, because, in it we answer to the Divine Nature, which has love and sincerity not as attributes, but as its very essence, and so we are the tools of love, and by its supernatural strength do that which no mere creature can." * This is doubtless Luther's thought. But there is no answer to our question there. Gottschick shows rightly how Luther, in this way, made it clear that in the Christian man religious experience and moral energy are two forms of the same eternal life. On the other hand, it would be false were we to hold that, in this manner, we can clearly show the process in which religious experience passes over into moral activity of the will. One could only think so if one held that the spiritual good that lies away beyond in the active sphere of moral energy could, at the moment of moral decision, be completely visible to us, rousing our emotion and drawing us upwards. But the human morality that we know shows another course, even in the Christian. Even if in certain directions it becomes more and more an effortless accomplishment of the good, it remains on the whole a struggle. The task of attaining moral mastery over the situation of each moment in all its relations is always too much for the strength we have hitherto won. For the good that is to come to us through the accomplishment of the good lies beyond the horizon of our inclinations, and, therefore, of our practical reason. The moral task, therefore, when it is completely understood, always produces once more the impression of being an impossibility. And so, indeed, it must be if the moral law is to elevate our existence, and if through the narrow gates of the law we are to enter into a life, the glory of which is at present beyond our ken. It can

* Gottschick, "Katechetische Lutherstudien," Zeitschrift für Theologie u Kirche, 1892, p. 455.

become clear to us how the problem lying here is overcome through religious faith only if we see how faith
becomes the impulse to moral decision.   In order to do
so we make a starting-point of a familiar series of
religious thoughts.

" The life of the Christian is nothing but an abiding,
and awaiting, and a longing for the revelation of that
which is within us, and that we may lay hold on what
has laid hold on us ; as St. Paul says :—' I press on, if
so be that I may apprehend that for which also I was
apprehended of Christ Jesus;' that is, that I may yet see
what riches are laid up for me in the treasury of faith." *
These words refer, first of all, to the Christian's longing
for a revelation of that bliss which he already possesses,
yet which he cannot experience fully until after the
death of the body.   Luther explains in the following
words that the Christian who looks so confidently
towards future bliss is to experience in this present life
also that gracious power which comes to him through
his faith.   " Our awaiting and living on here after
baptism is ordained for the chastening of our body,
and that we may prove the power of His grace in the
fight against the flesh, the world, and the devil."
Through the renewal which is in faith, it comes to pass
" that a new man, a new species, a new creature comes
into being, one that thinks quite differently, loves, lives,
speaks and works quite differently from before."   In
Luther's view the language we use concerning the new
birth shows the *nature of faith*, to wit, " that we at
once receive grace fully, and are made blessed;" and

* Erlangen edition, vii. 174.

such grace can be, and is to be, experienced by the believer. " God's grace is indeed something strong, mighty and active ; it is not something that lies inert in our souls as those dream-preachers pretend, something that slumbers, or is borne about, just as a painted board bears its colours. Nay, not thus; it carries, it leads, it drives, it draws, it travels, it does everything in a man : it does indeed make itself felt and experienced. It is hidden, but its works are not hidden." The believer who has really had this experience will always long for its repetition. The Christian " has no joy higher than this treasure, that he knows Christ." Hence the Christian's spirit is " restless amid the highest rest, that is, in God's grace and peace ; so that he cannot be quiet and at leisure." * The motive to activity which is inherent in the Christian's faith consists in his longing to submit himself to the circumstances wherein he has experienced the power of God acting upon him.

This condition is always a state of suffering. " Therefore also it comes about that those who truly believe must suffer much, and even die, so that grace may manifest its nature and presence." † Hence, impatience under the cross, or the endeavour to escape the natural claim of the world upon us is opposed to faith. For our own fancies concerning divine things might indeed bloom amid such comfortable rest as has thus been gained ; but the power of the redeeming God and a real communion with Him are to be experienced only by bowing calmly to the inevitable. In death the Word

* Erlangen edition xlix. 113.   † *Ibid.* vii. 180.

of Life can show its power. " This is the reason why God lays the cross on all believers, that they may taste and try the power of God, which they have grasped through faith." *

Exactly the same holds good, and in greater measure, concerning submission to moral necessity. For, on the one hand, the constraint under which we lie at each moment is intimately connected with the moral demand the moment brings, and, on the other hand, duty is part of the Christian's cross, which he has to bear. Faith concerns invisible things, and so also the command to love sets the realm of the invisible before us, and it is from this that our lower nature shrinks. We are bound to exercise self-denial : yet self-denial is not something self-evident, even to those who have already reached a high moral level. As we solve each moral problem, there is an instant when we certainly see the necessity of what is good, but in which we nevertheless have to admit that we are not at home in it, but that it seems cold and unwelcome to us. Now our faith carries us through this inner trouble. It tells us that the same Will who is claiming our obedience, and so letting us feel how far we are from Him, becomes comprehensible to us in Jesus Christ as that Power over all things which desires to lift us to Himself, and while our faith shows us this fact, it makes us also grasp the hand of the redeeming God even in the unwelcome call of duty, and teaches us that He lets us feel the strange sublimity of what is necessary and eternal only in order that

* Erlangen edition, li., 474 ; cf. xv., 432 : " Faith is an almighty thing like the Eternal God Himself ; therefore God seeks to prove and try it."

we may see how little we understand of the wealth He
has still in store for us. Hence the very hardness of
duty, which hurts the feelings of the natural man,
becomes to the Christian a promise of hidden riches
which awaits him in endless profusion. But when we
recognise in each call of duty the God whom Jesus
Christ reveals, we experience a joy that makes us
morally free, for it identifies the vital instinct[45] in us
which longs for bliss with our indelible knowledge of
the necessity of the Good. In our struggle with moral
problems, a struggle always too great for us, we find
that we are lifted away beyond ourselves by our contact with God, in the faith He awakens and maintains.
*Duty seems to kill all the joy of life ; but certainty that
we are in the grasp of God turns this pain into a
promise of life.*

In such deaths and resurrections we have communion
with God, the Creator of life. Therefore faith, whose
only interest is to receive such a gift from God, must
for its own sake, desire moral activity. Faith does not
seek that cross which consists in painful combinations of
earthly relationships, but if the cross be there, faith still
patiently pursues its desire to commune with God. On
the other hand we are always confronted by the demand
that we shall gather what our duty is from the situation
of the moment. Just as incessantly does faith insist
that in moral conduct we receive God's blessing.[46] So we
may see how good works are really the fruit of faith.
Faith loves what is good because it finds God there, and
experiences God's redeeming power amid moral conflicts.
We can reply now to the question whether the moral

activity of a Christian interrupts his communion with
God, that on the contrary that activity itself belongs to
that communion since faith finds therein the experience
of God's life-giving power, and communion with God is
only experienced when we thus receive life at His hands.
Of course it goes without saying that all who are inclined
to mysticism will tell us that this inclusion of moral
activity in communion with God is simply dry morality ;
but on a little reflction they will, nevertheless, have to
admit that we can have no more intimate communion
with God than the experience of being actually touched
by Him and brought into a life in the eternal. The
thankful joy we feel in such experiences is true love to
God,* and this is the only worship that truly honours
Him. He who has this joy keeps perpetual Sabbath and
has the peace of God—the peace which abides through
all unrest. †

§ 29. *The Consequences of this further Development of Luther's Ideas.*

We have now reached a point where we must necessarily carry the description of Christian piety further
than Luther has done. Our discussion thus far may
indeed claim to be in essential accord with Luther, for
it is nothing else than a thorough explication of the
thought that good works are the fruit of faith. Good
works may be described as good only when they satisfy
faith's instinctive desire to find God Himself. But the
fact cannot be ignored that Luther remains on the lines

---

* *Cf.* Erlangen edition, xii. 285 ; xvi. 177, 182f.
† *Ibid.* viii. 83 ; vii. 132f.

of Roman Catholic tradition in so far as he usually speaks too indefinitely of the way in which good works proceed from faith. It was indeed a mighty step forward, a mighty turning towards reality, when the Catholic expression that true love is wrought in men by grace was replaced by the new doctrine that love proceeds *from faith*. For the work of grace in men is just the faith which God awakens in them, and so the new doctrine shows more plainly than the old what is the actual renewing which the Christian experiences. But now, if we wish to travel still further along Luther's road, then we must seek to unfold in clearer language those inner processes in which the life of faith expands into moral activity. Luther's imperfect solution of this problem has produced in his church a further development of the hurtful idea that some impersonal force, supposed to be concealed in faith, gives us the faculty of willing what is good. But it is really the Personal God, touching us in the historical Christ, who, as soon as we come to know Him, gives us the power and impulse to will aright.

If this be clear, then it follows that the Christian Church must not try to discover the ground of redemption in doctrines concerning the Person and Work of Christ, but must find that ground in Christ Himself. And then we shall come to understand that our spiritual possessions are the product of Christian faith, and that this actually gives us a new life of inexhaustible richness. This must help Christian theology to the only purification of its tradition which is possible and healthy. The more our thoughts are absorbed by the mighty fact that we commune with God in our faith, the more surely, even if imperceptibly, will those theological figments disappear which help us to see clearly neither the God who turns towards us nor the faith which receives His gifts. Our inner concentration on the one thing needful will set us free from the morbid craving for such things as the presence of the body and blood of Christ in the Lord's Supper,* without at the same time arousing in us the equally unhealthy clamour against them. The

* In the sermon which was first printed in 1523, and reprinted in 1532, but which is not given in the summer division of the sermons on the Gospels in the "Kirchenpostille" of 1543 (Erlangen edition, xi., 197ff), there is an excellent exposition of the conditions on which this idea may have a place in the proper use of the sacrament. Luther says, first of all, it is easy to persuade a man that the body and blood of Christ are in the sacrament ; even the devils and non-Christians might believe that. And so if any one desires to enjoy the wondrous feast, but is led by this idea alone, he had better stay away. "For if thou give the sacrament to such a man, it is much the same thing as if thou wert to stab a sow in the neck." The true use of the sacrament is that we should understand and accept the same as an expression of the forgiveness of sins. In this use of the sacrament the presence of the body and blood of Christ must necessarily be regarded as a means of expressing what God desires to say to the Christian through the sacrament. Hence, Luther calls it a "Wahrzeichen," or "sign," which is connected with the word of Christ, and, like the latter, must be understood in the sense it is intended to express, and not simply accepted. It is self-evident that such a use of the sacrament is quite another thing from a symbolical conception of it, i.e., the use of it as a sort of creed. But at the same time it is clear that the conception of the presence of the body and blood of Christ is not necessary. The one thing of importance is that the individual who partakes in the sacrament should be understood as receiving thereby an expression of the forgiveness of his own sins. Such an understanding of the sacrament is necessary ; it is of no use to make up one's mind to hold the doctrine that the reception of the sacrament has such a meaning, "for it must be a faith which God makes within thee." Modern Lutherans appear indeed to think that the conception above described, which even the devil and all non-Christians may have, is not of much account after

man who has come to understand the difficulty and seriousness of true faith—that faith by whose breathing, man is born into a new life—will be not simply indifferent but will be even patient towards such ways of thinking ; * they certainly do not belong to faith, but they need not disturb it. They are the grass that withers away, and so we may let them bloom as long as men rejoice in them. They have no part in what is eternal ; they do not claim any certainty, for they stand out of all relation to the exaltation of men to eternal life.

§ 30. *The Prayer of Faith.*

And now, finally, we can define the relation of Christian prayer to Christian faith. If the life of faith is itself communion with God, then " a true faith is nothing other than simple prayer." † " Therefore, where there is a Christian, there is also the Holy Ghost, and He does nothing else save pray continually. For even if the mouth be not always moving and uttering words, yet the heart goes on beating unceasingly with sighs like these: Ah ! dear Father, may thy name be hallowed, may Thy kingdom come, and Thy will be done ; and whenever there come sorer buffetings and trials and

all. For they can hardly fail to see that the Kenotic Christology, which most of them favour, excludes the conception of a presence of the body and blood of Christ in the elements in the Lord's Supper. (*Cf.* H. Schultz, " Zur Lehre vom heiligen Abendmahl," 1886, p. 86.)

* Luther himself says of the doctrines and commandments of the Papacy, that he would willingly leave his opponents undisturbed in them, yea, even support them if they would only leave this one thing free and unhindered, namely, the great truth that it is in the knowledge of Christ that we have eternal life. Erlangen edition, l., 184f.

† Erlangen edition, xiv., 52.

needs, then the sighing and supplication increase, even audibly, so that you cannot find a Christian who does not pray; just as you cannot find a living man without a pulse that never stands still, but beats and beats on continually of itself, although the man may sleep or do anything else, so being all unconscious of this pulse." * This inner unceasing prayer is faith itself in the form of a continual turning of the heart towards God, that goes on steadily amid all our work.† This faith, which is really a life in God, breaks forth when opportunity offers into spoken prayer, interrupting work with thanks and supplication.‡ But special prayer must always spring from a confidence already existing that a message from God has been received and understood.§ Without this it is not Christian prayer, and does not come before God at all.‖ "The best thing in prayer is faith."¶ "He who would pray, must first believe." ** The Christian is certainly to say to himself that he is commanded to pray; †† but he who makes prayer simply a way to reach God, "invents a god for himself, and one that does not hear." ‡‡ Hence the Christian must strive above all "to have his heart free unto prayer." §§ And he does this when he takes God's message to heart and lets its power lay hold of him.‖‖ In such receiving we do commune with God. It

* Erlangen edition, xlix. 115.

† *Cf. Ibid.* xvi. 165f ; viii. 291 ; x. 308.

‡ *Cf.* Ritschl, "Lehre von der Rechtf." Second edition, iii. 595.

§ Erlangen edition, xx., I., 248.   ‖ *Cf. Ibid.* vii. 131 ; l. 119.

¶ *Ibid.* viii. 36.   ** *Ibid.* xxlii. 240.

†† *Cf.* Ritschl, "Lehre von der Rechtf." Second edition, i. 351.

‡‡ Erlangen edition, xxiii. 18.   §§ *Cf. Ibid.* xxiii. 222.

‖‖ *Ibid.* l. 110 : " The foundation stone in prayer is confidence in God."

is then alone that we can talk with God, and this is something far above all difficult tasks or hard work,* for then the heart is kindled and lit up by the kindness of God.† Hence every prayer which is not a meaningless crying out into space is in its inmost essence an act of praise and thanks to the Almighty God, whose love has found its way to us before we have sought Him. And does not the Lord's prayer begin with thanks and praise on this very ground?‡ To be certain that we stand in the light of God's grace because of Christ's attitude towards us, and to bow in faith under this actual proof of God's love,§ this is prayer in spirit and in truth. Hence true prayer is a work of faith, and only a Christian can offer it.‖ True worship can take place only where Christ is so perceived that we come through Him into the relation of children towards God.¶

But it is not only true that Christian prayer must be an utterance of faith ; it is also true that faith must give birth to prayer. If faith has been awakened in us, then we are not to keep musing over the slender possessions of our own thoughts ; rather will the mastery faith gives over each event in life express itself in prayer, whereby God makes us richer than we were before. As we face and seek to master the particular trouble with which each step in life is burdened, we find

---

* *Cf.* Erlangen edition, xvi. 163.

† *Ibid.* vii. 130 ; xii. 158.

‡ *Ibid.* vii. 129 ; xi. 232, 242 ; xvi. 185. Ritschl, " Lehre von der Rechtf." Second edition, iii. 599. The so-called orthodoxy about us holds, as a rule, a different opinion.

§ *Ibid.* xv. 219f ; xvi. 231.   ‖ *Ibid.* xlix. 113ff, 316.

¶ *Ibid.* xlix. 130.

that there we always need something more; and the mere fact of what we have already received never helps us out of the inmost need of the moment. If we do so rely upon it, then the content of our faith becomes a dead possession and mere doctrine. But "it is not enough here that we have the Word and know and understand all that we ought to know, both the doctrine of faith and of comfort and victory in all our need another thing is wanting yet, namely, that all this teaching and guidance of our faith and knowledge is put into practice." * From these words of Luther's it is clear that faith itself loses its original character and power as soon as it is regarded as a settled gain, as a foundation on which we can proceed to build in our own strength. Luther knew well that the content of faith is not mere doctrine, and that, therefore, faith itself is not mere knowledge that is to be supplemented by action. For faith is itself life and activity.† It is a relapse into the delusion that a man can have life in himself, if we treat the strength and insight we have already gained from the gospel as a means given whereby we may help ourselves. In opposition to this view, which is already betrayed into distinguishing faith and work, Luther is certainly right in recalling us to the fact that a faith, which is regarded as a restful possession is of no help to us at all. Faith can continue to be a reception from the infinite fulness of God as it was originally, only if in every position in life it turns to prayer, and asks for the removal of its distress from the God of whose life and presence it is conscious. The declaration

* Erlangen edition, l. 105.   † *Ibid.* xiv. 86,

of faith within the soul, which expresses the inward
freedom wrung out of conflict, is certainly not a simple
logical conclusion from something we knew before.
That declaration or judgment always arises afresh as
a reception of blessing from God—a reception which
is of precisely the same nature as the first rise of faith.
The Christian who feels a burden at any moment, bows
at every such moment of the life of faith under the
good, kind hand of God, and this is prayer and nothing
else. Of course it is at the same time a fresh understanding of the gospel, because in such prayer we turn
to the God who is revealed in Christ. But this God is
not the mere contents of a doctrine; not the author of
an event long past. To us He is the Living God whom,
by the entrance of the historical Christ into our life, we
realise to be present in power.* When we receive comfort from God we are by no means simply drawing the
practical inference from some train of thought, but we
are turning to a Personal Power, with the confidence
that He will strengthen us beyond all our expectation,
and will lead us through the present darkness into a
marvellous light. "For God will have it that ye
recognise not the doctrine alone and what ye already
have to be given by Him, but ye are to seek in Him
also what ye still need and lack, and thus to experience
that nothing stands in your own power, but everything,
both beginning and ending, willing and doing, must be
sought in Him and given by Him." †

* Erlangen edition, xlvi. 216 : "In the Lord Christ the Christian
finds God at home in his own heart." *Cf.* xx. 1. 508.
† *Ibid.* 1. 107f.

If faith is not to be a mere play with words concerning God, it must pass into the form of prayer, and if prayer is not to be a play of fancy or an unmeaning travail, then it must be the application of faith to the definite circumstances of the moment. This must not be overlooked when we urge men to prayer. For the Christian regular prayer becomes a sacred rule. But for man, the most important thing is that he learns to pray from his own heart. And this he can learn when he experiences that revelation of God, which can be mediated only by the love of men who stand in God's presence. If, therefore, we desire to help a man to prayer, the most needful thing is that we pray ourselves and win through our prayer that power of love which may make us of service to him. Luther has reminded us that the promises made to prayer are made to those who pray in faith, and not as compensation for a prayer that is simply a work done without faith.* Moreover, Luther by no means recommends prayer as the chief means whereby we are to come to God. He knows that it is contrary to the Gospel for the clergy to teach that men are to enter heaven by fastings, prayings and such-like works.† He thinks that any one might indeed become a praying man by his own endeavour, but he could not so become a Christian man.‡ Praying is indeed a good work, but although any one were to pray day and night he would not thereby become a Christian.‖ Life consists not in much praying, but in Christ.§ It is by

* *Cf.* Erlangen edition, l. 124f.
† *Ibid.* xii. 377; xiv. 8, 172f.   ‡ *Ibid.* xvi. 452.
‖ *Ibid.* xiv. 335.   § *Ibid.* xv. 156.

understanding Christ that we enter into communion with God.*

§ 31. *Prayer and Willing Resignation.*

Now, if our prayer is based on this experience, it will be regulated from its very outset far better than even the most exact rules could regulate it. Such prayer is the result of the true confidence in God which He Himself has aroused by the tidings He has given us of Himself; and along with this trust, which God has won from us by the manifestation of His love, there comes a thankful joy. Hence the prayer that is thus inspired is first of all thanksgiving, even when it takes the form of a supplication; and since the prayer that springs from faith is of such a character, there will result a combination in living unity of two spiritual affections which no human endeavour could unite, namely, the heart-felt desire to receive special help from God, and the humble (*i.e.*, joyful) submission to God's will. It is fruitless to try to bring about this union by merely saying to a soul that it may indeed ask God for a definite gift, but it must also be always ready to find the gift denied. If we made such an attempt we should either make the prayer heartless, or we should pretend a resignation that was utter hypocrisy. On the other hand, in the prayer of faith this union follows of itself; for faith does not see in God an indefinite power that holds both good and ill fortune in its hand, and which may perhaps be influenced by men's stormy asking. Our faith sets us rather

* *Cf.* Erlangen edition, i. 359 ; ix. 232, 263.

before a God whose help is certain. This alone will moderate all that might be passionate in the prayer that is life's utterance of its healthy desire for blessing. The natural desire of the troubled creature to influence the will of God to its own advantage vanishes in Christian prayer, because we feel that our supplications are laid before a God who loves us more than father or mother can. These two tendencies, the natural desire and the divine gift of confidence, can be clearly distinguished in the real living supplication of a Christian. His prayer is an inward conflict, which should normally bring the Christian up to a higher plane of the inner life; the sign of the attainment of this goal is the dying away of the storm of desire into stillness before God.

§ 32. *Prayer for Earthly Blessings.*

Faith certainly does not prevent the Christian altogether from asking for earthly blessings. Such a fancied refinement of prayer would empty it of all its meaning. Whatever really so burdens the soul as to threaten its peace is to be brought before God in prayer, with the confidence that the Father's love understands even our anxious clinging to earthly things. "Hast thou a want or trouble which presses thee, then call to Him, and open thy mouth with good cheer, as a child will to its father: a father is pleased with all that his child does, so long as it clings to its father."* It is this attitude towards the Father who comes to us in Christ that first gives us firmness of soul

* Erlangen edition, xlix. 313.

in view of all the things that would hold us captive.
If we try of ourselves to get free from these, and so far
do not pray about them, we do ourselves a two-fold
injury. In the first place we make our prayer dead and
insincere; it is in truth not our own prayer at all, but
might be the prayer of a man placed in utterly different
conditions; and secondly, we do not really lay ourselves before the God who would be sought of us as
our Helper and Saviour; we rather imagine a God who
has a kind of love for the human ideal, but has no
sympathy for our needs. But if, on the contrary, we
turn to God with what really oppresses us, then the
confidence which He calls forth within us takes away the
burden from our soul. "A Christian knows that he is
not refused what he has prayed for, and he finds, also,
in fact, that he is helped in all troubles; and if he be
not delivered from them so speedily, yet he knows that
prayer is pleasing to God, and that it is heard, and
that God gives him power to bear his troubles and to
overcome them : which is just the same thing as taking
his trouble away from him, and making it no longer
misfortune or distress, seeing it has been overcome." *
In this way our prayer becomes a " tranquil prayer ; " †
not by our summoning up all our powers of renunciation, but through the impression within us that God's
love is turned towards us, and that we can calmly trust
this. It would be, however, a shameful misuse of
prayer if trifles which have really no significance for
our inner life were to be made the topics of our prayers.
A prayer offered in such a trafficking fashion, as it

* Erlangen edition, xlix. 316.   † *Ibid.* xi. 57.

were, would either be empty talk, or would keep us entangled by matters which ought to trouble no serious man : such conduct destroys prayer, because amid such gazing upon what has no reality we forget the soul's actual need.

Prayer may be perverted in another direction, if in it there be no turning to God at all, but only a determined concentration on the eager desire to obtain some particular thing. We sink into such earthliness when we view the power of God simply as a means whereby some difficulty may be removed, and which may be set in motion by the energy of prayer. In so doing we do not trust the God who is revealed in Christ ; we trust our own power of prayer ; we do not then pray in Christ's name, but in our own. "Those, however, who pray in their own name, such as those who presume that God must hear them or look upon them, since they pray so many, so great, so devout, so holy prayers—these deserve and obtain only wrath and disfavour."* The man who only thinks of an " *uti Deo*," that is, of how

---

* Erlangen edition, xii. 160. It is easy to understand how a passionate man like Luther might sometimes fall into this kind of prayer himself ; but such prayers as, *e.g.*, those for the deliverance of Melanchthon and Mykonius, surely fall under the condemnation of the words quoted above. It is therefore ingratitude towards the great champion to allow such sins, into which his very fight for the cause of God led him, to continue to have a ruling influence in the church, by praising them as being among the best prayers in the history of the church, as Luthardt does in his otherwise excellent book. *Cf.* Luthardt, "Vorträge uber die Moral des Christentums " (Lectures on the Morality of Christianity). Second edition, 1873, p. 224. The creature certainly does not become heroic when it ventures to say, like God Himself, " my will be done."

to use God, and not of a "*frui Deo*," that is, of how to enjoy God, knows nothing of the joy which Christ promises to him who prays.* We pray aright only when we have joy in God himself; and such joy in God, kindled in us by His revelation, is love to God; and "true love to God is having the heart disposed and the mouth opened to say: ' Lord God, I am Thy creature, do with me as Thou wilt, it is all the same to me; I am Thine indeed, that I know; and if it were Thy will that I should die this hour, or suffer any great misfortune, I would suffer it with a willing heart; I will never count my life, my honour and my good, and whatever I may have, as higher and greater than Thy will.' " † Of course, this is the ideal of prayer; and yet in the struggle of a prayer that really comes before God, joy in God necessarily pushes into the place that was at first filled with passionate desire, and so such desire is moderated. The natural desire that is born of the passion of the creature, and the joy in God and His will which He Himself awakens, must be blended together in a Christian prayer. But no advice, however careful, can direct us how to balance the two exactly in any individual instance. God alone solves the problem, by so touching us in His revelation to us that there comes upon us like a sunrise a wondrous pleasure and joy in life, out of which there is able to spring willing renunciation and patience under what we have to bear.

* Erlangen edition, l. 125.
† *Ibid.* xiv. 172f; *cf.* xiv. 8; xvi. 428.

§ 33. *The New Birth.*

Such is the picture of communion with God which Luther gives us as the testimony of his inner life, whenever his language is not fettered by any definite polemical task. Even those who have been led to accept some other form of piety will hardly deny that whoever stands towards God as Luther stood, realises Jesus Christ as the Mediator and Reconciler, and yet communes at the same time with God Himself.

When the Christian has become conscious that his faith is sincere communion with God, he will sum up all that has happened to him through God's revelation in one definite judgment regarding himself. He knows that he has been transplanted into a new existence which he regards as a miracle wrought by God. Empty and weak as his life has been hitherto, he observes now and for the first time the point where he has learned to understand the love of the Father in what is real round about him. The New Testament gives the fitting expression for this; it says the believer is a new creation of God; he has been born again. And everywhere, even outside the Christian Church, all really pious men know that the full certainty of God, or the consciousness of communion with Him, is not a product of human strivings, but that it is a work of the Almighty that lets men see something utterly new. We see men who are not Christians feeling this majesty of God's revelation, and we can know ourselves at one with them in that feeling. But the Christian knows more; the thought must arise in his mind that he himself has been born again. God reveals Himself to us, and by that act makes of the creature a new being. With the rise of faith in the Christian's heart a new life begins which brings with it a thorough change of purpose and in place of former impotence a life in the strength of God.

Hence Luther very often pointed out how the new birth is the new purpose and courage given by the faith which is based on the fact of the appearance of Jesus.* He finds an interpretation of the new birth in the words of John, that our faith is the victory that has overcome the world.† To be born again is the same thing as to come through Christ to the Father ; ‡ faith involves the new birth,§ or the divine birth is nothing else than faith itself.‖ Accordingly he sees the means whereby the new birth is brought about in the Word, namely in that message of God which awakens faith.¶ And baptism is regarded as " an accompanying sign," or another expression, of what God tells us through the Word.**

Nevertheless we may not say that the Christian can point to anything in his new inner life as the phenomenon in the realm of his experience which attests his new birth.[47] It would be a monstrous thought for a Christian

* *Cf.* Erlangen edition, v. 246 ; vii. 178 ; viii. 224 ; xv. 341ff, 362 ; xviii. 206 ; xxiii. 247.

† *Cf. Ibid.* viii. 226.   ‡ *Ibid.* li. 334f ; xxii. 17.

§ *Cf. Ibid.* viii. 284 ; x. 143.

‖ *Cf. Ibid.* x. 216 ; xx. II. 43 ; xlvi. 270.   ¶ *Cf. Ibid.* viii. 284, 291.

** *Cf. Ibid.* xii. 439 ; xlvi. 296 ; xi. 72 ; xx. I. 27 ; xx. II. 47 ; xxi. 269 ; xxiv. 65 ; xlvii. 207.

that he should hold himself born again on the ground
of what he can now do and of what he is conscious of
being.   His opinion that he lives as a new man by the
strength of God is based, not on the experience that he
himself accomplishes anything that is divine, but on
the fact that God is his refuge.   Nor was it by any
means Luther's view that he had had an actual experience of the new birth and so knew himself to be born
again because of what he actually was, or that he could
fully explain how the new birth comes about.   It is
true that he sees the traces of the new birth in the
power of his faith ; but nevertheless the new life that
he observes in himself would be to him no basis for the
certainty that he had been born again.   On the contrary,
his faith gained that power to overcome the world of
which he was conscious, not from aught within him,
but through his inferring from facts which he distinguishes from himself and his own life, the conclusion
that the almighty impulses of God's love were working
in him.   Hence he says concerning the new birth:
" This birth is neither seen nor grasped ; we only believe
in it." *   The Christian by no means sees in what he at
present experiences a full expression of what he has
become through the grace of God.   He knows rather
that his deepest life is still hidden even from himself.†
" Wherefore it is also called a life hidden from the
world and from Christians themselves, so far as out-

---

* Erlangen edition, xlvi. 276.

† *Cf.* " Krit. Gesamtansgabe " (Critical Complete Edition), I. 486 :
"Abscondit enim Deus omnem vitam sanctorum ita profunde, ut ipsi
eam scire non possunt " (For God hides all the life of the saints so
deeply that they themselves cannot know it).

ward beholding and feeling can go ; but yet it is a life
that is certainly there and well protected." * Thus the
life that springs from God, or the life of the man that
has been born again, is not a thing that we can behold
and study in any of the present experiences of our faith ;
we gain for ourselves the certainty that that very experience is at bottom a divine life, by a judgment of faith.

Indeed this could not possibly be otherwise. If the
Christian could look upon his new birth from God as
the spiritual riches now in his possession, then he might
be called a fruit fallen from the tree of life, but not a
branch of Christ the Vine. He would then have to seek
within himself the ground of his own salvation. But a
Christian cannot give ear to any such fancy. "If thou
wilt behold, then I will give thee even the life of St.
Peter, St. Paul, or St. John ; and yet with all that thou
shalt come to nothing. Wilt thou be holy in God's
sight ? Then set not store on thy having life, else thou
art lost ; for all must come from pure gift, mercy and
grace, and not from a life or work in thee. If it be in
thee, then forsooth has it happened for *thy* sake." "As
long as thou remainest in thyself, thou art not devout.
This means that our life is hidden up high, and far
above our feelings, heart, eyes and sense." † At every
moment Christ alone is the ground of our confidence.
"If I am not free from care and fear, yet He is free
from all care, and without fear ; let me then soar away
from myself into Him, and boast that I am devout in
Christ and through Christ." ‡ We gain assurance that

* Erlangen edition, viii. 210 ; *cf.* xi. 251.   † *Ibid.* xvii. 353.
‡ *Ibid.* xv. 416f.

we are born again only by a judgment springing from faith which is based on Christ. When a man puts clearly before himself what Christ means for him, namely, the God who turns towards him and fills him with a new mind for life,[48] then at the same moment he makes it plain to himself that he has become a new creature, full of strength that flows from the one great fact that God has revealed Himself to us in the flesh. Luther rightly finds this meaning in Colossians iii. 3. In that passage Paul wished to comfort those Christians that " felt little life and joy " in themselves, " as they gladly would have felt; they felt rather death and terror." He desires to show them " where they are to seek their life and grasp it with certainty." He means to say " An eternal glory which cannot pass away has actually been given to you. But you do not have this life in yourselves and through your own feeling, but in Christ and through faith. And thus Christ is called your life, which is not yet revealed in you but which is certain in Him, and so assured to you that no one can take it from you; and thus through faith in His life you must be preserved and shall have the victory." *

It is dangerous to give oneself over to the idea that the new birth can be experienced as a process in time. Those who cherish this conception think they are very strong Christians, while in reality they are lacking in that certainty of the new birth which is given us in Christ. Just as clearly is a theology perverted which

---

* Erlangen edition, viii. 221; *cf.* xv. 157: " It is not something disclosed in us, but in the Word alone, that through Him and in Him we must receive and hold life."

makes regeneration a process that can be traced by human enquiry. Those circumstantial investigations as to the way in which a man of God comes into being which Frank published[49] must be fruitless, and they betray a striking want of clearness concerning the tasks that are possible to science ; yet this is not their worst fault. Their most injurious feature is rather the fact that by such an undertaking the true character of the idea of regeneration is concealed : for it is a thought arising from faith, and applies to something that lies beyond all experience. Frank works out the old scholastic problem, How can a man be renewed by God " without injury to his human freedom ? " and he reaches only the same result which has already been seen in the schoolmen. He treats the freedom of man and the renewing grace of God as opposites which must be ground down till they seem to fit one another. But in reality neither the idea of freedom nor that of regeneration permits of such treatment. For a man to have his conscience in agreement with the law of God is for that man to be conscious of his freedom, and this thought allows of no limitation. And this is not a description of something that we can experience as real, but it is a statement of the fact that the divine secret of our nature lies beyond all experience now possible to us. Just as little can we take away any element from the idea of a new creation by God so as to make it fit into the idea of human freedom. So far as we undertake to do so we are on the way to semi-pelagianism. Men are very ready to assert the miracle of faith, and at the same time to set aside what they cannot understand in it. Surely we ought by this time to have had enough of this old and ingenious practice. Its supporters are very willing to acknowledge all possible miracles, regarding which faith can never become certain, and which have not the least significance for the inner attitude of the man towards God, as, for example, that of the magical working of the sacraments: but on the main point, where the only question is of man's submission to the God who reveals Himself to him, they try to avoid the very facts which their faith knows to be such. The man who has come to God through Christ finds arising in himself the thought that through the new environment into which he has been transplanted he has become a new creature. This remains to him a miracle which lies beyond all experience, inasmuch as he never exhausts its meaning in any moment of conscious experience; but, further, the fact which faith describes in the thought of regeneration is not something that can be dissected as we analyse the separate parts of a process. This thought means rather that faith, though it advances through victories and through defeats, receives everything at once if it only holds fast to Christ.

But now, on the other hand, it is possible for us, with Luther, to see the new life of the regenerate man in the workings of his faith, if we will only remember that other fact which Luther emphasised quite as strongly, namely, that the new birth from God is not something to be seen or grasped, but only to be believed in. For the workings of faith have the power of a really new life only when they are supported by the conviction that the invincible power of God works in them, and of this we gain ever fresh certainty from the attitude God takes towards us in Christ. Faith receives from its understanding of Christ both the power and the impulse so to regard itself; and the thought thus brought about marks the faith which manifests itself as a new life. The theology at present common among Protestants regards faith, however, in such a way that we must expect to hear the objection that such regeneration as we have described is a mere thought, a man's dream or poem, but not a real thing. To this objection we could answer in brief that it is always a sign of unbelief to desire some other proof of reality for the content of ideas that God creates in us through Christ than this their real foundation. But let us compare that conception of regeneration which is certainly considered within the prevailing orthodoxy, as having the church's sanction, with that conception of New Birth which we have derived from Luther.

§ 34. *Baptism and the New Birth.*

Undoubtedly it is counted orthodox to-day to believe that something remarkable takes place in a man when he is baptised, and that thereby in some way, as the Formula Concordiæ expresses it, a freed will is made out of one that was in bondage. This process is supposed to be the new birth. Naturally it is impossible to know anything of this from our own experience, and only in the rarest cases do men claim such knowledge. Hence it is assumed that the process has taken place, on the ground of some texts of Scripture in which it is supposed to be asserted that baptism has some such power. Now what does the Christian gain by such a supposition as that which men call faith in the regenerative power of baptism? Without doubt those who share this kind of faith are able to conceive of this questionable event with very sensuous distinctness; they regard it, as Luthardt would say, as something " objectively real." But it is of no service for the inner life; for even if we are firmly convinced that this change took place in us some years ago, yet the recollection of that will not at all diminish our present need, our present feeling of the slavery of our will, our discontent and despair where we should enjoy the glorious liberty of the children of God. A Christian who stands in such need as this will necessarily hear with indifference the assertion that he received a new life in baptism; in his anxiety for comfort he will say to the preachers of that doctrine; It may be so, for aught I know, but that does not help me. Of course it may be replied by way of proof that the doctrine is not without practical fruits, that what took place in that sacrament was a work of God which cannot be destroyed through our sin; it is there, and will help us if we will use it. Here an appeal is made to us to trust in the faithfulness of God, who will keep the promises He makes to man through Christ, and so will declare to us the sincerity of His love. Certainly this is the right course to pursue, to comfort ourselves and other Christians; but at the same time it is plain that this is a retreat from the doctrine of the regenerative power of baptism which was borrowed from the schoolmen, and it is an evident turning towards what faith really thinks concerning the new birth. For we come to trust the faithfulness of God because of the tidings He has given us which have for us this meaning, namely Christ alone in His word, *i.e.*, in His appearance in history. And there fore all we have to do is to look to Him when we desire to awaken our trust in God's faithfulness. If then we point to baptism, as to the work of God that is guaranteed by His faithfulness, are we not dispensing with Christ as the basis of our confidence ? This question certainly arises if we say that a miraculous change of the inner life results from baptism. In such a case men's thoughts cling to an event concerning which nothing more can be said than that it is miraculously effected and that it brings about a miraculous result. It would be foolish to attempt to deny that under the influence of these conceptions an emotion may arise which seems to afford a momentary relief amid trouble ; but this is not the comfort of Christ. Christ Himself is supplanted by this conception of a miraculous event, and moreover much of the meaning of the event may be the mere product of men's own imagination. Christ becomes a mere presupposition for the process in which men think the help has been given them ; and no one is bound to think much about this presupposition, for of course it has already done its own part in providing a redeeming fact for them.

It is self-evident that a Protestant Christian may not remain in an attitude towards this sacrament which is actually a turning away from the Redeemer Himself. So the only just view of baptism is that it is an expression of the love of God which is turned towards us in

Christ. *If we take this view, which of course is only possible when we have a Christian faith in Providence, then Christ, and the God revealed to us in Him, are really brought to us through baptism.* We take our comfort from Christ Himself if we understand baptism as a special promise from the God who through Him touches our inner life. And when we take this position towards Christ and towards the act of baptism which receives us into His brotherhood, then the doctrine that supposes baptism to effect a process of regeneration becomes a story that we can well afford to lay on one side. As Christ emancipates us, bringing us into a right confidence in God, He becomes so great and mighty in our sight that we can say, in some form or other, that to stand under His protection amounts to being a new creature born of the power of God. The marvellous power of the thought which Christ thus brings about within us is known to every believing Christian ; we experience it in the hours when our faith has been weak, when we keep our grip on the fact that God's love has made much more of us than we can understand, since we can only estimate in a very slight degree the power that Christ has given us to resist the powers of evil. It is not necessary to explain here how such a faith teaches us to understand that the baptism administered to us by the Christian brotherhood is a gift of God. For such an explanation we may simply refer men to Luther's Greater Catechism. But it is clear that this significance that his own baptism assumes for the Christian forces him to judge more leniently about any supposed magical effect of the sacraments. There may lie in that belief an expression of the fact that the gift of God is more than our comprehension can ever fathom. The only error is, then, that a conception capable of being grasped in its real sense only by a highly developed religious mind is treated as a foundation for faith, and that then an illumination of the mystery concealed there is at- tempted by means of a theological theory. And the error is not a small one. It helps on the profanation of the sacrament in its inmost meaning. For it makes it possible for an utterly profane man to believe in the sacrament as he might believe in any other magic. But, on the other hand, the mystery of the sacrament is pre- served if it is maintained that the proper reception of the sacrament is that which takes place in the conscious- ness that "it is as if God were letting me hear a new voice or a new sign from heaven and thus promising me grace" ("Apology of the Augsburg Confession" vii). This most simple religious interpretation is an impene- trable wall round about the mystery. For that experi- ence is impossible to the ungodly.

§ 35. *Science and the Thoughts of Faith.*

The thoughts of faith concerning the source and support of its own life cannot be made fruitful by seeking to get at what they mean by any merely sen- suous experience, and to make it comprehensible by reason in a theological theory. Men certainly fall into this error if they get these thoughts by learning them by rote from the apostles or from sacred Scripture. On the other hand, they become fruitful in us when they

arise in us just as they did in the apostles. If faith is
awakened in us through the actual power of the real
historical revelation, then in that impulse our thoughts
will be lifted far above the realm of experience that is
possible to us. What we thus hold to be possible by
the power of faith cannot be made even comprehensible
to the man who does not stand in the same faith. It
is not possible so to combine it with the results of
general philosophy as to build it up into a philosophical
scheme of that sort, or to establish it on a metaphysical
basis. Hence follows what the ruling theology of our
time calls "dualism," and which it abhors greatly,
because thereby its own beautiful alliance with science
is called in question, an alliance from which only a
worldly, grasping church could gain anything. Nevertheless, it is just as clear to the believer as it is to those
who are acquainted with science, that science has no
part or lot in the content of these thoughts. For these
things there is no theory of perception⁵⁰ In these
thoughts the believer breaks down every bridge between
his own conviction, and all that science can acknowledge to be real, simply because these thoughts have
grown out of the faith awakened by God's historical
revelation.

But the thoughts of faith are not thereby rendered
unfounded or worthless. Their worth lies herein, that
the soul that conceives them is set free from the world
and rises to God, reaches away beyond its present life
and is at home in another world. We certainly could
not find this in our thoughts concerning God's nature
and in all our other thoughts arising from faith, if these

could all be shown to belong to our ordinary knowledge of the world, or if they all simply expressed what we now experience. The thoughts springing from faith have their firm assurance in the faith itself from which they by a necessity arise, and therefore ultimately in the revelation which gives faith its existence and its certainty. For this faith itself we are ready to answer to science. It has its root in the fact that Jesus brings us by His appearance to confidence in the reality of a God who wills what is good, and who forgives us our sins. Thus two different powers combine to bring about the certainty of faith, one, the impression made upon us by a historical personage and fact which comes to us in time; and the other, the moral law whose eternal truth we learn to know at once when we are aware of that law. Religious faith in general arises when a man runs against an undeniable fact which compels him by force of what lies in it to recognise that in it God is touching his life. We begin to be Christians when we find the footprints of God in our life in the fact that the Person of Jesus has come our way. When once we have come to see that religious faith is not a thing concerned with the establishment of eternal truths, but rather with the actual elevation of men out of the life according to the flesh into eternal life, then we no longer think of gaining certainty of faith in any other way.

§ 36. *Our Attitude among the Theological Parties of the Present Day.*

We regard the theological divisions of the present day calmly and gladly because with our theology, founded as we have described, we stand firmly on the law and the Gospel; and because in this way we are equally free from dishonouring faith by a false subjection to science or by the conception that science must be shut up within its own limits lest any harm may happen to poor faith. Some day this emancipating knowledge will dawn on others also; meanwhile we rejoice in the thought of the joy which awaits them when God shall give them the strength to throw aside the monkish cowl of the scholastic theology.

SUPPLEMENTARY NOTES TO THE TEXT

Page

lxviii 1. The translator has chosen here and on p. 3 to render "christliches Volk" as "Christian democracy." This is probably an unsuccessful attempt to capture some of the richer nuances of *Volk* especially as this was used in Herrmann's day. Herrmann's own political views do not emerge clearly from his published works but in two essays one gets a glimpse of his position. In a lecture given on the Kaiser's birthday in 1884 ("Warum bedarf unser Glaube geschichtliche Tatsachen?," *Schriften zur Grundlegung der Theologie* I: 81-103.), Herrmann indicates that he shares the position of many political liberals that unification of Germany under Prussian leadership has concretely fulfilled the yearning of the German people for national self-identity. In a later essay written during World War I and prompted by reflections about British use of troops from "heathen" lands on the one hand and German alliance with the Turks on the other ("Die Türken, die Engländer und die Deutschen Christen," *Die Christliche Welt* 29: 218-24, 231-36), he makes comments about the distinctive character of German culture. In both of these essays he reflects the interpenetration of religious heritage, national self-identity, and hopes for the future peculiar to German thought in the nineteenth and twentieth centuries. When the term *Volk* is used, these nuances should be included.

lxviii 2. The phrase "those who desire to be sincere" renders the German original *"die wahrhaftig sein wollen."* It is well to call the reader's attention to the consistent use of "sincere" in this translation when Herrmann has written *wahrhaftig* (and the use of "sincerity" for *Wahrhaftigkeit*). For Herrmann the primary issue in theological controversy is honesty and truthfulness. His attack upon orthodoxy and creedalism is founded precisely on his insight that faith demands honesty and truthfulness and thus is violated when one is asked to bend to ecclesiastical dictation. *Wahrhaftigkeit* for Herrmann indicates the honesty and truthfulness which are the expression of personal integrity.

3 3. "Positive Christianity" can mean very generally as did positive religion for Schleiermacher the traditional character of the Christian

Page

church formed by its particular history. In the context of the next
few pages, however, it refers to party strife within the Prussian state
church of Herrmann's day. The parties were crystalized with the
promulgation of a church constitution in 1876. One, a non-Lutheran
party—thus a party of the Union church of 1817—but highly conservative in its defense of church dogma, discipline, and control of
education was called the Positive Union. Herrmann, although never
challenging the basic pattern of church-state relations, was a constant
critic of the conservative stance taken by controlling forces within
the ecclesiastical bureaucracy.

13 4. One should not overlook the fact that Herrmann's student, Karl
Barth, not only adopted this contention but made it the basis for
his response to critics of his commentary on Romans. See the preface
of the Second Edition by E. C. Hoskyns, *The Epistle to the Romans*
(New York: Oxford, 1933). [LEK]

23 5. This reference is to the German edition of Harnack's *Lehrbuch
der Dogmengeschichte* and not to the English translation of this
work, *History of Dogma* (New York: Dover, 1961). In the English
edition the reference is to be found in vol. 6, p. 105.

26 6. Adolf Lasson (1832-1917) was a philosopher perhaps most known
for his new edition of Hegel's works in the *Philosophischen Bibliothek,*
1905 and following. This work was actually completed by his son
Georg Lasson after his father's death. Lasson was one who tried to
save the classical theological tradition from creedal conservatives while
not surrendering it to critics like Harnack. A philosophy of religion
resulted which was based on the premise that Greek philosophy
provided the proper thought forms for reception of Christian
religious impulses. Lasson was also interested in Meister Eckhart
and was able in his thought to bring religion conceived as mysticism
into intimate connection with metaphysical schemes.

28 7. It is interesting to note in Herrmann's argument the choice of
Richard Rothe for a protagonist. Rothe was seen in the movement
of dialectical theology in the 1920's as epitomizing cultural Protestantism and continuous with theological liberalism. Indeed this was
in some measure true; Troeltsch delivered a lecture in 1899 in cele-
bration of Rothe's one hundredth birthday. Rothe was also patron
saint of the *Protestantenverein* founded in Frankfurt in 1863 as the
vehicle for reaching liberal goals in both church and state. Sharing
objectives with the National Liberals, the *Protestantenverein* stood
opposite the Positive Union in Prussian church politics. Rothe himself was a speculative thinker whose formative years prior to 1848
brought him under the influence of Hegel and Schelling. He was never
much influenced by the Tübingen school of historical-critical Biblical
study and retained many influences from the *Erweckungsbewegung*
he met in Berlin. The distinction Herrmann draws between himself

and men like Rothe is instructive about the character of Ritschlian liberalism. The issue is the nature of religious life including the place of thought and action in it. The distance the Ritschlians felt between themselves and men like Rothe is further to be seen in their aloofness from the *Protestantenverein*. Herrmann's friend and colleague Martin Rade strove always in his famous paper *Die Christliche Welt* to transcend the ecclesiastical political strife of the parties. By 1900, though, the aim of Rothe to see religion inform and shape the cultural life and institutions of man could be rearticulated without the speculative metaphysical scheme Rothe himself employed. It is Troeltsch who took up the task of Christian social ethics, and he also had roots in Ritschlianism. Furthermore, his influence is to be found on Rade and the direction taken by *Die Christliche Welt* in the last years of the Empire.

41   8. The term here translated as "Plan of Salvation"—also to be found on page 134—is the German word *Heilsordnung*. In the technical language of orthodox dogmatics this renders the Latin term *ordo salutis*. In Lutheran scholasticism it was customary to discuss the *ordo salutis* in connection with the third article of the creed and the work of the Holy Spirit. Herrmann finds such labor worthless since it is based on a mistaken understanding of the nature of faith.

49   9. Reference to German edition. Cf. English: vol. 7, pp. 173 ff.

56   10. The method which Herrmann here chooses in dealing with Luther is worth noting, for he stood well at the beginning of the Luther Renaissance which is still with us and shows no sign of letting up. In the pages which follow Herrmann notes the major textbooks of both Theodosius Harnack (Adolf Harnack's father) and Julius Koestlin. They were the major scholarly achievements in Luther study in the nineteenth century. However, Herrmann shares with his teacher Ritschl and with his colleague Harnack the search for the unifying thread in Luther's religious life which gives his theology significance outside of its dogmatic contents. Although not directly reflected in this discussion, the larger context for this approach to Luther is the question German philosophers and historians since Hegel and Leopold von Ranke had posed: what is the real significance of the Reformation as this occurred in Germany? The political dimensions of the problem are interesting too when one notices that Bismarck's campaign against the Roman Catholics which enjoyed much support from the National Liberals took place in the years 1873-1878. These cultural aspects of the question Herrmann posed here were taken seriously by Troeltsch, whereas the method which Herrmann represents was particularly well used by Karl Holl (*Gesammelte Aufsätze zur Kirchengeschichte,* 2nd ed. [Tübingen: J. C. B. Mohr, 1923], Bd. I.). The revival of interest in the dogmatic content of Luther's thought cannot be seen apart from the backdrop

Page

provided by the work of the Ritschlians. Here it perhaps is wise to recall these words from Harnack's *History of Dogma* which, although they were written before the turn of the century, remained in the fifth edition of that work published in 1931. "The fullest, most distinct, and truest account of Luther's *religion* is to be found in Herrmann's book . . . *The Communion of the Christian with God*" 7:184, n. 3.

66 11. This expression is to be found in Chr. E. Luthardt, "Zur Kontroverse ueber die Ritschl'sche Theologie," *Zeitschrift für kirchliche Wissenschaft und kirchliches Leben* 7 (1886):638. This is an essay devoted to a critique of the first edition of *The Communion* in which Luthardt answers many of the polemical asides which Herrmann had directed his way. That this whole front on which Herrmann fought largely gave way and thus the polemical references disappeared from the later editions is witness to the overall victory of Ritschlian theology. The new front was to be found between Herrmann and Kähler. Basically Luthardt and other Lutherans did not understand that Herrmann was not accusing them of being rigidly orthodox. Rather he was insisting in the short treatise mentioned in this footnote that the problem of updating an historical tradition includes the problem of history itself and that this problem arises when one seriously places himself at the mercy of the peculiar events surrounding the life, death, and resurrection of Jesus and thereby gains new perspective on and impetus for participating in the events of his own time.

70 12. More than any other contemporary theologian, Gerhard Ebeling has worked with this motif of Jesus as the "ground of faith." Whereas Bultmann concentrated on the question, How did the proclaimer become the proclaimed?, Ebeling concentrates on, How did the witness of faith become the basis of faith? See *The Nature of Faith,* trans. Ronald Gregor Smith (Philadelphia: Fortress, 1961), chaps. 4, 5; "Jesus and Faith" in *Word and Faith,* trans. J. W. Leitch Philadelphia: Fortress, 1963), chap. 7 and his book *Theology and Proclamation,* trans. John Riches (Philadelphia: Fortress, 1966). Ebeling, of course, does not simply repeat Herrmann; see the editor's discussion in the Introduction, pp. l-liv. [LEK]

72 13. It is not necessary to go beyond Herrmann's wishes and identify his protagonists. It is interesting to note that this footnote appears in the 1903 (4th) edition of the book. It is also interesting to note that he lines himself up against both liberal rationalists and conservative "positives." This indicates that his subtle understanding of history is misunderstood on both the right and the left. Perhaps it is also relevant to point out that his reference here to Lessing and the problem of how an eternal happiness can be based upon an historical event the reality of which can be only said to be highly

probable echoes the concerns of Søren Kierkegaard. Of the latter Herrmann seemed to be only peripherally conscious; his disciples—for example Ebeling—have followed the similarity in more detail.

75 14. Much critical study of the Gospels has made Herrmann's confidence in ascertaining the inner life of Jesus untenable, for precisely those passages in which Jesus speaks most explicitly of himself and of his mission are held to be Christian in origin (especially the "I am" sayings; cf. Bultmann, *The History of the Synoptic Tradition,* trans. John Marsh [New York: Harper, 1963], pp. 150 ff.). Moreover, Bultmann rebelled against the theological legitimacy of being interested in Jesus' inner life at all. On principle he does not want to know about it because that too is only a historical fact about Jesus, and "faith does not at all arise from the acceptance of historical facts." See his critique of Ebeling and Fuchs at precisely this point in "The Primitive Christian Kerygma and Historical Jesus" in *Historical Jesus and the Kerygmatic Christ,* Carl E. Braaten and Roy A. Harrisville, eds., (Nashville: Abingdon, 1964), p. 24. Although on p. 59 Herrmann appears to appeal to the factuality of Jesus as a faith-engendering reality, he takes pains to show that this is a gross distortion (p. 72). It is the power of Jesus himself, mediated by the New Testament record which is the reflex of his power. Hence on p. 75 the appeal to Jesus' inner life functions like a Kantian categorical imperative (see also p. 87), and especially pp. 102 ff. In other words Bultmann uses "fact" quite differently from Herrmann because he is denying its legitimating power; for Bultmann, only the kerygma has faith-engendering power. Bultmann himself discusses Herrmann's views in "On the Question of Christology," in *Faith and Understanding,* trans. Louise Pettibone Smith (New York: Harper, 1969), pp. 132 ff. [LEK]

77 15. The word "historical" here translates *geschichtliche.*

78 16. In the German text this sentence ends at this point. A new sentence then begins: "Erst aus der Freude. . . ." It would be more accurate to the emphasis Herrmann wishes to place on the movement from the experience of the personal life in Jesus' disciples to the New Testament to retain the German structure. The second sentence would then run: "It is first out of the joy and amazement that such a thing as personal life really meets us in the world that it becomes possible for the Christian religion to develop."

83 17. The choice of "minds intent on exercising our moral judgment and satisfying our religious need" to translate "innerlich gesammelt in sittlichen Verstaendnis und religiosen Bedürfnis" is certainly a possibility. It is complemented by the insertion of "in our hearts" in the text five lines below. Thus does the translator strive to retain Herrmann's meaning that one's very selfhood is involved in the experience of revelation and this only happens when one is morally

engaged. The reader is warned not to see "mind" and "heart" as technical terms for Herrmann.

84 18. "Portrait"=*Bild*.

95 19. For some reason the revised translation based in the German edition of 1903 does not include this important footnote from that edition: "Compare J. Weiss, *Die Predigt Jesu vom Reiche Gottes*, 2nd ed., 1900, and in connection with this W. Bousset, 'Das Reich Gottes in der Predigt Jesu,' *Theologishe Rundschau*, 1902, pp. 437-49." The first edition of Weiss's book appears in this Lives of Jesus Series as *Jesus' Proclamation of the Kingdom of God*, Richard Hiers and D. Larrimore Holland, eds. (1971).

97 20. In the fifth German edition the following lengthy passage is inserted at this point. It may be found in the 7th edition, pp. 77-79. "If we then yield to his attraction and come to feel with deep reverence how his strength and purity discloses to us the impurity and weakness of our own souls, then the impression of inexhaustible goodness can be brought to bear upon the men who are subjected to his power. In this way, however, we have the intuition (*Anschauung*) of that one power by which we can know ourselves both to be entirely overcome and yet freely surrendering, and which, therefore, we can alone think of as almighty. Out of the feelings of reverence and pure trust, with which the spiritual figure of Jesus fills us, rises to us the picture of the invisible God. Our God becomes a reality for us in that we perceive in this experience his message to us. That is the gospel which may not be transmitted through mere doctrine but resounds anew in every soul which awakens to real life. As such it is the Word of God grasped ever and again individually and addressed to those who wish not to vegetate but to do battle in history.

"This beginning of the consciousness of a living God who is actually above the world, that is, the particular and actual beginning of an inner subjection to him, is the entry way into the transcendent realm of religion. It is opened to no one by proofs. All science can lead one only to the threshold of this transcendent realm—in itself no mean accomplishment. Should he experience the miracle which takes him across this threshold, then he must wish in his own life to be truly authentic (*wahrhaftig*). However, the idea of a life of one's own in which a human individual wishes to exist and act as a thinking, willing person can only be true for him when it corresponds with that reality in which he can think himself a living participant. [The text is footnoted here as follows: Compare my explanations in the *Zeitschrift für Theologie und Kirche*, 1907, pp. 187-201. The reference is to the essay "Die Lage und Aufgabe der evangelischen Dogmatik in der Gegenwart" and the pages mentioned can be found in *Schriften zur Grundlegung der Theologie*, II. pp. 42-54.] That only happens when he recognizes something to which he knows himself entirely subjected. Every man seeks from day to day for such a lord over his soul or he would be dead on his feet. The more he raises this question for himself as the question of his life, the clearer it must become to him that such a reality opens for him only in the impulses of pure reverence and trust and that he can encounter them therefore not in things but only where he senses a personal life conquering. When this question burns in our own hearts, we knock on the door of another's heart. Moral earnestness can bring us no further. We hear from all religious people the promise that the door will be opened to us. But we must experience this happening.

"We believe we can find traces of this experience outside the context of a living Christian community. Everywhere where men come to the intuition of personal life aroused by reverence and trust can these experiences become so strong that these men gain a view of the real power over their lives and thus the power over everything. Therefore they also stand in the peace of religion. We have only this one advantage over other religious people: that we have before us in Jesus the spiritual power whose incomparable character we have sought to indicate. However, for us also no doctrine, no historical (*historischer*) or dogmatic proof can procure that which makes Jesus a revelation of God for us. Everyone is to be carefully warned against trying this since he will find no ground for it at all in his own individual experience. For here the spiritual power of Jesus actually brought him to subject himself freely and in subjecting himself he found all his inner uncertainty and impurity dissolved.

"If that has happened to us, then we find help first of all in the powerful claim which Jesus, according to the tradition, raises. Otherwise this claim must make the impression of coercion which our souls should reject. For one may not allow himself to be coerced but may only become subject when he can freely surrender. But when we center that experience upon the person of Jesus, then we learn to share his invincible confidence that he can uplift and bless perfectly those who do not turn away from him."

101   21. "Historical movement in which the good wields ever greater sway" translates part of the phrase "dass wir in einem zusammenhaengenden Wachstum des Guten stehen." So long as one does not weight the words "historical movement" too heavily, this is adequate.

102   22. "Historical fact" renders "geschichtliche Tatsache."

113   23. What Herrmann here attributes to the power of Jesus' inner life, Bultmann restricts to the kerygma. [LEK]

118   24. It is significant to notice that what the translator renders by "collect our thoughts" is the German phrase "uns auf uns selbst zu besinnen." *Selbstbesinnung* is something of a technical term for Herrmann meaning to be aware of one's self. He chooses to use it

Page

normally rather than *Selbstbewusstsein* which means much the same thing and is usually translated "self-consciousness." When Herrmann uses this term, he is avoiding many of the connotations of "self-consciousness" that lead one to associate it with a reflective or passive moment in human experience. The self-awareness of which Herrmann speaks refers to active moments in human experience in which one disposes of himself responsibly. Perhaps one can call a man then "self-possessed."

133 25. The terms "sincerity and truthfulness" render "Ernst und Wahrhaftigkeit."

146 26. Cf. *The History of Dogma* 7:168-80.

154 27. At this point in the text of the second edition of 1892 Herrmann had an extensive footnote dealing with his interpretation of Luther's Christology. Since this is replaced in the later editions by the paragraph of text which follows, it is not necessary to reproduce it in full. It is interesting to note, however, that criticism of his interpretation of Luther by A. Kohlrausch in the journal *Beweis des Glaubens* [72 (1891):209-26, 257-74] under the title of "Professor Herrmann's Luther Quotations" caused him to distinguish more and more carefully between the implications of Luther's understanding of Christ as the ground of faith and the content of his statements about orthodox Christology. When one reflects upon this lengthy section of *The Communion,* so out of proportion to the others of the book, he is led to feel that this whole issue troubled Herrmann considerably. His instinct to see Luther as the foremost articulator of the real essence of faith was constantly chastened by the realization that Luther could not by the very nature of the times in which he lived carry out its theological consequences.

157 28. Herrmann here refers to those led by G. Thomasius who developed a particular kenotic Christology in the middle third of the nineteenth century. Cf. the discussion of Claude Welch and the texts in translation in *God and Incarnation in Mid-Nineteenth Century German Theology* (New York: Oxford, 1965). The fundamental difference in theological method used by Herrmann and that of the so-called mediating theologians is no more apparent than here. Orthodox dogma is not to be recovered by new schemes of understanding. It is rather to be known only as the way faith once came to speech.

163 29. The text between here and on page 169 is dropped from the fifth and subsequent editions of the book. In its place appears the following conclusion to the paragraph begun and the beginning of the next: "Thus the method he follows as a rule is simply to set the passages of scripture which according to the traditional interpretation witness to the deity of Christ together with the doctrines of the fathers and to infer that Christ is true man and true God

in one. However, he goes further in seeing in the notion of the deity of Christ only the content of an old doctrine which each one if he wishes can say is true. He also comprehends the notion of the deity of Christ religiously, that is, as the expression of the fact that we find in Jesus God himself—the power which brings us to subject ourselves freely to it in spite of our feeling of guilt and our anxiety in the face of death. His explanations are often marked by traces of the new awareness that the deity of Christ means more to the man of faith than the presence of divine substance in him. *The one personal God thinks, speaks, and acts in and through Christ.* Thus only a monotheistic piety which focuses upon itself can understand the deity of Christ. The idea that the essence of God is a substance in which a number of subjects can take part is polytheistic. For monotheism the essence of God is necessarily the one spiritual power which reveals itself to us through its work upon us as the omnipotent one. If we can say to ourselves that we meet this one power which takes captive our inmost self in that which we experience in the person of Jesus, then we believe in the deity of Christ.

"Because Luther understands the notion of the deity of Christ religiously, he gives the old dogma which he wishes to retain a new content." (Seventh ed., p. 133.)

164   30. The following footnote was printed in the second edition of 1892 but removed from the fourth and subsequent editions. "To the first edition of this work objection is often made that I have missed this fact. I grant gladly that my exposition could have caused this objection for the point, for me, was not to give a complete representation of Luther's teaching style but to pull together the thoughts which in his religious practice quite differently than in the catholic ones find a place in his communion with God. However, I do not conceive that this reproach has been again repeated when Luthardt says, on the contrary, that I indeed hold to the reformer in Luther and not to the scholastic." (Page 131.)

168   31. This motif has been developed recently by Wolfhart Pannenberg, *Jesus—God and Man,* trans. L. L. Wilkens and Duane Priebe (Philadelphia: Westminster, 1968); Pannenberg speaks of a "christology from below." [LEK]

172   32. In the fifth and later editions the following footnote appears. "In the earlier editions I sought in the context of these explanations to demonstrate that Luther in several places in his reflection about the origin of faith had distinguished the man Jesus as the experience-able fact which grounds faith from the notion of divine sonship in which faith expresses itself. J. Gottschick (*The Churchliness of the so-called Church Theology* [1890], p. 28) seconded me in this. However, after the appearance of K. Thieme's work, *Luther's Testament against Rome in his Schmalkald Articles,* 1900, he communi-

cated to me that he would give up this interpretation. I also grant to Thieme and J. Koestlin, who likewise in the second edition of his *Luther's Theology*, 1901, questions my reading of these passages, that from the beginning that distinction was improbable for Luther because for him the deity of Christ was on the ground of the Holy Scripture an unshakeable presupposition which he saw formulated in the dogma. I have had, therefore, to be satisfied now with demonstrating that Luther's understanding of the deity of Christ can serve a Christian to whom a doctrine handed down to him cannot be the foundation of the confidence of his faith. This can only come from a fact which he himself experiences. Thieme correctly says that Luther could never have seen the personal life of Jesus without the "cloud" of deity. But the knowledge of the deity of Christ meant for Luther in distinction from the dogma the knowledge of the one God living and effective in Christ. In distinction from the way of thinking which expresses itself in the dogma it is characteristic for Luther that being taken captive by the person of Jesus and knowing the God who turns to us in him are inseparable in experience."

198   33. This sentence appears already in the second edition of 1892. In fact it is in this context that Herrmann's words about the official theology of the church are most meaningful, for 1892 was the year of the struggle within the church over the use of the Apostle's Creed. Although the reading of the creed was required at baptism, a pastor Christoph Schrempf in Württemburg did not do so. He was disciplined and Adolf Harnack was drawn into the controversy. The storms which then broke about Harnack involved many of the Ritschlians. They met at the instigation of Harnack and under the leadership of Rade to discuss the matter and this association led to the organization of "The Friends of the *Christliche Welt*." In its ranks were the leaders of German liberal theology until it was eclipsed by the Barthian movement and the traumas which led to the end of the Weimar Republic. Herrmann in this and the next two years published several articles relating to the *Apostolikumsstreit*. Cf. Bibliography.

203   34. "Historical circumstances" renders "*geschichtliche Wirklichkeit*." The original carries the sense that human existence is real in its historicity, and only in connection with this historicity is speaking of God meaningful.

205   35. Note the non-eschatological character of the Kingdom of God in this formulation. Note also that Herrmann turns the discussion into one about love, as Fuchs frequently does. See, e.g., "Jesus' Understanding of Time," in *Studies of the Historical Jesus*, trans. Andrew Scobie ("Studies in Biblical Theology 42"), (Nashville: Allenson, 1964), pp. 104 ff. Fuchs too minimizes the apocalyptic character of Jesus' message. [LEK]

212 36. Cf. Herrmann's article on *"Andacht" Realencyklopaedie für protestantische Theologie und Kirche*, 3rd ed., I: 497-501. This is reprinted in *Schriften zur Grundlegung der Theologie* I: 186-92.

217 37. "New being" renders *"ein neues Wesen."* This could be as well translated "a new person."

221 38. "Historical figure" renders *"geschichtliche Gestalt."*

243 39. The echoes of Schleiermacher's emphasis on "absolute dependence" are manifest throughout this discussion. Bultmann, on the other hand, denies flatly that faith is a state of consciousness. "Liberal Theology and the Latest Theological Movement," in *Faith and Understanding*, p. 50. [LEK]

252 40. The last sentence of the German original is missing from the English translation. It reads thus: "All methodism is of the devil (vom Übel)." I choose not to capitalize this in translation although this is certainly possible, since Herrmann meant, I believe, something more (and perhaps less) than Methodism as a specific ecclesiastical body. The reader should be aware that German Methodism was a very small movement in nineteenth-century church history and was understood to be related to the Herrnhutters in origin and the *Erweckungsbewegung* (nineteenth-century Pietism) in its contemporary expression. Thus it is what might better be called in America "revivalism" toward which this polemical aside is directed. It is evident that Herrmann's interest in religious experience is informed by Ritschl's critique of Pietism.

292 41. The German text has this footnote which is missing from this English translation. "Compare H. Hoffmann, *Eins ist not* (Halle, 1895), pp. 153-54."

307 42. Between here and the paragraph break on page 325 lie the pages which were added to the second edition of this work and represent Herrmann's further exposition of the way in which the idea of faith leads naturally into the question of ethics.

312 43. This footnote from the original text is missing: "Compare, Thieme, op. cit., p. 271."

320 44. This footnote from the original is also missing: "Compare, Soden, 'Die Ethik des Paulus,' *Zeitschrift für Theologie und Kirche*, Vol. 5 (1892), p. 115."

327 45. This is not quite adequate to convey the force of the German original *"Lebenstreib."* It is the drive of life itself which is brought together with the knowledge of the necessity of the good in moral freedom.

327 46. This footnote from the German original is missing: "Thieme raises the objection that a love of neighbor which wishes to be nothing else but love of God could not at all come to focus whole-

Page

heartedly upon the neighbor himself. I am of the opinion that our neighbor first becomes truly dear to us when we seek God in him."

343 47. The non-phenomenal character of Christian existence is a theme emphasized by Bultmann. See, e.g., "Revelation in the New Testament," in *Existence and Faith,* trans. Schubert Ogden (New York: Meridian, 1960), pp. 72 ff. [LEK]

346 48. "Mind for life" renders *"Lebensmut."* When one remembers one English usage of mind, e.g., "he has a mind to do that," then he will be able to sense the meaning in this translation of the German original.

347 49. Referred to here is the work of F. H. R. Frank entitled *System der christlichen Gewissheit* written in two volumes and published in two editions (1870-73 and 1881-84).

354 50. "Theory of perception" renders *"Erkenntnistheorie."*

INDEX OF NAMES

Aquinas 24, 223
Aristotle xxvi
Athanasius 156, 174
Augustine 35, 175, 211
Baier, J. W. 218
Barth, K. xvi, xliii, 358
Baur, F. C. xx
Bergson, H. xxv
Bernard 278, 279
Bismarck, O. 359
Bornkamm, G. xlix
Brieger, Th. 224
Buddha 92
Bultmann R. xlii-xlvi, l, lix, 360, 361, 903, 367, 368

Cohen, H. xxiv
Collingwood, R. G. xlv
Cremer, E. 8

Darwin, Ch. xviii, xix, xxxi
Dante 35
Denifle, S. 28
Dieckhoff, A. W. 52
Dilthey, W. xxv, xlv

Ebeling, G. xlii, xlvii, l-liv, lix, 361
Eckhart, 358

Feuerbach, L. xvi
Fischer-Appelt, P. xxiv
Frank, F. H. R. xxix, 10, 222, 347, 368
Fuchs, E. xlii-lii, lix, 361, 366

Gallwitz, H. 104
Gerhard, J. 223
Gogarten, F. lii
Gottschick, J. 8, 224, 323, 365
Gregory of Nyssa xv, 174

Harnack, A. xx, xxi, 8, 23, 146, 358, 360, 366
Harnack, Th. 359
Hegel, G. F. W. xvi, xvii, 359
Heidegger, M. xliv, xlv, xlix, 360
Hilary, 174
Hoffmann, H. 112, 367
Holl, K. 359

Jesuits 132, 133

Kähler, M. xxxvii-xlii, xlvi, 176, 360
Kant, I. xxiii, lv
Käsemann, E. xlix
Kierkegaard, S. xvi, 361
Kohlrausch, A. 364
König, E. 222
Köstlin, J. 149, 359, 366
Kübel, R. 166, 183

Lasson, A. 26, 358
Lessing, G. E. 72, 360
Lipsius, R. A. xxix, 10, 172, 177
Luthardt, C. E. xxix, 10, 66, 182, 340, 350, 360, 365

Mahlmann, Th. xxv, xxxvi
Marx, K. xvi, xviii, xix, xxxi, lx
Meinhold, Th. 153

Melanchthon, P. xliv, 223, 224
Mueller, J. xv

Natorp, P. xxiv
Nietzsche, F. xvi, xviii, xxxi

Ogden, S. xlvi
Oppenrieder, A. 234
Overbeck, F. xvi

Pannenberg, W. 365
Plato xxv, 92

Quenstedt, J. A. 217

Rade, M. xx, xxi, 359, 366
Ranke, L. von 102, 359
Ritschl, A. xv, xx-xxii, xxviii, xxxiv, 131, 209, 210, 224, 239, 246, 250, 264, 268, 272, 273, 280, 281, 332, 333
Ritschl, O. xxviii
Robertson, F. W. 109, 112

Robinson, J. xxviii, xlix
Rothe, R. 27, 28, 358, 359

Schleiermacher, F. xvi-xviii, 357, 367
Schmidt, H. 218
Schmidt, W. xix
Schrempf, C. 366
Schultz, H. 139, 149, 331
Schweizer, A. 295
Smith, W. C. lviii
Socrates 93
Soden, H. von 367

Thieme, K. 310-17, 365-67
Tholuck, F. A. G. xv, xix
Thomasius, G. 364
Timm, H. xxii
Troeltsch, E. xxi, liv-lxi, 358

Weiss, J. xli, 362
Welch, C. 364
Wilhelm II xvi

INDEX OF SCRIPTURE REFERENCES

Psalm 5	168
Matthew 7:15-23	161
Matthew 22:39	274
John 1:4	189
John 10:1	60
John 14:23-31	152

I Corinthians 1:30	94
I Corinthians 12:3	129
Ephesians 3:12	324
Colossians 3:3	293
I John	299